D1044560

HIKING

the

JERSEY

HIGHLANDS

Wilderness in Your Back Yard

GEORGE PETTY

New York-New Jersey Trail Conference

Library of Congress Cataloging-in-Publication Data

Petty, George, 1928-
Hiking the Jersey Highlands : wilderness in your back yard / George Petty.
p. cm.
Includes bibliographical references and index.
ISBN 978-1-880775-49-3 (alk. paper)
1. Hiking--New Jersey--New Jersey Highlands--Guidebooks. 2. Trails--New
Jersey--New Jersey Highlands--Guidebooks. 3. Natural history--New Jersey--New
Jersey Highlands--Guidebooks. 4. New Jersey Highlands (N.J.)--Guidebooks. I.
Title.
GV199.42.N5P48 2007
796.5109749--dc22
2007010429

Published by:
New York-New Jersey Trail Conference
156 Ramapo Valley Road
Mahwah, New Jersey 07430

Cartography: Mike Siegel, Staff Cartographer, Dept. of Geography, Rutgers,
The State University

*Front cover photo: Viewpoint across Echo Lake; front and back cover photos by Marilyn Katz.
Color insert photo credits appear on page 420.*

For Marilyn

Sine qua non

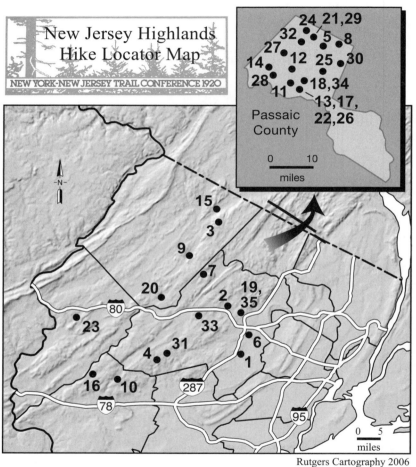

New Jersey Highlands
Hike Locator Map

NEW YORK-NEW JERSEY TRAIL CONFERENCE 1920

Passaic County

Rutgers Cartography 2006

Contents

Acknowledgments

First of all, I am most grateful to my Project Manager, Ruth Rosenthal, editor, grammarian, fact checker, and general supervisor who brought the many details of this book together. Ruth found expert readers for the introductory sections on geology, wildlife, and plants. She contacted all the field checkers and assembled their reports. She obtained the latest information from state and county park officials. She insisted on consistency of presentation in the text, the maps, and the pictures. All of these tasks are magnified for a first edition of a new book, where there is no template of an existing edition to follow. Her careful attention to detail, and her willingness to tackle all sorts of technicalities of contemporary computerized book production, raised the standards of this work far beyond what I could have achieved by myself.

I am also grateful to Daniel Chazin, Chair of the New York-New Jersey Trail Conference Publications Committee, for sharing his encyclopedic knowledge of the trails, and for showing by his example just how careful a hike description should be.

Every one of the trails described in this book has been hiked by the author, but I was never alone. I always had with me my constant companion in the woods and in my life, Marilyn Katz, who, when she wasn't walking beside me with her digital camera, was at the telephone making sure I got home safely. And I had with me my good friend and colleague from Montclair State University, Bob Whitney, an excellent photographer, who lugged his tripod and lenses through the Highlands to record my enthusiasm for wildflowers, rocks, and long views.

I must also express my appreciation for the professionalism and patience of our cartographer, Mike Siegel, staff cartographer for Rutgers, the State University, Department of Geography. Though he knew that every time I called or sent him an e-mail, I was bringing trouble, he always seemed glad to hear from me, and ready to produce the best maps possible.

When I began this project three years ago, I supposed I knew enough about hiking in the Jersey Highlands to complete it by myself. I had tramped the Farny Highlands as a youngster, walked Highlands trails with my own kids, and could write a list of 35 good Highlands hikes that I knew well from hiking each one several times. But that was not enough, not even close.

Trails change: they become eroded, and rerouted; trees grow and obscure viewpoints, new trails are built, new views become accessible, blaze forms are altered. To be complete and accurate, I should have hiked each trail two or three times in the past month. Obviously I needed help, and a lot of it.

I found help in generous supply among the experienced and dedicated hike leaders of local hiking clubs and organizations, and especially from the trail supervisors and maintainers of the New York-New Jersey Trail Conference. These men and women field-checked the drafts of my trail descriptions, took the papers with them into the woods, made detailed, up-to-date corrections, and opened my eyes to landmarks and trail features I had either missed or forgotten. They taught me a lesson, which, for someone who has always been a loner both in the woods and out of it, was very hard to learn: a project like this cannot be an individual creation, it has to be the group effort of many skilled volunteers and observant trail walkers.

Every one of the hike descriptions in this book has been field-checked at least once, and some two or three times, to record trail improvements made while the manuscript was being written. The result is a collection of very complete and accurate hike descriptions, and though I am listed as author, the book is the work of this team of hikers who love the woods and ridges of the Jersey Highlands. They did their best to keep me straight, and if there are errors, they are my own entirely. The field-checkers are listed below in alphabetical order, but this hardly begins to thank them enough.

Field-checkers are from the New York-New Jersey Trail Conference unless otherwise noted.

Estelle Anderson
Suse Bell
Bob Boysen
Daniel Chazin
Ellen Cronan
David Epstein, Executive Director, Morris County Land
    Conservancy
Gene Giordano
Bob Jonas
John Jurasek
Al Leigh
John Mack
John McKay
John Moran
Brian Rogers
Bruce Thompson
Martin Treat

Dick Woolf, Hike leader for the Appalachian Mountain Club and the New Jersey Audubon Society Weis Ecology Center.

Advice on maps, history, trail development, and pictures:
David Helmer, Executive Director, Morris County Park Commission
Karla Risdon, New Jersey Audubon Society, Weis Ecology Center
Helen Maurella, Supervisor, Hopatcong State Park Forest Rangers

Readers for introductory chapters:
Genny Gauss, Environmental Education, Morris County Park Commission
Alexander E. Gates, Professor of Earth and Environmental Sciences, Rutgers University, Newark Campus
Susan Petty, CEO Black Rock Technologies, Seattle WA

Advice on history and trail development of the Highlands Trail:
Bob Moss, NYNJTC first New Jersey Supervisor, Highlands Trail
Glen Oleksak, NYNJTC current New Jersey Supervisor, Highlands Trail
John Myers, NYNJTC Land Acquisitions Director

I am very grateful to all of them.

—George Petty

CHESTNUT OAK

We chose the chestnut oak (Quercus prinus L.) to decorate the pages of this book not because it is the tallest, most noble tree in the New Jersey Highlands, but because we admire its strength and resilience. Unlike those of other Highlands oaks, the chestnut oak leaf is like that of the once common beautiful American chestnut, which, succumbing to a blight early in the last century, has disappeared from our forests.

The chestnut oak is a medium-sized tree, reaching a height of 50 to 70 feet, with a trunk diameter of 1 to 2 feet. The wood is heavy, tough, strong, and durable when in contact with soil. In the nineteenth and early twentieth centuries, the tree was logged extensively for construction lumber, railroad ties, posts, and fuel. Its thick, deeply-ridged bark resists fire and, was, in earlier times, a rich source of tannin for treating leather.

Also called "rock" oak, the tree thrives on dry rocky slopes at higher elevations, where it may be the dominant tree. It can regenerate from roots and stumps when cut or burned, and along Highlands trails, you will see many chestnut oaks with two or more trunks, "coppiced" trees, growing out of stumps left by loggers.

Although exposed on hilltops to long-term drought, wind, and weather, chestnut oaks persist when other species give up, though often becoming stunted and bent on thin-soiled rocky ridgetops, where small twisted trees may be a century old. The chestnut oak is an appropriate symbol of the New Jersey Highlands, which having survived the assaults of the nineteenth-century iron industry and the twentieth-century housing boom, are now, in the twenty-first century, capable of again becoming the wilderness in our back yard. For this hopeful possibility, we can thank courageous political leaders, visionary environmental organizations, dedicated citizens, and hikers like you who love Highlands trails.

EDGEWALKER

for Marilyn

In the city she was a steady-ender.
For her playmates the turning rope
opened to rhythmical joy;
for her it threatened dirt and danger,
scuffed shoes and torn skirt,
her mother's pained silence;
she grasped the loose end
to keep it calm, and turning for others.

So many careful years—
her spirit locked in a child's cabinet,
until a surprise love smuggles her the key.
Out she flies to a tall mountaintop,
overlooking a river far below;
bounds down over boulders
to the last edge of the cliff,
turns with one hand on her hat,
waves with the other,
her dark salted hair blowing in the wind,
her new boots rock-scuffed and dirty,
and laughing, shouts, "Take my picture!"

—George Petty

Introduction

SCENES FROM A HIGHLANDS MOUNTAINTOP

It's a sultry June day on the summit of Wyanokie High Point, 960 feet high in the northeast corner of the New Jersey Highlands. People in the towns below swelter, and to the east the New York City skyline steams in the humid air, but here a steady breeze drifts in from the higher mountains to the west. Hikers come here in all seasons, under different skies; sometimes the air swirls, bursts in gusts, or tries to carry you away, but always it moves, like the tides of an invisible sea.

Those tides run back into all kinds of histories, whose consequences are part of the scenery. To the northeast on the ridge of Ramapo Mountain, you can see recent housing developments, and lines of townhouses along Skyline Drive. The great Wanaque Reservoir to the east, completed in 1930 to supply the growing cities of North Jersey with essential water, covered 70 homesteads, farms, and commercial buildings of the Wanaque River valley. Streaks of

The summit of Wyanokie High Point, looking to the northeast toward Windbeam Mountain.

rusty color in the rocks of High Point summit show the iron content of Highlands gneiss, which in rich veins was a source of iron ore for the rebellious colonies and the thriving nineteenth-century iron industry of New Jersey. The smooth summit of High Point was polished about 15,000 years ago by the abrasion of ice and rocks embedded in the mile-thick Wisconsin Glacier, and an examination of the summit rocks reveals small flecks of crystalline quartz and feldspar formed during a continental collision thousands of millions of years ago, just as visible life was beginning to appear on our planet. Hundreds of millions of years of erosion by water and wind have worn them down to the crystalline rock foundations you sit on now.

Although the view from the top of High Point will seem much the same next week, and even next year, the world of the Highlands is not static, but rather the product of processes of change proceeding on time scales ranging from decades to eons. Every day, grain by grain, water and wind erode the rock of High Point summit, carrying it down to the soil below, into brooks and streams, and finally to the sea. There it is deposited on the continental shelf and pushed deep into the crust of the Earth to form new sedimentary rock, which awaits the next collision of continents to be raised into mountains again.

On this mountaintop, where you sit quietly in a soft breeze, you are part of many natural cycles that create new forests, watercourses, mountains, and civilizations out of the remains of the old. And every year, in another important cycle, new hikers, young and old, make their way to the summit of Wyanokie High Point to appreciate the beauty of the Highlands and to wonder how their generations may influence its future.

THE EXTENT OF THE JERSEY HIGHLANDS

The New Jersey Highlands are 1,250 square miles of rugged hills in a narrow triangle extending about 100 miles from the New York State border to the Delaware River. The Highlands are 23 miles wide and 1,300 feet high between Vernon and Mahwah in the north, diminishing to 8 miles wide and 500 feet high at Phillipsburg in the south. From the air, the Highlands today are a mostly forested swath of steep hills and valleys, dotted with hundreds of ponds, lakes, and reservoirs, and an increasing number of growing suburban communities.

HIGHLANDS TOPOGRAPHY

The unusual geology of the Jersey Highlands offers the hiker opportunities and challenges not found in other areas of the state. The tectonic faulting of the Highlands bedrock, ages of erosion, and recent

The first falls of Posts Brook in the Wyanokies, where several hikes begin, is called Otter Hole.

glaciations have produced a tightly packed series of broken ridges, separated by narrow valleys with small running streams feeding into larger watercourses. Because the Highlands have been so broken and folded, the hiker can find in them both short and long hikes offering varieties of terrain and views. A short Highlands hike of an hour or two can take you through moist slopes, dry ridgetops, long views from bedrock ledges, glacial boulder fields, changes in vegetation, and startling geological surprises. Every hike in this book offers a scenic water view, perhaps of a vast reservoir, a glacial lake or pond, a waterfall, or a substantial stream. When you have completed one of the longer hikes, you will have been up and down more times than you can remember, been physically tested, and enjoyed many beautiful and varied views along the way.

THE SURVIVAL OF THE JERSEY HIGHLANDS

The history of the Jersey Highlands records the complex interaction between the economic exploitation of its natural resources, the protection of its watersheds to supply growing cities, and the more recent desire of urban and suburban populations for homesites and recreation with access to its nearby natural beauty.

From earliest times, the topography of the Highlands has made it resistant to farming. The Native Americans of North Jersey, the Minsi, made their permanent agricultural settlements in the Upper Delaware

The Blue Mine, on the Mine Trail in the Wyanokies (Hike #18: High Point–Iron Mines Loop), was worked continuously from 1765 to 1855 and finally abandoned in 1905.

River Valley, and used the rugged hills mostly for hunting. The colonists bypassed them in favor of level and fertile land to the south and north. During the American Revolution and for most of the nineteenth century, the Highlands forests were leveled to provide wood fuel for a thriving iron industry, and industrial settlements grew up around the forges (see the remains of the Hibernia Mines on the Wildcat Ridge Loop, Hike #2, and the Long Pond Ironworks on Hike #21). But western competition gradually forced the mines to close, allowing the depleted forests to regenerate.

The Highlands in the early twentieth century was an area of a few small rural towns, some small commercial and subsistence farms and dairy operations, and declining iron towns and abandoned forge complexes. The hills began to develop slender forests in various stages of recovery. The first edition of the New York-New Jersey Trail Conference's *New York Walk Book*, published in 1923, quotes a surveyor saying of the Wyanokie Highlands that they are "too wild and too worthless to be taxed," and that "in these areas it is possible for a man to get thoroughly lost while still in sight of the Woolworth Building."

As late as 1950, an aerial photograph shows suburban growth stopping at the eastern rise of the Highlands. In spite of the incursions of agriculture and iron industry, for 200 years the rugged topography had preserved the Highlands from becoming part of cities and their suburbs.

SUBURBAN DEVELOPMENT ENTERS THE HIGHLANDS

Beginning in the years after World War II, both federal and state governments invested large amounts of money in improved highways. At the same time, the need of expanding city populations for family housing put pressure on undeveloped areas of the state.

Townhouse development along Skyline Drive, on the west slope of Ramapo Mountain, seen from Wyanokie High Point.

Gradually, the insistent growth of the suburbs spread along the new roads, breaching the natural defenses of the Highlands. By the end of the twentieth century, Highlands forests in New York and New Jersey were being consumed by housing development at the rate of 5,000 acres every year. The conflict between developing the Jersey Highlands and preserving them had reached a crucial stage.

PRESERVING THE WILDERNESS IN YOUR BACK YARD

The New Jersey state government, in a bipartisan collaboration, began responding to this situation in 1961 by proposing a bond issue to provide funds to purchase farms and woodlands statewide to be preserved from development for their historic or recreational value.

Called the Green Acres Program, the proposal was approved by the voters, who have in the past 45 years overwhelmingly approved nine bond issues for the same purpose. The Green Acres Program has announced that the Highlands will receive special attention in its acquisitions planning: "Serving as a spectacular green belt around some of the nation's most densely populated cities and suburbs, the majority of the Highlands' mountains, ridges, forests, and fields are privately held and therefore are vulnerable to development. Preservation of the greenbelt is critical to ensuring the integrity of New Jersey's water supplies and maintaining the state's biodiversity."

Private individuals also led opposition to unrestricted housing development in Highlands hills and forests. In a typical case, Mrs.

Ryker Lake and 2,000 acres around it was saved from development by the efforts of an organization of local residents called The Friends of Sparta Mountain, with the cooperation of the New Jersey Green Acres Program, the Victoria Foundation, and the New Jersey Audubon Society.

Lucy A. Meyer of Montville organized local opposition to the development of nearby Pyramid Mountain. She was able to gain support from local officials to delay approvals for construction, and eventually put together a coalition of state, county, municipal, and private funding sources to purchase the land for a fair price from the developer. In 1987, the area was turned over to the Morris County Park Commission to become one of the most popular hiking areas in the Highlands. Her work is commemorated in Lucy's Overlook on the Pyramid Mountain Loop (Hike #6). A similar campaign by concerned citizens helped preserve the land around Ryker Lake (Hike #10). In all such campaigns, patience and dedication is required; it took 20 years of constant effort for Lucy Meyer and her colleagues to win their battle.

In 1988, a group of conservation organizations, including the New York-New Jersey Trail Conference, formed the Highlands Coalition to advocate legislation to prevent further uncontrolled development in the entire Highlands area from Connecticut to Pennsylvania. At the latest count, 110 organizations have joined the Coalition. In 2004, the Highlands Coalition efforts, with the support of then Governor James McGreevey, a Democrat, led to the passage of the Highlands Water Protection and Planning Act by the New Jersey Legislature.

The demand for urban water resources made the preservation of the Jersey Highlands a public issue of the first importance. In Congress, Representative Rodney Frelinghuysen, a Republican of the 11th District, led the effort to have a federal study define the importance of the Highlands resources, and subsequently introduced legislation to authorize funds to help preserve the Highlands. This law, the federal Highlands Conservation Act, was passed in 2004, and signed into law by President George W. Bush.

As a result of these public and private efforts, the equitable long-term preservation of the Jersey Highlands is within reach. The conflicts continue, but the legal machinery for preservation is in place.

According to the Highlands Coalition, 25 million people live within a two-hour drive of the Highlands. We hope this book will encourage all of those citizens to appreciate and help preserve the resources and recreational opportunities offered by this wilderness in their back yard.

THE NEW YORK-NEW JERSEY TRAIL CONFERENCE AND THE HIGHLANDS

In 1920, the New York-New Jersey Trail Conference (NYNJTC) was formed to encourage hiking and to organize the creation and maintenance of hiking trails in the metropolitan area. Today, the Trail Conference and about 100 affiliated hiking organizations have over 10,000 active members who walk the trails in New Jersey. The Trail Conference maintains more than 400 miles of Jersey Highlands trails in three maintenance districts, and publishes maps of northern Highlands trails from the New York-New Jersey border to NJ Route 23. It also has committed its resources to land acquisition, public advocacy of wilderness conservation, and education for hiking and other forms of passive recreation. The Trail Conference is a founding member of the Highlands Coalition, the advocacy group that helped promote New Jersey's Highlands Water Protection and Planning Act of 2004. The publication of *Hiking the Jersey Highlands* supports the Conference's education program by introducing the public to the outdoor recreation resources of the Highlands.

THE HIGHLANDS TRAIL

The last section of our book is devoted to a brief history and description of the Highlands Trail, which was designated New Jersey's

The Highlands Trail is blazed with painted teal diamond blazes, or with a plastic teal-on-white logo like this one.

Legacy Millennium Trail in 1999 under a nationwide program initiated by the administration of President Bill Clinton to encourage outdoor recreation. The Highlands Trail begins near Storm King Mountain in New York State. It enters New Jersey on Big Beech Mountain in Passaic County (Hike #21) and continues 110 miles toward the Delaware River near Phillipsburg.

Many of the hikes in this book have been selected because they follow parts of the Highlands Trail, and our description of the Highlands Trail will refer to those hikes. Our descriptions of sections of the trail not covered by our numbered hikes will be sufficiently detailed to direct the hiker through turns and intersections. We provide a small-scale overall map of the trail, but for more detailed maps and continuous trail directions, the hiker should go to the website of the New York-New Jersey Trail Conference, www.nynjtc.org, and click the "trails" button.

HOW TO USE THIS BOOK

We intend this book to be an introduction to recreational hiking in the Highlands, both for people who think of woodland walking as a relatively new experience, and for those who have hiked elsewhere but aren't familiar with the Jersey Highlands. For most residents of metro area cities and older suburbs, the Highlands trails described here offer access to woodlands within easy driving distance. We have selected hikes from the northern Highlands close to the New York-New Jersey border, down to the southern end in Hunterdon County. Those who live in suburbs farther from city centers may find the wilderness of the Highlands almost in their back yards. In some cases, the trails are accessible by public transportation. Hikers willing to take a bicycle on a train or in the baggage compartment of a bus could reach all of the trailheads without driving a car. Of course, there would be some long uphill pedaling involved.

Because the rugged Highlands terrain cannot be described completely on a trail map, a hike book like this one is particularly useful. We have chosen and combined trails to provide long views, seasonal wildflowers, interesting history, varied terrain, and beautiful water. Our descriptions will point out the physical obstacles to be encountered on the trail, and provide careful navigation guides. The book can be studied at home to help you choose a hike appropriate for your experience and capabilities. And it is small enough to be carried on the trail to call attention to interesting features and views, to reassure you at trail junctions, and to remind you how far you've come and how far you have to go. Where possible, the hike descriptions suggest ways to cut a hike short in case heavy rain surprises, or the day grows dark. Our maps try to show these options, and they may be supplemented for many hikes by consulting the detailed and comprehensive map set of North Jersey Trails published by the New York-New Jersey Trail Conference and available from its office at 156 Ramapo Valley Road, Mahwah, NJ 07430, (201) 512-9348, www.nynjtc.org.

Every step of the trails described in this book has been walked by the author and two wonderful hiking companions. All of us have gray hair, and believe in taking enough time on a hike to really see what's there. We like to stop occasionally to examine a wildflower, a mushroom or a rock, listen for a bird (we try to identify them by their song, but we aren't very good at it), to admire a view, or to take a photograph. Every photograph in the book was taken on a trail in the Highlands by one of us, or a hiking friend, because we wanted you to know that the rocks, flowers, animals, and beautiful views we write about really exist on the trails. The book is written not only to tell you how to complete a hike, but to show why you might want to walk there in the first place.

We usually stop briefly to take a drink every half hour, and we try to start our hike so we can snack or eat lunch at an interesting lookout. We walk at a reasonable pace, on level track, about 2.5 miles per hour, and on steep climbs up and down about 1 mile per hour. We are sometimes passed by younger legs scissoring along at 3 to 4 miles per hour, and we admire them, but we are convinced we come home with more of the Highlands in our memories than the speedy hikers. For this reason, the times allowed for the hikes described here may be a little long. If you beat them, we are satisfied; there are as many ways to walk in the woods as there are walkers.

We have acquired some other trail habits over the years, which hikers may find they want to adopt. We carry a backpack with a wool sweater, raingear, flashlight, small first-aid kit, compass, a multi-use trail knife, food, a quart of water for every three hours on the trail (more in hot weather), and a trail map. We all wear waterproof hiking boots to provide ankle support and good traction over rocks, and to get through the occasional seasonal wet spots without soaking our socks. However, we do know that with the improvement in athletic shoe construction, for some of the less demanding hikes a good strong pair of sneakers with wide treads will do very well. We like to carry hikers' trekking poles to provide balance on edges, and to

Hiking in winter on a bright day when the leaves are down offers vistas not available in green seasons. This overlook is on Hike #13, Wyanokie Torne.

cushion the impact of climbing down steep trails. Two of us always wear lightweight artificial fiber long pants and long-sleeved shirts to defend against insects, especially ticks. The third one opts for shorts in warm weather, and relies on a swim or shower to wash off the ticks. But he has had his brush with Lyme disease, and the others have not.

Each season in the woods has its pleasures; we walk year-round to enjoy them all. Most hikers prefer to walk in spring or fall, when the weather is mild and colors delightful. Summer hiking is attractive, too, as long as the temperature and humidity don't climb too high. We have learned to enjoy walking on a cool, dry winter day, without snow or ice on the ground. Then the leaves are down, and you can see deeper into the woods to the hills, rock outcrops, and contours that may be hidden in green seasons.

As part of our hike descriptions, we often mention wildflowers

we have seen along the trail. To help you understand these references, we provide sixteen pages of color pictures of common woodland wildflowers, and some of the more interesting uncommon ones
as well. Every one of these pictures was taken on a trail described in
this book. We have included enough examples so that for the first
year or two you won't have to carry a book-length wildflower guide
in your pack. The flowers are presented in seasonal sections, and
grouped according to color. Wildflowers are very fragile; they will
not survive long after being picked or removed from their habitat.
We hope you will enjoy recognizing them and leaving them for the
next passing hiker to see.

The hikes described in this book are graded from "Starter
Hikes" to "Longer Hikes, Climbs, and Scrambles" to "Challenges."
The starters are appropriate for new hikers, for families with young
children, or for seniors looking for manageable outdoor exercise.

Cardinal flowers blooming in August at Otter Hole. Photo: Dan Chazin

There are some difficulties involved in the Starter Hikes, but in general, people capable of enjoying a walk from the lake in Jersey City's Lincoln Park to the corner of Bergen Avenue and Montgomery Street, or from Newark's Broad Street railroad station to Springfield Avenue and 16th Street, or across New York City's Central Park and back, should be able to enjoy these hikes. There are some differences, of course; the footing on woodland trails is not always secure, and any snacks you eat along the way you will have to carry in with you, and carry the wrappers out. Within the "Starter" category, the hikes gradually become a little longer and a little more strenuous.

If you have completed and enjoyed one of the longer Starter hikes, or one similar to them, you should be able to enjoy one of the "Longer Hikes, Climbs, and Scrambles." A climb here means an ascent of at least 100 feet in 0.1 mile horizontal distance, for an average grade of close to 20%. A scramble is a climb over rocks requiring the use of hands and knees as well as feet. The urban equivalent of a climb is to walk up ten flights of apartment building stairs at a slow but steady pace, carrying on a conversation as you go. As for the scrambles, if you can carry a modest-sized TV set

A scramble is a climb where you might have to use your hands as well as your feet to get up and over. This one is on Hike #13, the Wyanokie Torne Loop.

from the bedroom to the living room, or hoist yourself up into the bed of a pick-up truck, you're ready.

Similarly, if you have completed and enjoyed one of the more strenuous "Longer Hikes, Climbs, and Scrambles," you should be ready to try the "Challenges." These hikes add distance, more frequent ups and downs, or more difficult climbs and scrambles. They are for fit hikers with some experience, and, because they wander farther into the woods, should not be attempted alone.

The forest provides favorable habitat for deer, turkey, and grouse, and is open to seasonal deer hunting (firearms and bow) in specified zones by permit only. Deer seasons usually are scheduled from the end of September to the end of January. Hunting seasons for turkey and other game birds usually last from the middle of April to late May. Hunting is prohibited on Sunday everywhere in New Jersey. If you are in the woods during hunting seasons, you should wear bright orange outer clothing. For specific information about New Jersey hunting regulations, areas, and dates in state Wildlife Management Areas, contact the New Jersey DEP Division of Fish

The three companions who together hiked every step of the trails in this book (from left): Bob Whitney, George Petty, and Marilyn Katz.

and Wildlife office at the Pequest Trout Hatchery Natural Resource Education Center, (908) 637-4125, or check the website: www.njfishandwildlife.com. For trails in state parks, you should call the office of the park superintendent, listed in the back of this book under "Organizations of Interest to Hikers." For Morris County Parks, contact Morris County Park Police, (973) 326-7632.

A Hiker's Geology of
the Highlands

Hikers in the Jersey Highlands will encounter both spectacular beauty and imposing rock formations that make a walk in the woods more exciting than a walk in the park. The trails traverse frequent ups and downs, some of them steep and rocky, with exposed bedrock walls and summit rock outcrops smoothed to a shine by ages of glaciers. There are cliffs to climb and fields of boulders to step through. The hills hold sparkling streams, hundreds of lakes and ponds, wetlands perched in the middle of dry ridgetops, and vast reservoirs. We provide some background here to help appreciate the sensory excitement, the occasional physical challenges, and the geological surprises found only in these mountains so close to the megalopolis of New York-New Jersey.

FORMATION OF THE HIGHLANDS

The Jersey Highlands are a part of an ancient mountain range whose eroded remains extend from the Green Mountains of Vermont through the Blue Ridge Mountains of Virginia and the hills of eastern Tennessee and Georgia. At the New Jersey-New York state line, the Highlands are just over 1,300 feet high and 23 miles wide between Wawayanda Mountain in Vernon and a steep margin near the Ramapo River in Mahwah. They diminish gradually to 500 feet high and eight miles wide at the Delaware River near Phillipsburg. The Highlands disappear under overlying sedimentary rocks near Reading, Pennsylvania, leading some geologists to call them the Reading Prong. They re-appear above the surface at South Mountain in Pennsylvania.

Most of the ridges and rock outcrops we see in the Highlands are "basement rocks," formed between 1.0 and 1.3 billion years ago during a collision between the North American and South American continents in what geologists call the Proterozoic Eon, when whatever life existed was either of microscopic size or had neither shells nor bones. During the collision, rocks of all kinds at the edge of the continental plates were pushed down, heated, folded, and contorted, lifting surface rocks above them into a range of mountains.

After the continental collision and the creation of the mountain range, the North American continental plate, of which these mountains were the eastern edge, split and separated from the South American land mass, a movement propelled by convection currents deep in the semi-solid mantle. Another cycle of collision and separation between North America and Africa occurred in the Paleozoic Era, during the creation and break-up of the super-continent Pangaea between 450 and 200 million years ago. The consequent mountain building produced a second North American east coast range, the Folded Appalachians, which extends from Newfoundland to Alabama. In New Jersey, this range forms the Ridge and Valley Province just to the west of and a little higher than the Highlands, with the long Kittatinny Mountain as its principal feature.

HIGHLANDS RIDGES
AND HOLLOWS

The faulting and contorting of the Jersey Highlands caused by slow continental collisions produced an underlying hard rock mass with an uneven surface. The valleys created by these faults were filled by softer sediments made from the erosion of material from the second east coast mountain range. Although continual erosion of the basement rock since it was first exposed and subsequent glacial grinding have modified the terrain, the Highlands of our era are a series of narrow ridges and valleys more tightly packed together than other land forms in the area. These topographical features are aligned perpendicular to the stress of the continental collisions that caused them, and parallel to the edge of the North American plate. The edge of that plate is now positioned in a northeast-southwest direction, and the Highlands follow this line from Vermont to Georgia.

For the hiker, this means that the main ridges and valleys of the Jersey Highlands follow this northeast-to-southwest line, and when the trail turns across that direction, you may face a series of short, steep rocky ridge climbs and descents, often with small streams or wetlands in the hollows between. The ridges may vary from 10 feet to 600 feet high, and many do not appear on trail maps designed to show contours of 100 feet or more. First-time hikers on trails in this area should allow a little extra time to deal with these features. You may be surprised at how much energy is required to traverse an east-west line that on your map seems to be relatively level. As a reward for your extra effort, you will find the topography of the Highlands always interesting, with varied plant communities and dramatic overlooks and lake views.

HIGHLANDS ROCKS

During the continental collision, the rocks of the oceanic floor between the continents were pushed (subducted) to depths of up to hundreds of miles below the surface. The deepest rocks were subjected to such heat and pressure that they melted and mixed together, so that the minerals of the original rock were reconstituted into a liquid known as magma. Rocks melted completely by this process are called igneous, from the Latin word for fire.

Igneous rocks develop when magma cools as it rises through the crust above and forms mineral crystals, much as water forms ice crystals when its temperature goes below freezing. Some magma forces its way through cracks in the broken crust, reaching the surface as volcanoes or other lava flows. There it cools very quickly, so that its mineral crystals cannot grow beyond microscopic size before the rock solidifies. However, when igneous rocks are contained below the surface, as they form beneath rising mountains they cool more slowly, and mineral crystals have time to grow to visible size, locking tightly together and making the rocks very hard and more resistant to erosion than other rocks. After hundreds of millions of years, when the mountains over these rocks erode away and the basement rocks are exposed on the surface, hikers can see their crystals with the unaided eye.

The crustal rocks that were pushed down far enough to melt became a more or less homogeneous mass of new minerals called granite. Granite has a chemical composition corresponding to the average distribution of elements in the continental crust, as might be expected, because it is formed by the mixing of all kinds of rocks from that crust. It consists largely of the minerals feldspar and quartz, with hornblende, mica, and small quantities of iron oxide and other metals. All of these minerals except the iron are silicates, compounds of silicon and oxygen, joined with light metals like aluminum, magnesium, potassium, sodium, and calcium. Silicate minerals are the most abundant of all naturally occurring inorganic compounds. In granite, the mineral crystals will be distributed randomly, and the rock will have no recognizable structure of lines or planes of different materials. Granite is not very common along these trails; in the Jersey Highlands about 10% of the crystalline bedrock we see is granite.

G N E I S S

Much of the rock involved in a continental collision does not quite melt, but becomes a semi-solid ductile mass. In this state, its minerals can be completely changed into new compounds. Such rocks are

This large gneiss boulder sits in a relatively flat hollow, far from higher ridges; it was probably carried there by a glacier. Notice the bands of quartz crystals, raised because they are harder and more resistant to erosion than the rock around them.

called metamorphic, from a Greek word meaning transformed. Because metamorphic rocks are semi-solid, they cannot flow to the surface. Kept below at depth, they cool very slowly, form networks of visible crystals, and become hard and erosion resistant. During this process, the rock mass may be subjected to more stress from one direction than another, as the continental plates move together. If the rock does not melt, but undergoes change as a ductile solid, its new minerals will not be homogeneously mixed, and its crystals will not distribute themselves randomly, but form bands or sheets perpendicular to the applied stress. When the rock is exposed on the surface, the bands appear as visible lines of color in the rock. Such banded rocks are called gneiss. You can see this gneissic banding on rock outcrops and boulders along the trail. The bands generally form long parallel lines, but sometimes they are folded and contorted.

The chemical composition and appearance of gneiss varies slightly according to the composition of the rocks from which it was formed. Highlands gneiss is highly metamorphosed, formed close to the conditions of melting, and has a coarse-grained crystal structure much like granite, except that it retains the banded texture caused by differential stress. Highlands gneiss comes in many varieties; it is basically mottled gray, with slight differences in color depending on the distribution and the chemical makeup of its crystals. Gneiss in the Wyanokies usually contains potassium feldspar, which produces a pink cast to the exposed bedrock. Most of the bedrock seen by Highlands hikers is gneiss of one kind or another.

In the average piece of rock you pick up on the trail, the visible crystals will be tiny milk white or gray rectangles of quartz, irregular dots of white or light pink feldspar, small black dots of hornblende, and flakes of shiny black biotite mica. If you have trouble seeing the small crystals, you might try looking through a magnifying glass.

DIFFERENTIAL EROSION

Often on an exposed bedrock slab we see small raised ridges perhaps a quarter of an inch high and half an inch apart extending in parallel lines across the rock. These lines may seem to be the same as the rock, but a close look shows they are slightly different in color. Because most of us know that glaciers scoured the Highlands 15,000 years ago, we may want to say these lines are glacial striations. But they are not grooves in the bedrock; these lines are actually raised above it to a fine edge, not a probable result of glacial grinding. The better explanation is they are gneissic bands of quartz or other silicate crystals. The glacier smoothed the whole slab evenly, but since that

A quartzite glacial erratic with calcareous bands, on top of Jenny Jump Mountain. The calcium carbonate bands, being softer than the host rock, have eroded more quickly, producing the deep indentations of differential erosion.

time the crystalline bands have resisted erosion to a greater extent than did the rock around them, and as a result they now stand out above their surroundings. This differential erosion is a small model of the larger process that over hundreds of millions of years has produced the ridges and valleys so characteristic of the Highlands.

R O C K   C O L O R

Most of the rocks a hiker sees in the Highlands have a gray exterior, no matter what their interior color may be. The gray outside comes from the formation of surface compounds of metallic oxides caused by the chemical effect of water, and also from the growth of lichen on the rock. Lichen is a combination of algae and fungus in which the algae obtain energy by decomposing the rock, and the fungus in turn gets energy from the algae. The result is a grayish growth attached to the rock; in common varieties it is shaded with green or yellow, or streaked with white. The natural interior colors of a rock may be visible in exposed locations where the

This lichen has grown on a gneissic boulder. The small gray or milky dots are crystals of quartz or feldspar, and the darker dots are hornblende or shiny biotite mica. The bands characteristic of gneiss can be seen just below the bottom edge of the lichen.

The gneiss bedrock on the summit of High Point in the Wyanokies is shot through with white quartz veins.

constant water-wash, wind, and animal or human wear and tear keep the gray coverings from growing. Or you may find a piece of recently broken rock whose fractured face will show interior color, which you can enhance by dipping the stone in water.

QUARTZ VEINS

Hikers will often see boulders or bedrock outcrops streaked with jagged veins of white crystals, like lightning streaks. These streaks occur where, during the formation of the host rock, physical stress created spaces, which were then filled by an available mineral dissolved in fluid. The most likely mineral to fill these spaces was

Puddingstone bedrock of the Schunemunk formation overlooks Terrace Pond.

quartz, pure silicon dioxide, which crystallizes late in the cooling process, and whose constituent, silicon, is the most plentiful solid element in the earth's crust. Quartz dissolved in water squeezed from source rocks filled the spaces and crystallized as the rock cooled, making the streaks of white we see when the rock is exposed.

BEARFORT MOUNTAIN PUDDINGSTONE

Several hikes described in this book follow trails along Bearfort Mountain, the long ridge overlooking Greenwood Lake from the west that extends southwest until it disappears under Clinton Reservoir. Bearfort Mountain is an unusual geological feature of the Highlands because its visible bedrock is not gneiss, but rather a conglomerate rock of quartz pebbles in a fine-grained purple sandstone matrix, known locally as "puddingstone." This ridge is an extension of a formation that begins on Schunemunk Mountain in New York. The formation is part of a series of sedimentary rocks laid down before the building of the Folded Appalachians. The puddingstone was made from fine sand eroded from mountains to the east at the edge of a shallow sea, into which quartz pebbles were mixed along the shore. As other sediments formed on top of it over millions of years, the pebbles and silt were pushed deep into the earth and became puddingstone layers.

When the Appalachians were formed, these sedimentary layers folded into waves of rock. Under tectonic pressure, a part of the underlying bedrock slipped down in what is called a normal fault just west of Bearfort Mountain, separating a fold of the sedimentary layers from its equivalent formation to the west. After these layers eroded down to the level of the basement rock of the Highlands, this fold of sedimentary rock remained in a slot made by the fault in the middle of the gneissic hills. This erosion-resistant puddingstone formed the glacially smoothed ridges of Bearfort Mountain. Alongside the ridges, layers of dark red, gray, and black shale, some tilted almost vertical, have eroded more rapidly, forming hollows that often trap water and create wetlands with small groves of hemlock trees or moisture-loving hardwoods perched near the summit outcrops. The center of the fold provides depths for West Pond at the north end of Bearfort Mountain, and Terrace Pond farther south. Boulders, cobbles, and pebbles of puddingstone were quarried by glaciers and carried all over the Highlands, where you will see them along the trail, in stream beds, and boulder fields, and on glacial depressions in rock outcrops.

GLACIAL ERRATICS

Besides the topographical effects of tectonic mountain building and subsequent erosion, the Highlands have been scoured at least four

This large "glacial erratic" boulder, rounded by glacial abrasion, was left perched on a rock outcrop as the glacier retreated over the exposed ridge of High Point in the Wyanokies.

times by continental glaciers. The most recent advance began about 20,000 years ago and ended with the retreat of the ice about 15,000 years ago. As it melted, the glacier left at its southernmost extent an elongate 250-foot-high mound of sand and boulders; this is known as a terminal moraine. The moraine crosses the Highlands on a line from the Jenny Jump Mountains, past the southern tip of Lake Hopatcong, to just north of Dover, turning south behind Morristown. As it retreated, the glacier left the ridges and valleys of the Highlands bare of trees, plants, and soil. The hillsides were lined with boulders and debris from small moraines formed on the sides of glacial tongues. On flat surfaces, large boulders, transported by the ice from farther north, settled gently through the melting ice onto the bedrock below.

Today we see these "glacial erratics" standing on bare rock overlooks or alone in the woods, looking hugely out of place. A sure sign that a boulder is an erratic is that it differs in composition from the nearby bedrock, exactly as does the great gneiss boulder left on a puddingstone rock ledge just off the blue trail going west from Terrace Pond. Or an erratic can be left surprisingly balanced on smaller rocks, as is the famous Tripod Rock on Pyramid Mountain near Boonton.

BOULDER FIELDS

Boulder fields, those collections of rounded boulders in or near streambeds in the hollows and valleys of the Highlands, lie across many trails described in this book. With a little experience, hikers learn to enjoy the care and agility required to find a way through them. After all, a hike should not be a walk in the park. But why are there so many in the Highlands, and from where do they come? The Highlands have more than their share of boulder fields because differential erosion over hundreds of millions of years produced in its topography the many corrugations which collect traveling boulders, and four successive glaciations have pried loose the many boulders to fill them. Rocks left on bare hillsides in lateral moraines of retreating glaciers will easily slide or fall downslope to a streambed. Later, when vegetation has returned to the slopes, rocks will continue to be dislodged from rock outcrops higher up by freeze-thaw action or by the erosion of finer supporting material, and either fall or work their way down to the streambed by soil creep, the pull of gravity on everything lying on a slope. Highlands soil is notorious for being full of glacially rounded boulders. An accumulation of organic matter may cover up a collection of such rocks, and a change in water flow may uncover them again and push them together. The Otter Hole-Wyanokie Crest Loop (Hike #17), has a particularly extensive boulder field on the climb away from Posts Brook, but every trail in this book crosses at least one such feature, and usually several.

An entirely different kind of boulder field is formed by a rock-slide at a fault, a place where two sections of the Earth's crust move against each other, causing a tremor that shakes rocks loose from a high outcrop and casts them suddenly all together down a slope. On the southwest face of Point Mountain in Hunterdon County, at the beginning of the Point Mountain Loop (Hike #16), there is such a rockslide. On the trail, there we found an example of "slickensides," a piece of rock rubbed smooth by the stress of crustal movement along a fault exposed near the overlook at the top of the first climb.

GLACIAL RIDGETOPS

The ridgetops of the Highlands were scraped clean and smoothed by the Wisconsin Glacier, which retreated 15,000 years ago. Hikers will often find themselves standing on polished rock outcrops, or walking on long, smooth mountain "sidewalks," particularly on Bearfort Mountain, where the outcrops are narrow and frequent. The glacier came from the northwest and crossed the Highlands toward the southeast, making grooves and scooping out small hollows in the bedrock in the direction of its advance. Such glacial "striations" can still be seen in the Highlands. On the north side of rock outcrops the glacier rubbed away sharp edges and left smooth contours, but on the south end of rocky ridges it pulled away boulders, loosened joints, and left rugged cliff faces to be exposed when it retreated. For example, on the Wyanokie Torne Loop in Norvin Green State Forest (Hike #13), the hiker at the top on the north end faces steep smooth rocks that can be slippery when wet, and on the south end, during descent, must negotiate rough ledges with cracks, edges, steep faces, and loose boulders all around the trail.

IRON ORE

Small quantities of iron oxide and other metals are randomly distributed in all rocks, but useful ore forms when geological and chemical processes collect the iron into much higher concentrations. In one such process, melting of crustal rock deep in the Earth forms iron-rich magma, which rises through volcanic action or along cracks in the country rock, and cools into long veins of iron oxides. In another process, during rock formation, iron oxides dissolve in hot fluids and are transported along faults and fractures where they are deposited. As a result of either of these processes, after hundreds of millions of years of erosion, the veins of iron oxide appear at the surface in concentrations which can be mined efficiently.

The iron ore in the Jersey Highlands is mostly magnetite, a black, shiny mineral that is visible in the rocks at the mouth of the Roomy Mine, on the yellow-dot-blazed Mine Trail in Hike #18. The Blue Mine, a quarter of a mile farther along the trail, was active until the late nineteenth century. The U.S. Geological Survey says of the minerals in the discarded rocks around this mine: "The rubble includes masses of pyroxene gabbro, biotite, hornblende, magnetite, and pyrite. Much of the ore was processed in a furnace near the location of the Weis Ecology Center's swimming pool (now the public Highlands Pool), but it was dismantled many years ago. The ore deposits are similar to numerous other magnetite-rich veins in the granite and gneiss of Late Proterozoic time throughout the Highlands province, and are probably a product of the intense regional metamorphism and deep crustal igneous intrusions that occurred during the Grenville Orogeny, the crustal collision that built the Highlands." Magnetite carries its own magnetic field and can attract a compass needle. This was a useful property for early prospectors, but is a hazard for hikers today, who may find both compass and cell phone disturbed in Highlands hollows. These are more likely to function properly on the ridgetops, but there are no guarantees.

L A K E S

Every hike in this book offers a view of at least one important water resource, and most provide views of a lake or reservoir. Some of these lakes, such as West Pond, Surprise Lake, and Terrace Pond on Bearfort Mountain, are natural lakes formed in a Highlands geological feature. Most of the natural lakes in the Highlands are found north of the terminal moraine of the Wisconsin Glacier. Some reservoirs and their feeder ponds, such as those in the Pequannock Watershed, are natural lakes that have been raised by artificial dams to increase their storage capacity. The Wanaque Reservoir was created in an inhabited valley by damming the vigorous Wanaque River. Early iron furnaces were built near natural lakes to supply power for running bellows, as in the case of Long Pond, now Greenwood Lake (Long Pond Ironworks State Park: Big Beech Mountain Turnaround, Hike #21), and Split Rock Reservoir (Split Rock Loop South, Hike #19, and Split Rock Loop, Hike #35). Some Highlands lakes were formed by the damming of streams by glacial deposits, as in the case of Lake Hopatcong and Greenwood Lake, where glacial moraines blocked the southern ends of these lakes. In modern times, many small lakes have been made by damming streams for recreational purposes. For the hiker, the Highlands lakes and streams are a resource of beauty and pleasure. We hope, by popularizing trails in the Highlands as an interesting option for metro-area hikers, we may develop support for the continued protection of its water resources.

Spring

1. Wood anemone *Anemone quinquefolia*

2. Rue anemone *Anemonella thalictroides*

3. Trailing arbutus *Epigaea repens*

4. Canada mayflower *Maianthemum canadense*

5. Bloodroot *Sanguinaria canadensis*

6. Dwarf ginseng *Panax trifolium*

7. Early saxifrage *Saxifraga virginiensis*

8. Solomon's seal *Polygonatum biflorum*

9. False solomon's seal *Smilacina racemosa*

10. Dutchman's breeches
Dicentra cucullaria

11. Spring beauty *Claytonia virginica*

12. Deerberry *Vaccinium stamineum*

13. Large-flowered trillium
Trillium grandiflorum

14. Mountain shadbush *Amelanchier bartramiana*

15. Mayapple *Podophyllum peltatum*

16. Foamflower *Tiarella cordifolia*

17. Starflower *Trientalis borealis*

18. Spicebush *Lindera benzoin*

20. Trout lily *Erythronium americanum*

19. Wild oats *Uvularia sessilifolia*

21. Lousewort *Pedicularis canadensis*   22. Marsh marigold *Caltha palustris*

23. Downy yellow violet *Viola pubescens*   24. Golden Alexander *Zizia aurea*

25. Wild geranium
Geranium maculatum

26. Herb Robert *Geranium robertianum*

28. Toadshade *Trillium sessile*

27. Pink lady's slipper
Cypripedium acaule

29. Fringed polygala
Polygala paucifolia

30. Wild columbine *Aquilegia canadensis*

31. Pinesap
Monotropa hypopithys

33. Round-lobed hepatica
Hepatica americana

32. Pinxster flower *Rhododendron nudiflorum*

34. Common blue violet
Viola papilionacea

35. Forget-me-not *Myosotis scorpioides*

37. Jack-in-the-pulpit *Arisaema atrorubens*

36. Wild sarsaparilla *Aralia nudicaulis*

38. Indian cucumber root *Medeola virginiana*

Summer

1. American fly honeysuckle
Lonicera canadensis

2. Wild madder *Galium mollugo*

3. Black snakeroot
Cimicifuga racemosa

4. Bouncing bet
Saponaria officinalis

5. White campion *Lychnis alba*

6. Bristly sarsaparilla *Aralia hispida*

7. Garlic mustard *Alliaria offinallis*

8. Strawberry *Fagaria virginiana*

9. Hedge bindweed *Convolvulus sepium*

10. Tall meadow rue
Thalictrum polygamum

11. Meadowsweet *Spirea latifolia*

12. Hoary mountain mint
Pycnanthemum incanum

13. Indian pipe
Monotropa uniflora

14. Striped wintergreen
Chimaphila maculata

15. Daisy *Chysanthemum sp.*

16. Sweet pepperbush *Clethra alnifolia*

17. Turtlehead *Chelone glabra*

18. White water lily *Nymphaea odorata*

19. Whorled aster *Aster acuminatus*

20. Daisy fleabane *Erigeron annuus*

21. Tall buttercup *Ranunculus acris*

22. Dwarf cinquefoil
Potentilla canadensis

23. Cypress spurge *Euphorbia cyparissias*

24. Evening primrose *Oenothera biennis*

25. Fringed loosestrife *Lysimachia ciliata*

26. Butter-and-eggs *Linaria vulgaris*

27. Hawkweed *Hieraceum sp.*

28. Panicled hawkweed *Hieraceum paniculatum*

29. Agrimony
Agrimonia gryposepala

30. Thin-leaved coneflower
Rudbeckia triloba

31. Whorled loosestrife
Lysimachia quadrifolia

32. Jerusalem artrichoke
Helianthus tuberosus

33. Yellow stargrass *Hypoxis hirsute*

34. Spotted jewelweed
Impatiens capensis

35. Black-eyed Susan *Rudbeckia serotina*

36. Canada lily *Lilium canadense*

37. Frostweed *Helianthemum canadense*

38. Cynthia *Krigia biflora*

39. Yellow sorrel *Oxalis europaea*

40. Rattlesnake weed
Hieraceum venosum

41. Nodding bur marigold *Biden laevis*

42. Purple gerardia
Gerardia purpurea

43. Winged monkey flower *Mimulus alatus*

44. Bull thistle *Cirsium vulgare*

45. Crown vetch *Coronilla varia*

46. Purple loosestrife *Lythrum salicaria*

47. Wandlike bush clover
Lespedeza intermedia

48. Bee balm *Monarda didyma*

49. Chicory *Cichorium intybus*

50. Pokeweed *Phytolacca americana*

52. Indian poke *Veratrum viride*

51. Stout blue-eyed grass
Sisyrinchium augustifolium

Fall

1. Pearly everlasting
Anaphalis margaritacea

2. Sweet everlasting
Gnaphalium obtusifolium

3. Nodding ladies' tresses
Spiranthes cernua

4. White wood aster *Aster divaricatus*

5. Goldenrod *Solidago sp.*

6. White snakeroot
Eupatorium rugosum

7. Silverrod
Solidago bicolor

8. Cardinal flower
Lobelia cardinalis

9. False Solomon's seal (fruit) *Smilacina racemosa*

11. Partridgeberry *Mitchella repens*

10. Jack-in-the-pulpit (fruit)
Arisaema sp.

13. Great lobelia *Lobelia syphilitica*

12. Bottle gentian *Gentiana clausa*

14. Wavy-leaved aster *Aster undulatus*

Highlands Habitats: Typical Plants and Trees

Hikers will encounter four different plant communities in the Highlands: wetlands, moist uplands, dry uplands, and ridgetops. Wetlands are areas where water stands above the surface for at least part of the year; moist uplands are slopes where water is present under the surface but doesn't accumulate; dry uplands are steeper, usually higher slopes where moisture drains away quickly; and ridgetops are dry, exposed, thin-soiled areas where bedrock is close to the surface. Each environment hosts a special group of trees, shrubs, and herbs, forming a plant community, which, with a little practice, hikers may come to recognize. In this section we try to fit what we have seen ourselves in the Highlands woods into the careful descriptions provided by scientists who have studied them.

WETLANDS

The Jersey Highlands is famous for its many streams, ponds, and lakes, which supply water to a third of the population of the state.

These watercourses were established by the underlying structure of the mountain bedrock and often modified by glacial activity. The glaciers formed new streambeds for meltwater runoff, created hollows in bedrock or depressions (kettles) in softer surfaces, and restricted streamflow with glacial debris. Although the volume of water has decreased radically since the retreat of the glaciers, and many ponds have been filled with silt and decaying vegetation, these wetlands still create environments for special water-loving plants.

MARSHES

At the start of the Laurel Pond Loop (Hike #3), in Wawayanda State Park, in the open areas on each side of the spillway from the Wawayanda Lake wingdam, tall reedy phragmites plants line the brookside, and nearby thickets provide nesting areas for ducks and yellow warblers. An area of year-round standing water such as this,

The marsh at the north end of Ryker Lake. Trees and shrubs will not grow in standing water like this. The area attracts birds, and produces colorful spring wildflowers such as marsh marigold and yellow iris.

where no trees and few shrubs will grow, is called a marsh. On our Highlands hikes, marshes may be seen in open, wet areas around ponds and lakes or along unshaded, slow-flowing streams.

On top of Bearfort Mountain in the southern end of the Terrace Pond Loop (Hike #27), stands of phragmites and water-loving shrubs like alders and sweet pepperbush mark a small marsh environment at one edge of a silting glacial pond. Similar treeless marshes have formed around the edges of beaver ponds along the trail on the Wildcat Ridge Loop (Hike #2), the Lost Lake Turnaround (Hike #33), and the Split Rock Loop (Hike #35). Wildflowers we have seen in small Highlands marshes include swamp loosestrife, purple loosestrife (an invasive alien plant), marsh marigold, jewelweed, boneset, and Joe-Pye weed. The red-winged blackbird loves to nest in marshes, and great blue herons, green herons, and mute swans will nest there, too. The beautiful large yellow iris, and the blue iris called blue flag, like to grow in larger marshes, as they do in the marshes at the north end of Ryker Lake (Hike #9), and along the Black River in a marsh beside an old railroad bed in the Black River Wildlife Management Area near Chester. In the rugged forested slopes of the Highlands, however, extensive marshes with these plants are not common.

SWAMPS

Many Highlands hikes begin at the bottom of a forested slope near a stream or other water source, which you must cross to begin your climb. At the start of the Terrace Pond Loop (Hike #27), the trail crosses two forested wet hollows on puncheons (board or log footpaths). In each of these wetlands, a small stream wanders slowly past boulders, tree trunks, tufts of tussock sedge, and clumps of moss and ferns. In wet seasons, the water stands in quiet pools and sometimes rises over the level of the puncheons. Such an area of standing water formed by the slow drainage of a running brook in a level forested area is a swamp. The trees found in Highlands swamps are typically red maples, yellow birches, and hemlocks, with an understory of alders, arrowwood, pussy willow, and spicebush. Common low plants of Highlands swamps include skunk cabbage, jack-in-the pulpit, Indian poke (false hellebore), and a variety of ferns. Because hemlocks make the soil and water acid, where they are numerous not many soft-stemmed ground plants can survive, and wildflowers are scarce. However, if hemlocks are absent or few, red maples, sugar maples, and yellow birches will take their place, and shrubs and wildflowers have a better chance to grow.

The eastern hemlock, which has thrived so well on cool, moist slopes and in hollows of the Highlands, is under attack from the hemlock woolly adelgid, an Asian insect accidentally introduced into the United States. The adelgid sucks juices from the hemlock needles, and mature hemlocks infested with them weaken and die within 3 to 5 years. Along the trail you will find many hemlocks with bare branches, and often all the trees in a grove will show signs of this infestation. In many hemlock groves dead trees litter the forest floor. Although individual trees can be saved by expensive treatment, no remedy is known to save hemlock groves or forests.

Where banks and slopes rise above the water, the wetland environment grades into the more prolific moist uplands described below, and many more shrubs and wildflowers can grow. This is the case in the Morris County Tourne Park Wildflower Walk and the Tourne Loop (Hike #1), where the walk begins beside a running stream and proceeds to a small area of standing water in a moderately sloping terrain. Because the trail passes through wetlands and moist uplands with only a few evergreens, a large variety of plants thrives through all green seasons. At Otter Hole in the Wyanokies (Carris Hill Circuit, Hike #22), the trail begins by crossing a running stream at a waterfall, where along the banks there is often standing water. Small spring wildflowers have been crowded out here by perennial summer plants and vines, including thick poison ivy, but interesting plants do grow: the special pink lady's slippers, and a marvelous display of cardinal flowers rising in the water in late August. During spring run-off and other wet seasons, Highlands brooks will rise and sometimes overflow their banks. On sloping hillsides, this doesn't produce what we think of as a swamp, but along these watercourses, particularly those flowing through level ground, the trees, shrubs, and herbs are often similar to those found in swampy wetlands. On the High Point-Iron Mines Loop (Hike #18), during the descent from High Point to Blue Mine Brook, you will cross two streams where the vegetation changes abruptly from dry uplands to the red maples, yellow birches, and occasional hemlocks typical of moist land. The Highlands hiker will encounter such changes in vegetation wherever the water table regularly rises close to or above the surface, which occurs frequently along these trails.

Swamps and small floodplains can also be found at the top of a ridge, as happens frequently on the Terrace Pond Loop (Hike #27), the Hanks Pond Circle (Hike #28), and the Bearfort Ridge Loop (Hike #32). These areas are sometimes called perched wetlands, to emphasize the special circumstances of their appearance at higher altitudes. Where the perched wetland is on a large, level tract, there may be evidence of nineteenth-century farming: stone fences, domestic trees and shrubs (typically, gnarled apple trees, barberry hedge, Japanese honeysuckle, and winged euonymous bushes), woods roads, and signs of forest regeneration from open fields. The glacial pond on the Terrace Pond Loop (Hike #27), described above as an example of a marsh, also has swampy edges. As organic matter and silt fills the pond, its edges retreat before small, young hardwoods, mostly red maples and yellow birches, and thickets of alders and willows. The water level of this glacial pond was raised long ago by a dam; its surroundings have all the indications to suggest that this level hilltop was farmland a century ago.

On the north ridge of Bearfort Mountain (Bearfort Ridge Loop, Hike #32; Surprise Lake Loop, Hike #24), swamps have formed in high glacial hollows between ridges, where water is retained by small bedrock basins near the surface. It is a surprise to find hemlock groves and other wetland plants surviving high on the dry mountaintop in small depressions protected from wind and weather by the northeast-southwest ridges.

STREAMS

Often your trail will start by crossing a running stream with a boulder field in dense woodlands and an uphill slope on one or both sides of the water, as it does in these three hikes: Otter Hole-Wyanokie Crest (Hike #17), Pyramid Mountain (Hike #6), and Bearfort Ridge (Hike #32). In these locations, trees such as red maple, sugar maple, and yellow birch will grow; understory shrubs may include maple-leaved viburnum, winterberry, arrowwood, pinxster flower, and spicebush. A variety of herbs may cover the ground. Wherever you find them, stream banks are attractive sites for spring and early summer wildflowers, including trout lilies, dwarf ginseng, turtleheads, violets, blue flag, lousewort, and occasionally pink lady's slippers.

UPLANDS

As your trail climbs away from a stream, you enter the upland forest environment where the terrain slopes, often steeply, in the Highlands. Upland environments are of two kinds: moist slopes and dry, well-drained, usually higher slopes.

MOIST SLOPES

On moist slopes, standing water is infrequent, although the water table in wet seasons comes close to or above the surface, and during a climb or descent you may find muddy stretches along the trail. In the Highlands, the most common plant community in these environments is the mixed-oak forest, made up of red oak, white oak, and black oak, in order of frequency. Along with the oaks, other hardwoods include American beech, hickory, red maple, black birch, ash, and sugar maple. Moist slopes often produce understory groves of flowering dogwood trees; their flat drifts of white blossoms make the May woods look as if there had been a snowstorm. Other second layer trees include shadbush, sassafras, black cherry, and ironwood. Shrubs in these areas include maple-leaved viburnum, mountain laurel, rhododendron, pinxster flower, highbush and lowbush blueberry, and spicebush.

Cool, moist uplands on low northern slopes and on hillsides beside moist hollows often support a hemlock-mixed hardwood forest, in which the hemlock is the most abundant tree, accompanied by northern hardwoods such as black birch, yellow birch, red maple, and beech, but not so many oaks. With the attack on the hemlocks by the woolly adelgid, the dominance of this species is rapidly being reduced. Moist uplands can also support a mixed hardwood for-

Shadbush, or, as some call it, "serviceberry," is a relatively short tree with a rounded crown, whose white blossoms appear in early spring before its leaves sprout. The flowers bloom at the same time as the shad return to the Delaware River to spawn, a coincidence that gives the tree its name.

est in which the wide-leaved sugar maple, rather than the hemlock, is prominent.

We have seen sugar maple groves beside Laurel Pond (Hike #3) and the South Branch of the Raritan River (Hike #10), beginning near the water and extending up the hillsides. Sugar maples also grow in clusters on some higher Highland uplands, for example, on top of Cupsaw Mountain (Hike #8), on Sparta Mountain (near, but not on Hike #9), and in protected perched wetlands on ridgetops (Hike #32), but do not dominate their surroundings.

In places where the acidic hemlock is absent, this moist upland environment is the most productive for our spring woodland wildflowers. In April and early May, along the trails you can see glades and hillsides in moist uplands dotted with hepaticas, spring beauties, anemones, several varieties of violets, and, near running water, mats of trout lilies and Mayapples. Among boulders and in moist rock outcrops, in May, you can still find the scarlet and yellow trumpets of wild columbine in this terrain. These early wildflowers bloom on moist hardwood uplands before the tree leaves are fully formed, when some sun still filters through the bare upper canopy. At the end of May and in early June, the pink lady's slipper, our most prevalent woodland orchid, will appear. This beautiful flower isn't limited to one kind of soil or shade, however. We have seen them growing happily near wet boulder fields, in moist uplands, on dry slopes and even on ridgetops. Pink lady's slippers bloom just off the trail on the slightly protected shore of Surprise Lake high on Bearfort Mountain (on Hike #24), and on the thin soil beside the exposed gneiss bedrock of Wyanokie Torne (on Hike #13). One of the main reasons for the gradual decrease in the number of these plants is their beauty, which makes people covet them. However, there is no point in attempting to dig them up to take them home to your garden. They depend on nutrients found in the wild, particularly near oak trees, and will not survive out of the woods.

Perhaps because there is usually more light, wildflowers often grow close to trails. It is hardly ever necessary to go tramping off trail to find them. If you glimpse a patch of color through the trees, just keep walking slowly so as to look carefully, and usually the same kind of blossom will soon appear close by. It's part of the serendipity of walking in the woods, as if the flowers know how pretty they are, and want to make sure you don't miss them completely. But you have to walk in the woods to see them; they don't compromise on that issue.

WELL-DRAINED SLOPES

As you climb higher and away from woodland streams, the slopes are drier, and the vegetation begins to change. The forest becomes dom-

These sugar maples grow on a moist slope on the east side of Laurel Pond in Wawayanda State Park. They are replacing a grove of mature hemlocks that has been destroyed by the woolly adelgid.

inated by oaks, including the noble white oak, with light discolorations in its bark and upward arching branches, the more common red oak with horizontal branches and spiky leaves, along with the less common but similar black oak, and the chestnut oak, so-called because its leaves resemble the leaves of the American chestnut, a tree eliminated from our forests by a blight brought here on Asian saplings in the early 1900s. American chestnut saplings sprung from old stumps still can be found in the Highlands; however, after reaching a height of 15 to 20 feet, they succumb to the blight. In lower elevations, the oaks are joined by beech, hickory, and occasional red maple, tulip poplar, and ash.

As you climb higher, where the soil is thin and dry, the dominant tree is the chestnut oak, which is able to thrive in such conditions. In the dry uplands, the chestnut oak forest also has some red oak, hickory, black birch, and black cherry. Trees near the

A well-drained Highlands upland slope in winter. The large straight-trunked, gray-splotched tree in the left foreground is a white oak. Its 16-inch diameter suggests it is about 60 or 70 years old. Behind the oak, a beech sapling retains its coppery leaves through the winter, though mature beeches have lost all their leaves. In the background, the slender trees are part of an early successional forest on what probably was a cultivated field, 30 or 40 years ago.

mountaintops of the Highlands have been stressed in recent years by gypsy moth infestations, long-term drought, and the hazards of ice and snowstorms that break off branches. For these reasons, the forest canopy at higher elevations is not as complete as it is below, and the trees are neither as thick-trunked nor as tall. There are many more blowdowns here; trail maintainers work hard to clear the debris and replace lost blazes.

The understory trees of the dry uplands are shadbush, chestnut oak saplings, and the occasional red maple. Lowbush blueberry, mountain laurel, and some wild azalea and sheep laurel, are the lower level shrubs. Wildflowers are not profuse on these slopes, although occasional examples of the flowers found on moist slopes will turn up in higher and drier areas. More commonly in summer, hawkweed, rattlesnake weed, wild sarsaparilla, and whorled loosestrife appear; in late summer and early fall, the white snakeroot and white woodland aster will bloom in the shaded woods. In edge habitats and open glades where some sunlight leaks through, varieties of goldenrod thrive.

RIDGETOPS

At the top of Highlands ridges, bare rock outcrops smoothed and scoured by the glaciers are exposed to wind, winter weather, and extremes of temperature. It takes a long time for plant life to overcome such environmental stresses. Where successional plant communities have produced a little soil in and around the rocks, specially adapted trees, shrubs, and herbs struggle to survive. The most prevalent tree of this environment is the pitch pine. In the pine barrens of South Jersey, this tree can reach 30 or 40 feet in height, but on the Highlands ridgetops it is usually stunted by the difficult conditions. It rarely grows more than 20 feet high, and its trunk is typically twisted and bent. Even though small, it may be quite old, often over a century in age. Other kinds of trees that can survive these conditions include chestnut oak, black birch, black cherry, scrub oak (a bushy oak with several stems no more than 10 feet tall), and shadbush (also called Juneberry and serviceberry). Ridgetop trees tend to germinate in rock crevices where soil accumulates; often their roots writhe like snakes into and over the rock looking for nutrients. Sometimes an expanding root will split a crevice apart, making it seem as if the tree grew up through the bedrock.

A small group of shrub species can survive on the ridgetops. The most common are lowbush blueberry, mountain laurel, sheep laurel (a low laurel with deep pink flowers and small, slightly toxic leaves), and sumac. No spring wildflowers bloom on the ridgetops, but in summer you find the pink and yellow trumpets of pale corydalis and sprawled white blossoms of bristly sarsaparilla growing in the rock crevices. Later in the year in patches of soil, hoary mountain mint will bloom, and at the end of summer, some goldenrod appears.

The habitats described here are not abruptly divided from

A pitch pine growing out of a crack in the rocky face of Indian Cliff, which overlooks Split Rock Reservoir in the Farny Highlands.

one another, but grade into each other gradually, as soil and moisture conditions change. For example, you will run into streams high on the side of a mountain that produce patches of moist vegetation where you don't expect them. The water level of many Highlands lakes has been raised by dams for water collection or recreation, so the shorelines are not naturally moist areas but more like dry upland, uncomfortable with the strange stuff lapping at its edges. As you walk these trails, you will begin to notice such surprises and enjoy figuring out why the textbook generalizations don't always apply.

OPEN FIELD PLANTS

Occasionally your trail may cross an open, treeless area, perhaps a once-cultivated field now in the process of regenerating into forest, or a tract under power lines that has been repeatedly cut. In these spaces open to the sun, a different group of shrubs and wildflowers grows. The Kinnelon-Boonton Trail in Morris County's Pyramid Mountain Natural Historic Area (Hike #6) passes under power lines, and offers (among others), in their seasons, Canada lilies, Jerusalem artichokes, gerardia, meadowsweet, steeplebush, monkeyflower, wood betony, turtleheads, ladies tresses, bottle gentians, and cardinal flowers. An abandoned open field near the Kay Environmental Center in Morris County's Black River Park (Hike #31), seen in early September, hosted examples of clematis, tall blazing star, turtleheads, and other more common flowers attractive to migrating warblers and butterflies. Hikers may learn to see these open fields as opportunities to observe plants they will never find in the shaded woods. Such openings are not always blessings, however. The tract under power lines along Beaver Brook on the Lost Lake Turnaround (Hike #33) is so over-grown with brambles, poison ivy, and dense thickets of small shrubs, that no flowering herbs can thrive.

SUCCESSIONAL FORESTS

For 150 years, from 1750 to 1900, the forests of the Highlands were logged mercilessly for fuel for the iron industry. Photographs of Ringwood at the end of the nineteenth century show the hillsides with hardly a tree standing. Wood to make charcoal was so scarce in the 1830s that the Morris Canal from the Delaware River to the Hackensack River was dug to bring in Pennsylvania coal to fuel the iron furnaces. According to state records, the destruction of Highlands forests reached its peak between 1850 and 1860. The New Jersey iron industry succumbed to competition from the open pit mines of Minnesota and began to close down about 1880. Although the northern and central Highlands were considered unfit for farming, forests in the southern Highlands and the slopes of its narrow valleys were affected by the clearing of hillsides for dairy pasture and for commercial truck farms. Dairy farms continued to be worked in northern New Jersey until the 1950s, when improved highways permitted western New York milk producers to undersell Jersey farms. The abandonment of Highlands iron manufacture and farming left the harvested slopes free to become forests once again, through natural regeneration. Thus, the forest has returned and held its own against increasing development. According to reports of the New Jersey State Geologist, forests comprised 46% of state land in 1899. In 1987, it was 42%.

When a cultivated field is abandoned, wild plant life begins to re-establish itself in a regular pattern called succession. At first annual herbs appear, followed by perennials like goldenrod and aster. Later, trees such as red cedar or gray birch establish themselves. These pioneer species then provide shade and shelter for the young saplings of red maple, wild black cherry, and sassafras, taller species that eventually shade out the pioneers. Subsequently, oak and tulip poplar move in, and in 50 or 60 years, or up to 100 years, the field has become a forest. Hikers who see a grassy hillside dotted with short triangular red cedars can surmise that ten or twenty years ago that field was either an open pasture or under cultivation, and will eventually become forest again. There are no old growth forests left in the Highlands; what we see from the trails are forests in one stage or another of successional growth.

Under the best growing conditions, forest trees like red oak or red maple will grow to a thickness of perhaps two and a half feet in about a century. If you walk through a forest on a south-facing moist upland slope and see that the oaks, maples, or beeches have trunks no more than a foot or so thick, you can suppose that this forest was seeded 50 or 60 years ago, perhaps after the slope had been clearcut or burned over, and, is now in the first few decades of succession from a cultivated field. Immature forests of slender trees will be bare of fallen trunks on the forest floor. Only after the trees have reached a mature height and thickness, are they subject to the hazards of destruction from storms and age. The absence of blowdowns is an indication of the youthfulness of a forest.

Occasionally along the trail you may see a tree with four or five large trunks growing out of a wide, old stump. Some trees like red maples and red oaks have the capacity to send up new shoots from existing roots when the trunk is cut, burned, or toppled. The resulting growth is called a coppiced tree and can reach surprising height and width. On the first climb up the Bearfort Ridge Trail (Hike #32), we passed a coppiced red maple with five trunks, each about two feet in diameter, approaching 100 years of age. By drawing an imaginary circle through the center of each trunk, we could estimate that the original tree from which they grew was about five feet in diameter, or close to 200 years old, when it was felled 100 years ago. We were looking at trees whose roots first took hold well before the American Revolution. It is an interesting romantic speculation to imagine a colonist in 1750 gazing at Bearfort Mountain covered with such trees five feet thick and 150 feet high. Here and there in the Highlands, a few individual old growth trees do survive. In the Farny Highlands,

The largest of the five trunks of this coppiced red oak on the Echo Lake West Trail is about 16 inches in diameter. The base trunk from which it grows was originally more than four feet in diameter, close to two hundred years old when it was logged perhaps 60 or 70 years ago.

the well-known Sentinel Oak on the shore of Split Rock Reservoir, two miles from the end of the Split Rock Loop (Hike #35), is five feet in diameter.

Years ago, on the Echo Lake East Through Hike (Hike #12), in a mixed oak forest about 50 or 60 years old, we passed a white oak four feet thick growing beside a tumbled stone fence. Its branches occupied a horizontal space greater than the height of the tree. It could not have sent limbs out so far if it had grown next to other trees in a forest. It must have grown unobstructed in an open field, and for that reason such a tree is called a pasture tree, or sometimes a "wolf tree." It is a sure sign that the land it grows on was an open farm field during the time it reached maturity, perhaps 175 to 200 years ago. The forest has since grown up around the tree, and the wide horizontal limbs have been shaded out and have fallen off, leaving their large stubs on the trunk. The tree's rounded crown has grown straight up, seeking the sun among the surrounding tall trees. It doesn't look much like a pasture tree today, but the evidence of its history is lying on the forest floor around it. Historians say that the glaciated northern end of the Highlands was unsuitable for farming, and this is generally true. But every once in a while along the trail, you will pass evidence, either man-made or natural, that tells you this was not entirely so, that on a few wide, level ridgetops with a water supply, farming continued until as late as 60 or 70 years ago.

With a little practice, the hiker can learn to recognize the main forest types in the Highlands: the swamp forest of red maple, yellow birch, and hemlock; the moist upland mixed oak forest; the hemlock-mixed hardwood forest; the sugar maple-mixed hardwood forest; the dry upland chestnut oak forest; and the ridgetop pitch pine and scrub oak forest. Each plant community has its characteristic understory trees, shrubs, and herbaceous ground plants, which you can identify and fit into their expected places. You will know you have become an experienced woods walker when you begin to notice things that break the pattern. We are great believers in watchful hiking; not strolling, but as you walk at a good pace, focusing so that your curious eyes and ears can enjoy what the woodlands have to show you.

Wildlife Along the Highlands Trails

In the detailed descriptions of these hikes, we occasionally mention animals we have seen along the trails. We don't expect them to be waiting for you at exactly that same spot when you walk by, but we do think it's important for you to know that beautiful and surprising wildlife is part of the hiking experience. The hills swarm with animals; to list them all, large and small, would be overwhelming. We have seen over a hundred species of birds, to say nothing of mammals, reptiles, amphibians, butterflies, and other insects. Among the animals you are most likely to see, some of the more interesting ones we describe here, telling where, when, and under what circumstances we encountered them.

It is our experience that woodland animals prefer to have nothing to do with people, even kind-hearted hikers who have the sympathetic impulse to speak softly to them and pet them gently. Touching or feeding a wild animal is never a good idea; many carry diseases, parasites, and secretions that are unhealthy to humans, and most of them live in places you would not want to touch, even with a long walking stick. When encountered, these animals, large and small, normally will "leave at their own chosen speed," unless they are provoked. Let them go, and be happy for glimpses. The line between the human and the wild, though approachable and fascinating, can be crossed only at the peril of both sides.

M A M M A L S

The **black bear** in New Jersey has proliferated in the past two decades, and as a consequence there are more recorded encounters with people, both in the woods and near houses and towns. They eat small animals, fish, carrion, nuts, insects from rotting stumps, the

A black bear photographed near a Highlands trail. Encounters between bears and hikers are becoming more common. Bears are not normally aggressive, but hikers should become familiar with safe behavior toward them.

inner layer of tree bark, brushy vegetation, and fruit, and have learned to steal birdseed from feeders and food from garbage cans. In the fall, they search more aggressively for food before seeking winter shelter and becoming dormant in forest caves, hollow trees, and brush piles. They are mostly nocturnal, but do move around during the day, particularly near dusk. Females are very protective of cubs in the spring, when they emerge from their winter den. In the past decade, we have met three bears on the trail during daylight. One, a yearling of about 150 pounds, emerged in mid-afternoon from the thick brush below the wingdam of Wawayanda Lake as we sat on the bridge watching birds. He crossed the brook about ten feet from us, but was intent on following his nose toward food at a park campsite and paid us no attention whatsoever. Friends and colleagues have told us of other harmless trail encounters.

The only aggressive bear behavior in the woods toward someone we know came about in spring, when a lone hiker's small dog barked at a couple of cubs, and the sow moved to protect her offspring. The hiker, a woman, did not turn and run, which would have indicated she was prey; instead she faced the bear, stretched as tall as she could, and made a lot of noise. The bear stopped between the dog and her cubs, and eventually moved away with them into the woods. A few aggressive bear encounters reported in newspapers have been associated with the behavior of dogs, which may be one reason for the state park rules requiring that dogs, where permitted on trails, be kept on six-foot leashes. That incident also suggests that hiking alone in the deep woods is unwise; for many reasons, you are safer in a group.

Here are some suggestions about encountering a bear on the trail:

> As you walk, make some noise; talk to your companions. Making noise lets a bear know you are nearby, and it will most likely avoid you.

> If you see a bear, keep your distance. People are not part of a bear's diet, but if you have food or items that smell like food,

a bear may approach. It may snap its jaws, make a "huff" noise, or swat the ground. These are warnings, not a sign that the bear is going to attack.

Stay calm and don't run. A bear can easily outrun you. Avoid eye contact, stand up tall, back up slowly, and, in a calm, firm voice, tell the bear to go away.

Do not climb a tree. Bears are excellent climbers. Instead, move slowly to a car or building if one is nearby.

Do not play dead. Remember that black bears eat dead things.

Never feed a bear. Bears that learn to associate food with people can become dangerous and may have to be destroyed.

The **white-tailed deer** has recovered from its early twentieth-century decline, caused, according to some observers, by over-hunting, and according to others, the elimination (by a fungal blight) of its favorite food, the American chestnut. The New Jersey herd has grown to such numbers that it is now often found grazing in suburban gardens. For the hiker, deer are a common sight in the woods. Fertile females produce one or two reddish-brown and white-spotted fawns in the spring. Deer tracks are a two-inch split oval hoof-mark. Bucks often scrape the bark from small trees, practicing fighting moves and strengthening their neck muscles. A deer is usually nervous at the smell and sound of people, and flees quickly, raising the white underside of its tail to wave goodbye. However, we met with an unusually curious first-year buck, which approached us to within ten feet on the Mahlon Dickerson Reservation: Highlands Trail— Headley Overlook Through Hike (Hike #7). We stopped and spoke quietly to him as he walked toward us, stood for a few minutes, showed us his new fur-covered antlers, and then walked slowly away, as if he'd just passed the time of day with a neighbor. Antlered bucks have been known to run at moving cars, so hikers should make no moves to provoke them. Along with the white-footed mouse, the

This young buck approached to within ten feet of us in Mahlon Dickerson Reservation. Close encounters with wild animals should be avoided whenever possible.

white-tailed deer is a host for the Lyme disease tick and bacterium.

Beavers are found once again in the Highlands. There was an active beaver pond at the dam of Buckabear Pond on the Buckabear Pond Loop (Hike #14), one in the marsh at the north end of the Ryker Lake Circle (Hike #9), and another six miles into the woods on the Split Rock Loop (Hike #35). Beavers are active year-round at dusk and at night, so day hikers are not likely to see them. But their lodges of mud and branches, sometimes reaching a diameter of twenty feet, stick up out of the water in a six-foot dome. Around the edges of their ponds, saplings and small trees lie felled, with conical stumps roughened by tooth marks. If the trees have been felled recently, the bare wood will be light yellow; if the wood is gray, the beavers have probably gone to a new pond.

Other mammals we have seen along the trail:

Raccoon (common, mostly nocturnal)

Red Fox (uncommon, nocturnal, except in winter, especially in snow, when it may appear during the day)

Coyote (now spread to the east through Canada, nocturnal, but we saw one trotting along a woodland edge in the early afternoon)

Striped Skunk (common, nocturnal)

Beavers are nocturnal animals, and hikers rarely see them, but their handiwork will be noticed on many trails near water. Beavers have girdled this stout red oak sapling near Ryker Lake. They will probably wait for the wind to blow the tree over.

A woodchuck, sometimes called the Eastern marmot, photographed near a Highlands trail.

Opossum (fairly common, nocturnal)

Woodchuck (common, mostly found in fields, roadsides, and open spaces)

Little Brown Bat (common, nocturnal) Most likely to be seen swooping quickly after insects at dusk.

Gray Squirrel (very common) Out and about during the day, nests in trees.

Red Squirrel (uncommon, smaller than gray squirrel)

Chipmunk (common) Out during the day, has a little chirpy "bark" that can sound like a bird, lives in round burrows in the ground.

Eastern Cottontail Rabbit (common) Out during the day, prefers open fields to woods.

Mammals can carry rabies, a serious disease for humans. Do not feed squirrels or rabbits, or any wild animals, no matter how cute and friendly they seem; they may bite your finger accidentally as they chew. Rabid animals lose their natural fears and act strangely. A nocturnal animal out in full daylight is exhibiting unusual behavior; give it a wide berth. If you are bitten, see a doctor immediately.

REPTILES

Ten to twenty years ago, scientists were concerned about the gradual decline of the populations of reptiles and amphibians; they suspected it was a sign of habitat deterioration for all species of animals. Whether the efforts of conservation organizations have been successful, or some natural cause has intervened, it is our impression that some of these animals are beginning to return to their woodland habitats. Last year, we saw more of them than the year before, and this year noticeably more than last. This is not a scientific sample, but it's good enough for encouraging conversation.

SNAKES
In the Highlands, only two snakes are venomous: the timber rattler, and the copperhead. We have not seen any rattlers, but we have come across two mature copperheads sleeping in the cracks of a rock outcrop. Trail builders have reported rattlesnake dens far from the trails on Windbeam Mountain and Ramapo Ridge.

> **Timber Rattler.** A very rare, thick, 4½ or 5-foot venomous gray snake, with dark, curvy marks outlined in light gray on its back. Its head is triangular, unmarked, and larger than its body. It has a dark tail with hard rings that rattle as a warning when alarmed. It is usually not aggressive. It lives on rocky upland hillsides, and stays away from human activity.
> **Copperhead.** A rare, wrist-thick, 2½-4 foot (maximum), orange-brown venomous snake with hourglass markings: narrow on

A timber rattler photographed near a trail on Kittatinny Mountain, to the northwest of the Highlands. Photo: Paul Tedesco

the back and broader along the sides. Its head is wider than its body. Usually very quiet, it likes to stretch out in cracks in sunny rock outcrops, but we have seen it coiled loosely beside the trail on moist ground under a bush. It is not aggressive, and unless you step on it or poke it with a stick, it will ignore you. On a rock outcrop viewpoint, we came upon two hikers eating their lunch contentedly, until we identified two copperheads sleeping in a long, deep crack a few feet from them. We all left, quickly and quietly, as we should, but the hikers could probably have finished their lunch without being interrupted by the snakes. These snakes will normally flee from people; if you come upon one in the middle of a trail, stand still to give the snake a chance to move away, and give it a very wide berth as you quietly walk on.

Black Rat Snake. Fairly common. This long (4+ feet), dark gray snake can wriggle up a steep slippery rock faster than most hikers can climb. After swallowing a meal of a rodent, it will coil quietly under a bush and be still.

A black rat snake near a trail in the Highlands. Notice the white patch under its chin. This snake is not poisonous; it is a constrictor that eats small rodents. Photo: Paul Tedesco

Northern Water Snake. A dark brown, fairly heavy snake with reddish black-edged bands encircling its body. If seen at all, it will be found along the shoreline of a lake or pond, swimming with only its head above water.

Common Garter Snake. A very common snake, small and slender with three yellow stripes from head to tail and black spots along its side.

TURTLES

Painted Turtle. This small, colorful red, yellow, and black turtle is fairly common; it can be seen basking in the summer sun on logs and rocks in Highlands ponds.

Common Snapping Turtle. These large muscular turtles thrive in the muddy bottoms of Highlands ponds. They don't usually bask on the edges, but we have seen some swimming, heads just above the water. When provoked, they are aggressive. Some say they will bite, others say no, but that jaw is big and powerful, so if you do see one don't fool with it.

Eastern Box Turtle. In recent years we have seen only one of these beautiful yellow-marked woodland turtles, walking across a trail in early morning. Sixty years ago it was fairly common, but since then this turtle has declined so much that it has become rare.

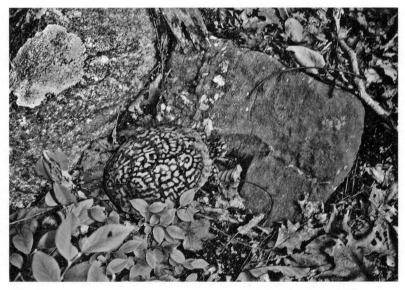

This box turtle was crossing the Split Rock Loop Trail while we were hiking north. It had been a long time since we had seen one, as their population has declined.

AMPHIBIANS

Eastern Newt. This red-spotted salamander begins life as an aquatic, legless, gilled larva, becomes for 1-3 years an air-breathing four-legged land-dwelling red eft, and finally matures into a four-legged aquatic animal. It is in the eft stage, as a narrow 3- to 4-inch smooth-skinned orange land animal (with 10-12 black ringed spots) that hikers will see this salamander along the trail in late spring and summer, particularly on moist days.

Yellow-Spotted Salamander. This 7-inch mole salamander breathes through lungs and lives in moist soil under logs and stones. It is increasingly scarce, and is likely to be found only accidentally under rocks and alongside lakes and ponds. We have seen only one in the past few years, under a rock we kicked over beside Echo Lake.

A red eft seen on the white trail near Terrace Pond.

American Toad found along the Otter Hole Trail (Hike #18), in the Wyanokies near Weis Ecology Center.

American Toad. A gray-brown toad with black spots on its back, some of those spots having small raised warts. Found in leaves and hopping across trails in upland woods. Touching or picking up the toad may irritate the skin of some people, though it has not affected the author, as you can tell from the picture.

Green Frog. Uncommon, but returning. These small, 2-inch inhabitants of woodland brooks declined in numbers in the second half of the twentieth century, but we have seen a few more of them lately. They are a shiny, greenish-gray color with black spots, and a kind of flat raised band extending from the neck down along the back. They live in water and swim quickly to hide under rocks whenever people come near.

BIRDS

We love the many species of birds that live in or pass through the Highlands, but we aren't birdwatchers who keep lists. We are hikers who delight in the sights and sounds of birds when we come upon them. We admit paying more attention to birds with beautiful colors or lovely songs than to the crows and buzzards. But there are so many wonderful birds in these woods, we find many occasions to stop, listen, and look. We report here on some of the interesting birds we have seen or heard on hikes in this book. You may see and hear many other birds we don't discuss. We urge you to take a birder's field guide into the woods, and see if you can identify species we have passed over.

MIGRANT WATER BIRDS

The spring migration of water birds begins in March and continues through April. They land to rest and feed in large ponds and lakes, and some of our hikes place you near bodies of water where you are likely to see them, such as Echo Lake (Hikes #11 and #12), Monksville Reservoir (Hike #29), Deer Park Pond (Hike #20), and Split Rock Reservoir (Hikes #19 and #35). You can look for these birds whenever you pass a large body of water during migration seasons.

Breeding Migrant Water Birds: April–October

Great Blue Heron. Our largest and, some would say our most beautiful wading bird, fairly common, fishing on long stilt-like legs along the shores of streams, ponds, and lakes. Some blue herons over-winter in New Jersey.

Great Egret. A large, completely white bird, with long stilt-like legs, also fairly common in marshes and along lakes, shores, and ponds.

Green Heron. A smaller heron, dark green on back and wings, brown on the neck, increasingly to be seen on the marshy shores and islands of ponds and lakes.

Migrant Ducks:
March-May, September-October

DABBLERS
This group of ducks feed by turning their rumps up and their heads down under the water to find aquatic vegetation.

Mallard. Our most common dabbler. Mallards breed in many Highlands lakes and ponds. The male has a dark green head; the female is a mottled brown. Both have a small patch of dark blue hidden at the back of their wings.

Green-winged Teal. Occasional during migration

Blue-winged Teal. Occasional during migration

A male mallard in breeding plumage has an iridescent green head and a bright yellow bill. Mallards are our most common breeding duck.

DIVERS

These ducks swim underwater to feed on small aquatic animals and plants.

Ring-necked Duck. The most common Highlands migrant diver. Male has a white ring around its bill, a dark purple head, and a large comma-shaped white patch at its shoulder.

Bufflehead. Common, our smallest diver. The male has a dark green head with a white patch at the back of the neck, a black back, and a white chest and under parts. From a distance, it looks mostly white, with dark head and back.

Ruddy Duck. Frequent, but not common. In breeding plumage, the male's back is reddish brown, the top part of the head is black, the lower part white, and the bill is a light grayish blue.

Common Merganser. Frequent, but not common.

Red-breasted Merganser. Occasional.

Hooded Merganser. Uncommon, but uncommonly beautiful when its white hood is spread.

Common Goldeneye. Occasional.

Wood Duck. This uncommon migratory duck may perch in trees alongside ponds and lakes. The male has a very colorful head, decorated in iridescent greens, purple, blues, with white streaks, a wide laid-back crest, and red bill.

RESIDENT RAPTORS

Red-tailed Hawk. A frequently heard and seen raptor, with a "keeeerr" cry. In mature plumage, its red tail is broad, fan-shaped in flight, and narrow and long when perched.

Bald Eagle. Uncommon, but increasing. Our largest raptor, with a six-foot wingspan. In mature plumage it has a brown body and wings, a white head and neck, and broad white tail. Most often seen circling high on thermals, wings straight and motionless. Now breeding in the Highlands. We startled one roosting on a tall tree as we walked in the afternoon along the

A juvenile red-tailed hawk perched on a bare branch beside a Highlands trail.

north edge of Echo Lake.

American Kestrel. Uncommon. Our smallest hawk, crow-sized, but very colorful, with orange back, gray wings, pale breast, and black neck stripes. Prefers open fields and valleys. We see two or three each year, recently one on the Ringwood Manor Loop (Hike #5).

Great Horned Owl. Nocturnal, but sometimes seen during the day.

Barred Owl. Nocturnal, hoots at dusk: "Who cooks for you? Who cooks for you-all?" Heard several times near the trailhead of Terrace Pond (Hike #27).

PERCHING BIRDS, COLORFUL SONGSTERS

Migrants Passing Through: April-May, September-October

Rose-breasted Grosbeak. Uncommon. This may be the most

beautiful East Coast bird, in color, and especially in song. Its striking mark is a deep fuchsia triangle at the top of its light gray or white breast. It has a big pale conical beak, black head and back, white rump, and black wings with small white patches and one white wing bar. Seen from the rear or flying away, it is simply a black and white bird. Its song is a melodic flute-like serenade; once heard, you will never forget it. The female looks like a large sparrow, but its big conical beak helps to identify it. A pair used to nest near Laurel Pond in Wawayanda State Park (Hike #3); after a few years of absence, we heard two birds (both males and females sing) singing for territory there from the tops of tall pines along the Laurel Pond shore. Though we stayed a long while and tried hard, we could not catch a glimpse of them. We also heard grosbeaks singing, and saw several, on the west shore of Ryker Lake (Hike #9). We heard one along the forest edge on Pyramid Mountain (Hike #6), but couldn't see that one at all.

Warblers. A wide variety of these small, often yellowish, active birds that flutter through trees and bushes as they pass through the Highlands during spring and fall migration. They have mostly high-pitched squeaky, buzzy or twittery calls; their colors are often spectacular. Every spring we have seen a variety of warblers, including yellow rumps, black-and-whites, redstarts, yellow warblers, and northern waterthrushes, along the brook flowing from the wingdam at Wawayanda Lake. Identifying warblers by sound and sight is a common game among outdoors people. We urge you to get a field guide to birds, and try your luck. We love these pretty birds and enjoy the identification game, but for some reason we don't have the talent to become really expert at it. We always see or hear more warblers than we can identify at a spring bird site, so we do have to be very certain when we claim to know the name of a bird we notice.

Indigo Bunting. Uncommon. A beautiful sparrow-sized bird of the finch family. The male's body is a deep iridescent blue all over. The female is a brown sparrow-looking bird with no wing bars or eye stripes, with the typical finch's conical beak. Books say they breed in the Highlands, but they nest in open brushy slopes or meadows with no trees, and there isn't much of that habitat to be found on our hikes. However, we have often seen them during spring migration on the ridgetops and along forest edges, most recently on Pyramid Mountain (Hike #6) and Wyanokie High Point (Hike #18).

Eastern Bluebird. Fairly common during migration. The male is blue on its back, rusty like a robin on its throat, breast, and sides, with a small patch of white on its lower belly. The female is similar, but its colors seem suffused with brown, particularly from a distance. New Jersey bird counts confirm that their numbers are increasing. They breed in our area, and we have seen some nesting; they prefer open level fields with scattered trees, and won't nest in the forested mountains. As you drive on country roads in the Highlands, you may see bluebird nest boxes in fallow fields near the hills. In April or May, you might pull over and stop to see if they are occupied. We often find bluebirds on the ridgetops during spring migration. They move in small flocks of a dozen or so, and usually pass through very early in the season; we have seen them in the first week of February.

Colorful Migrants Nesting in the Highlands: Spring to Fall

Baltimore Oriole. Fairly common. The male is a gorgeous bird with black throat, head and back, black wings with white streaks and one white wing bar; the rest of the body is flame-orange. In size, it varies from a little larger than a sparrow, to almost robin-sized. Its song is a lovely melodic whistle. Orioles nest in trees in woods and near houses, and like to sing as they move steadily upward, climbing through leaves to the tree tops.

Scarlet Tanager. Uncommon. The male is a striking, almost iridescent, bright red sparrow-sized bird with black wings and tail. Its song sounds like the repeated "cheery-up" of the robin, but raspy, as if it had a sore throat. Although scarce, it isn't shy. It likes to make itself visible on an exposed bare branch and sing for a while without moving, as if giving a performance. We saw one singing its heart out on a tall snag near the parking lot of Pyramid Mountain (Hike #6), another on a bare branch in the deep woods coming down from Buck Mountain (Hike #26), and two the same day on a woods edge near Terrace Pond (Hike #27). We see about three or four every year on Highlands trails, and hear perhaps a dozen others that we never see.

Red-winged Blackbird. Common. Nests near water among reeds and shrubs, arriving in early spring. Song: "choncharreee." The male's wing has a small, bright red patch near the shoulder, often with a similar yellow streak just below it.

Eastern Towhee. Uncommon. Numbers down in past years, but increasing recently. A robin-sized woodland bird; the male is black on the throat, head, back and wings, with a white belly and rusty dark orange sides. The tail has white streaks on each side, which flash as it flies away. The female is similar, except where the male is black it is brown. Its song sounds like "drink your tea," and its call is a shrill whistle, "tweee," which gives it its name. It frequents low limbs of woodland secondary trees and shrubs, and forages in the underbrush. We have heard five or six each year for the past two years, and have seen one or two. Our most recent sighting was on Pyramid Mountain (Hike #6).

Year-Round Residents, Colorful and Cheerful

Wild Turkey. Turkey numbers are increasing, the bird having been re-introduced by the New Jersey Department of Environmental Protection in 1977. They are now often found strutting through the woods, sometimes in flocks of twelve to twenty. They will fly quite well when surprised. Because there are such a large number of them, the state has established turkey-hunting seasons in fall and spring. These birds are not stupid; they know how to stay hidden, and are not often fooled by artificial turkey calls.

Blue Jay. Common. This beautiful blue and white streaked bird, with perky crest and screechy voice, prefers to live near towns, where feeders help them through the winter. But you will also hear and see them in the woods.

Mockingbird. Common. A robin-sized, gray-backed bird, with white wing bars, a pale belly, and white streaks on its long tail.

These wild turkeys have spread their tail feathers in a courting gesture.

It is one of the few birds that will sing loudly in the dark of night, especially on moonlit spring nights, sometimes for hours. Its beautiful song includes amazing imitations of other species, usually repeated four or more times.

Cardinal. Common. Our lovely all-red bird (male), with crest and big conical red bill. The female is also beautiful, though with subtler coloring: a buff-brown body tinged with red, and an orange bill. The male has several pretty whistled songs, including the repetitive "What cheer, cheer, cheer, cheer" and the 2-note "birdy, birdy." He will announce spring early, at the first real thaw, hopping to the top of a tall tree to let his lady and the world know what he's thinking. Cardinals are happy living near people, but some of them remain in the woods. A striking winter scene is to see a blue jay and a cardinal foraging together on top of new snow.

Tufted Titmouse. Common. A small gray bird with a lighter breast, a crest on its head, and a surprisingly loud whistling voice. The song, a repeated "peter, peter, peter, peter," is heard all year, and is a welcome cheerful sound on a cold winter morning. It forms small flocks with chickadees and juncos in winter, foraging through bushes together.

Black-capped Chickadee. Common. A small bird with black throat, head and neck, white cheeks and upper breast, buffy sides and lower belly, and gray wings and tail. Its colors always seem bright and new, and it's a hopping, flittery bird when winter weather gives it a chance. One of its vocalizations is its name, "chick-a-dee-dee-dee;" another is a plaintive, drawn out, tiny "feeee-beee." It forms small flocks with titmice and juncos in winter, flitting through bushes together.

Dark-eyed Junco. Common. A small dark-gray bird with a white belly and a slender white stripe along each side of its tail, that shows when it flies. It forms small active flocks with titmice and chickadees in winter.

White-breasted Nuthatch. Common. This small perky bird typically climbs down tree trunks head first in its search for insects. The male has a black head, a white face dotted with tiny dark eyes, a white breast, and blue-gray back. The female is similar but its head is blue-gray. Its song is a repeated note on one tone, something like what you might expect from a woodpecker, but smaller and higher, "whi whi whi whi whi . . ." many times, echoing shrilly through the woods.

American Goldfinch. Common. New Jersey's state bird. A small, bright yellow bird with a black cap, wings, and tail. It has an excited song, "perchicory, perchicory," often sung in flight. In fall and winter, its golden feathers become dusky olive gray. One of the first signs of spring is to see, in late January and early February, the goldfinch's feathers begin to turn gold again.

WOODPECKER SPECIES

Downy Woodpecker. Common. Year-round resident. A small, 6-inch bird with white back, black wings with white spots, white belly, and black/white striped head. Male has a small red patch at the back of its head.

Red-bellied Woodpecker. Common. Year-round resident. A robin-sized woodpecker, with black and white striped "ladder-back," and a buff belly. Male has a wide red stripe from forehead to base of neck. Female has a smaller red stripe at the back of the neck. Call, a whirring "Chirrrr."

Hairy Woodpecker. Uncommon. Exactly like the downy, except a couple of inches longer.

Pileated Woodpecker. Uncommon. Year-round resident. Spectacular and very large (up to 20 inches). This is the large red-crested, big-billed woodpecker exaggerated in movie cartoons. Its back is black, and its rump white. Its forward underwing feathers are white. It appears black and white as it flies.

The male's red crest is very tall. Its sound is a loud repeated "kik-kik-kik-kik …," similar to the flicker's, but in uneven rhythm. Within its territory, in trunks of dead and dying trees you will see large squarish holes, 3-4 inches high, 2 inches wide, and 2 inches deep. No other bird makes such holes. We have seen the bird's holes on most of our hikes, and heard it often, but have actually sighted it only a few times in the past two years.

Common Flicker. A once-common resident migrant, now declining in numbers. A large bird (12 inches), it has a brown back with black bars and spots, a broad black bib above a buff breast spotted with black, a long bill, and a telltale white rump which is visible as it flies away. The male has a red patch at the nape of its neck. Its song is a loud and long repeated "wick-wick-wick-wick."

A pileated woodpecker, with its tall red crest, is a startling sight in the woods. These birds are resident year-round in the Highlands.

Pink lady's slipper. Photo by Tina Schvejda, Morris Land Conservancy.

LADY'S SLIPPER

for Barbara

On the island, when I was a small kid,
there was a spot where a lady's slipper grew.
I knew it by its leaves, wide and close to the ground
on the wet bank in the moss,
but it never bloomed.

Oh, it grew each year, put out its leaves,
and I took a liking to it.
There was a special thing between me and that plant;
kids that small aren't supposed to care,
so I kept it to myself,
and believed in it every spring.

One year—I was much older—
I had a scratchy growth of beard—
it bloomed.
I saw it through two birch trees,
bounded by a laurel and the lake,
in a ray of sun, tall, slender, straight,
and I fought an impulse to run and tell the world
I told you so—that wasn't the point.
The important part was not seeing it bloom,
but all those years knowing what it was
without flowers.

—George Petty

from *The Chapbook*, a collection of prize-winning poems,
The Deep South Writers Conference, 1991

STARTER HIKES

Up to 4.3 miles, 3½ hours

Wildflower Walk and the Tourne Loop

2.0 miles • 1½ hours

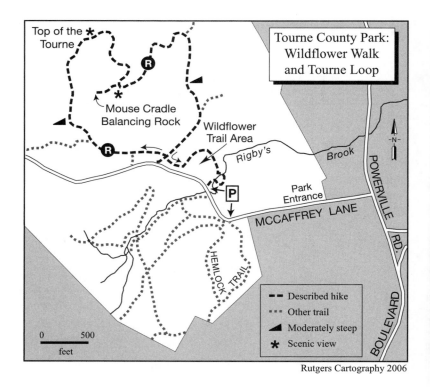

Top of the Tourne

Mouse Cradle Balancing Rock

Wildflower Trail Area

Rigby's

Brook

Park Entrance

MCCAFFREY LANE

POWERVILLE RD.

BOULEVARD

HEMLOCK TRAIL

Tourne County Park:
Wildflower Walk
and Tourne Loop

-N-

0   500
feet

- - Described hike
··· Other trail
◄ Moderately steep
* Scenic view

Rutgers Cartography 2006

ELEVATION: Low: 527 feet; High: 897 feet.

BLAZES: Red, unblazed, red again.

CLIMBING: A wide gravel path climbs steadily 370 feet to the top of the Tourne at an easy 10% grade and descends in a similar way on the opposite side of the hill.

PERMITTED USES: The Emily K. Hammond Wildflower Trail is for foot traffic only. About 0.2 mile up the mountain, the trail becomes a multi-use path for bikers and horses, although we have rarely seen horses on it.

OVERVIEW

This hike is a popular walk for families with kids, an exercise walk, or a jog with the dog. You will not feel alone in the deep woods on this trail. At the start, you will experience a nature walk through labeled examples of most of the native wildflowers and trees of the Highlands. Once past the Wildflower Trail area, you will see typical Highlands woodlands, gneiss rock outcrops and boulders, ridgetop bedrock smoothed by glaciers, and excellent long views both east to New York City and west across the Rockaway Valley to other hilltops. Check the trail map of the park for other hikes. Trail maps are usually available at a kiosk on the south side of the large parking lot on McCaffrey Lane, and can be obtained from the Morris County Park Commission, P.O. Box 1295, Morristown, NJ 07962-1295; (973) 326-7600, www.morrisparks.net.

ACCESS: From I-80 westbound, take Exit 42B (Parsippany/US 46) onto Cherry Hill Road. At the second traffic light, turn left onto US 46. At the second traffic light on US 46, turn right onto the Boulevard in Mountain Lakes.

From I-80 eastbound, take Exit 42C, continuing to the first traffic light at Parsippany Road, where you turn left toward US 46. At

US 46, turn left (west) and drive up Fox Hill to the third traffic light, where you turn right onto the Boulevard in Mountain Lakes.

On the Boulevard, drive 2.3 miles to a fork, where the Boulevard goes right and you bear left (carefully) across traffic. In 300 yards, you will see a sign on the right pointing to Tourne County Park. Turn left onto McCaffrey Lane and continue to a large parking lot on your right.

DETAILED DESCRIPTION

Walk 0.1 mile to the right downhill from the parking lot to a turnout for four cars on the right side of the road. You will see a triangle of three red blazes, which marks the trailhead of the Red Trail, near the gate in a fence put up to protect the wildflowers from deer. The Red Trail proceeds to the left (uphill) toward the top of the Tourne. Turn right, away from the Red Trail, on the other side of the gate, to begin

A snow trillium blooming beside the Wildflower Trail.

a walk through a native woodland wildflower and fern display carefully tended by local volunteers from the Rockaway Valley Garden Club. Flowers bloom throughout the summer and early fall, but are especially colorful in spring. The trail crosses and recrosses a brook on wooden bridges. After crossing the bridges, when there is an option, always take the right fork to see the best flowers. Not only flowers, but typical Highlands upland trees are labeled as well. Here, in spring, we have heard and seen some of our most colorful songbirds, both migrating and resident species. Flowers are most plentiful and migrating birds can be more easily seen when the trees have opened their leaf buds, but before the branches are densely covered. Early flowers can then still bask in the sun, and birds cannot hide themselves so completely in the foliage. The nature trail emerges at 0.3 mile onto a wide gravel road, the route of the Red Trail, where you turn right, and let yourself out through a gate in the fence.

The trail leads uphill (west) passing a junction where the return trail comes in on the right. As you climb at an easy 10% grade, you come to a fork at 0.5 mile. Here the red blazes head to the left, but you go to the right. A sign points to the "Top of the Tourne," and you now follow the unmarked DeCamp Trail uphill. You soon pass a typical Highlands gneiss rock outcrop on your right. The great Wisconsin Glacier of 15,000 years ago approached from the northwest, grinding the north-facing bedrock round and smooth on top, and plucking boulders from the south ends of ridges as it moved on. Often hikers will encounter loose boulders and steep, rough rock faces on the south slopes of Highlands hills, as you see here on this ledge. The glacier reached its southern limit a few miles south of this hill. As it retreated, it dropped a 250-foot-thick mound of sand, gravel, and boulders, known as a terminal moraine, on a line running through Dover and Morristown and down to Perth Amboy.

The forest on these slopes was logged at least two or three times between the Colonial years and the late nineteenth century, either to supply fuel for the thriving iron industry, or to clear land for farm-

A rough cliff face of gneiss bedrock on the south shoulder of the Tourne.

ing. Most large trees you see in these woods are between one and 1½ feet thick, indicating that the land was clear until perhaps 70 or 80 years ago, then abandoned to the natural regrowth of forest. The present woodland is typical Highlands dry upland oak-beech-hickory forest, with an understory of viburnum species, spice bush, shadbush, and both highbush and lowbush blueberry.

As it climbs, the trail bends around the side of the mountain; about halfway up, there is a bench for those who need a breather. At 0.9 mile, a view opens to the west over the Rockaway Valley toward Bald Hill and Green Pond Mountain beyond. The trail reaches the top of the Tourne at 1.1 miles in a clearing where there are picnic tables and a rock outcrop with views to the south and east. Continue on the wide path over the crest, past a memorial to those lost in the attack on the World Trade Center twin towers, which were visible from that spot. From the memorial you have a good view of the Manhattan skyline to the east and northeast.

The trail winds down to the left, at 1.2 miles passing a group of shagbark and pignut hickories, whose nuts you might notice on the pathway. As the trail bends back down to the right, you may find some seasonal wet spots and take note that the trees are larger on this side of the hill, perhaps because of extra moisture on the north face. At 1.8 miles, the trail reaches the intersection where you started to climb. You may retrace your steps to the left through the gate onto the Red Trail, or continue out to the road, turn left, and walk on the pavement. Either way will bring you back to the parking lot after a hike of 2.0 miles.

Overlook to the west toward Bald Hill and Green Pond Mountain.

Wildcat Ridge Loop

2.3 miles • 1½ hours

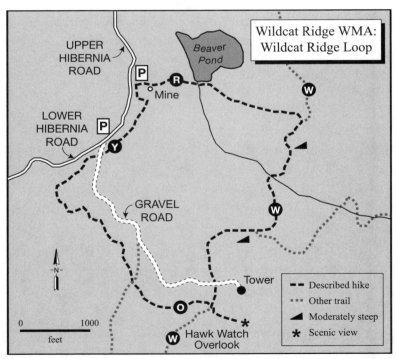

Wildcat Ridge WMA:
Wildcat Ridge Loop

UPPER
HIBERNIA
ROAD

Beaver
Pond

Mine

LOWER
HIBERNIA
ROAD

GRAVEL
ROAD

-N-

0   1000
feet

Tower

Hawk Watch
Overlook

- - Described hike
· · · Other trail
◀ Moderately steep
✳ Scenic view

Rutgers Cartography 2006

ELEVATION: Low: 755 feet; High: 1,045 feet.

BLAZES: Red, white, orange, yellow.

CLIMBING: Most of this walk has very gradual ascents and descents. On the Four Birds Trail, from the end of the Beaver Pond Trail to the Hawk Watch overlook, the trail descends 140 feet in 0.2 mile to a stream hollow and climbs back up to Wildcat Ridge, a moderate gain of 290 feet in 0.5 mile.

PERMITTED USES: Hiking only.

OVERVIEW

An easy walk past a beaver pond to the Wildcat Ridge Hawk Watch overlook, with a wide view of the Rockaway Valley and much of the Farny Highlands. You will find interesting seasonal wildflowers and birds, and glimpses of relics of the Hibernia Iron Mines, which were active during and after the Civil War.

ACCESS: From I-80, take Exit 37 (Rockaway/Hibernia) and turn left (north) toward Hibernia at the exit ramp onto County 513 (Green Pond Road). Drive 6.4 miles, passing the Green Pond Golf Course on your left. Opposite the Marcella Community Center, turn right onto Upper Hibernia Road. Drive 2.5 miles to the end of the paved road, turning into a gravel parking turnout on the left.

DETAILED DESCRIPTION

A loop hike including the Wildcat Ridge Hawk Watch lookout begins just past a private driveway at the east side of the parking area, on a woods road. The three red blazes of the trailhead of the Beaver Pond Trail are found immediately on a large boulder on the right side of the road. Watch for a Brown Hawk Watch binoculars logo. If

Ruins of Hibernia #12, the last working iron mine in the Highlands. It closed in 1920.

you look into the woods on your right, you will see decaying structures, the remains of the old Hibernia Iron Mine #12. This last oper-
ating mine of the Hibernia complex closed in 1920, leaving a small
city with a hotel, railroad repair yards, houses for officials and work-
ers, and a cemetery, all abandoned to the return of forest.

At 0.1 mile, the trail passes on the left a berm with mine tailings,
and then comes upon Beaver Pond, also on the left. On the far side of
the pond, red blazes show that the trail turns right into the woods on
a footpath and begins a slight climb. The trail passes several rock outcrops with broken boulders on the left. The woods here are relatively new growth, with few trees more than six inches in diameter,
suggesting this might have been cleared land as late as the 1940s.

After 0.5 mile of easy walking, the red trail ends at an intersection with the Four Birds Trail (white blazes). Turn right (south) on
the Four Birds Trail toward the Hawk Watch overlook. This trail
bends right, winds over a small rock outcrop and begins a moderate
descent of 140 feet into a hollow formed by the outlet stream from

Beaver Pond. After crossing the stream at 0.7 mile, the trail begins a 290-foot climb, moderated by the angling of the path to the right (west) across the contour of the hill. At 0.9 mile, the trail crosses a woods road. Near the top of the climb, the trail crosses a gravel access road leading to a communications tower up to the left. It reaches the summit of Wildcat Ridge at 1.2 miles, at an intersection with the Flyway Spur Trail (orange blazes). The Hawk Watch overlook, with excellent views to the east, is 0.1 mile to the left at the end of the Flyway Spur Trail. Local raptor enthusiasts often occupy the rock outcrop to observe and report on sightings of resident hawks and to count the amazing numbers of hawks drifting high overhead during migration periods. To the east from the viewpoint is Bald Hill, and to its left (north), the Tourne and Stony Brook Mountain. On a clear day, the New York City skyline is visible in the distance. We found interesting summer wildflowers, including woodland sunflowers,

Wildcat Ridge Hawk Watch overlook, with hiker Glenn Howanski, his son Stefan, and friend Ryan Tomasello.

mountain mint, and dittany, near the Hawk Watch site.

To complete the loop, return on the Flyway Spur Trail (orange blazes). The Flyway Spur Trail crosses the white-blazed Four Birds Trail at the kiosk, bears left at a fork with an unmarked path, and heads gently downhill on a footpath through mixed oak upland woods, with lowbush blueberry on the forest floor. At 1.5 miles, the trail crosses a wide woods road and passes through a laurel grove. After a short climb through a rock outcrop with broken boulders, you pass a pointed steel stake in the middle of the trail; this marks the old boundary of the lands belonging to the Hibernia Mines. At 1.8 miles, the trail crosses a shoulder of bedrock where the canopy is open to the sky, but long views are obscured by trees. As the trail begins a moderate descent, it passes several coppiced trees, with multiple trunks, each more than a foot thick, growing from one stump, suggesting that old growth trees were logged here perhaps 60 or 70 years ago.

During its gradual descent, the path parallels ditches that once held cast iron pipes bringing water for steam machinery used in the mine. At 2.1 miles, the trail reaches a gravel road from which the unpaved extension of Upper Hibernia Road is visible. Across the gravel road on a concrete block, three yellow blazes mark the trailhead of the short Connector Trail leading through the woods back to the parking area. Walk into the woods on this yellow trail, passing a large patch of raspberries, which ripen in early August. The trail passes ditches and excavations that were associated with iron mine activity, and finally comes upon the remaining structures of Mine #12. Here the trail turns left to avoid the ruins, then turns right, emerging at 2.3 miles near paved Upper Hibernia Road at the parking area where you left your car. Before leaving the parking area, examine its margins for interesting seasonal wildflowers.

Beaver Pond. Photo by Holly Szoke, Morris Land Conservancy.

Laurel Pond Loop

2.6 miles • 1½ hours

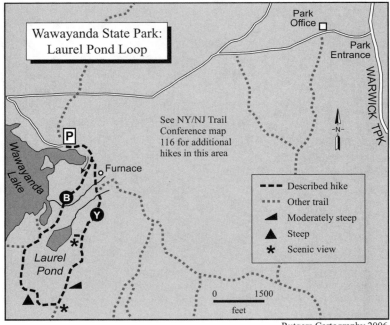

Wawayanda State Park:
Laurel Pond Loop

Park Office

Park Entrance

WARWICK TPK

See NY/NJ Trail Conference map 116 for additional hikes in this area

-N-

P

Furnace

B

Y

*

Wawayanda Lake

Laurel Pond

– – – Described hike

· · · · Other trail

◢ Moderately steep

▲ Steep

✳ Scenic view

0   1500
feet

Rutgers Cartography 2006

The blaze circles marked in primary colors (e.g., "R" for red) may represent a color on a white background (e.g., red triangle-on-white), as noted in the hike description.

ELEVATION: Low: 1,180 feet; High: 1,300 feet.

BLAZES: Plastic diamond blue-on-white logo, blue, yellow.

CLIMBING: One steep rocky climb of 100 feet and a few wet, muddy spots in rainy seasons.

PERMITTED USES: Trails in Wawayanda State Park west of Clinton Road, including the trails for this hike, are designated multi-use, which allows bicycles and horses. No motorized vehicles are permitted.

O V E R V I E W

A short, easy loop, beginning along Wawayanda Lake and near the end passing by the Wawayanda iron furnace. Mostly on wide old woods roads, it has one rocky steep climb to a grassy knoll with bedrock outcrops, and a return on a woods road that becomes muddy in wet weather. There is one partly obscured high westerly woodlands view and a spur trail to an overlook of pretty Laurel Pond. This hike is special for its spring wildflowers and birds. Near the end of the hike, in the swamp below a wooden bridge, we have more than once seen an oriole, a scarlet tanager, and a yellow warbler together on a small birch tree.

ACCESS: Head west on NJ 23 from the Kinnelon Road traffic light in Butler, and drive 5.8 miles to the Union Valley Road exit. Take Union Valley Road north to the second traffic light in West Milford, where it turns left and continues until it ends at Warwick Turnpike. Turn left and head west on Warwick Turnpike for 3.8 miles (passing Upper Greenwood Lake) to the Wawayanda State Park entrance on your left. From Memorial Day to Labor Day, there is an entrance fee, which you pay at a drive-by booth near the park office on the entrance road. From the booth, drive 1.8 miles until you see a turnoff for a large parking area beside the lake on the left, near the end of the paved road. Turn left to follow the parking entrance road past the first parking area, and park in a second area near a boat ramp used by fishermen. On warm summer weekends, the park can sometimes reach its capacity early in the day and then be closed to new entrants.

DETAILED DESCRIPTION

From the southeast end of the parking area (to the left as you face the lake), walk east (left) along a gravel road beside the lake. In spring, the roadside to the left here is covered with anemones and spring beauties. After 0.2 mile, you come to a fork, where the wide road goes left downhill toward a nineteenth-century iron furnace, and a small-er footpath heads to the right toward the wingdam. Take the path to the right, cross a new concrete dam, and on the other side, at 0.3 mile, find the trailhead of the Wingdam Trail, with its plastic diamond blue-on-white logo. The old painted blue rectangles are no longer being maintained.

The trail ahead is a wide woods road through a mixed oak and hardwood forest, with healthy stands of late June-blooming rhodo-dendron and small groves of dying hemlocks. Near the hemlocks, a group of mature sugar maples is beginning to produce many small saplings and in a decade or so might become a sugar maple forest. At 0.6 mile, the trail crosses a bridge over the outlet from the wingdam on your right, and soon Laurel Pond is visible through trees to the left. The trail next passes a woods road leaving to the right. As you go farther into the woods, the trail is more eroded and rocky. Along this section of trail in mid-May, we saw three varieties of violets, as well as starflowers and Indian cucumbers. At 0.9 mile, after passing another woods road leaving to the right, the trail bends left, at first on a woods road, then onto what once was a footpath, but is now an eroded swath almost as wide as a road. At 1.2 miles, the trail turns right and begins a steep 100-foot climb up a rocky, eroded path to a gneissic Highlands ridge. You reach the crest of the ridge at 1.4 miles. On the left of the trail in rocky crevices at the top, we found wild columbine in early May. In early April, on a grassy knoll well off the trail to the right, a few struggling plants of round-lobed hepatica may still survive. Hepatica is a lovely low plant, whose blossoms in shades of purple appear well before any spring leaves have opened.

This crest is the midpoint of the hike. From here, the blue-blazed Wingdam Trail climbs off the ridge to the left and ends at a T-intersection with the yellow-blazed Laurel Pond Trail. At this

Laurel Pond overlook amid dying hemlocks at the end of a spur trail.

The preserved Wawayanda Furnace, which used ore from nearby mines to produce iron ingots during the years from 1846 to 1857.

junction, just opposite the end of the Wingdam Trail, you can climb on top of a large boulder for a partially obscured outlook to the Wawayanda ridges to the southeast. You now follow the Laurel Pond Trail to the left (north) on a woods road, descending gradually through dense groves of laurel and rhododendron, which bloom in June: laurel first and then the larger-leaved rhododendron at the end of the month. Walking on the higher part of the trail is easy, but as you descend toward Laurel Pond, there are spots that will be muddy in spring and wet weather. At 1.8 miles, the trail reaches a plastic stake with a painted yellow rectangular blaze; this marks a spur trail to the left which leads in 0.1 mile, through low arching rhododendron, to a rock outcrop amid dying hemlocks on the high bank of Laurel Pond. In mid-May at this overlook, we heard two rose-breasted grosbeaks singing in the tops of trees, one on each side of the pond.

Returning to the yellow-blazed Laurel Pond Trail, continue left (northwest) downhill, passing two other unmarked spurs to the pond. You might slow down as you approach the brook that empties Laurel Pond and the dam spillway, because this is an excellent location for colorful birds. Every year, yellow warblers nest just upstream from the trail. As you cross the wooden bridge over the wingdam spillway at 2.3 miles, stop and look over the marsh to your right at a small gray birch tree, where we have often seen an oriole, a scarlet tanager, a rose-breasted grosbeak, a yellow warbler, and other colorful perching birds. They seem to congregate here, not all at once, of course, but sometimes two or three together at one time.

A little farther on, as the trail passes a mowed meadow and turns left uphill, you will see the well-preserved Wawayanda Furnace which, from 1846 to 1857, produced pig iron from ore mined at the nearby Wawayanda Mine. Continue uphill and retrace your steps to the right along Wawayanda Lake to reach the parking area and your car at 2.6 miles.

Rhinehart Loop

2.2 miles • 1½ hours

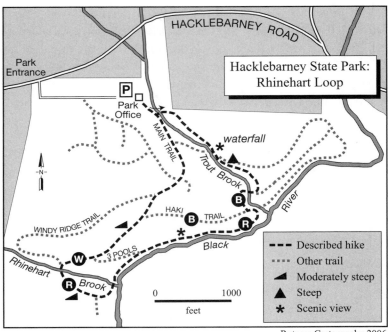

Rutgers Cartography 2006

ELEVATION: Low: 390 feet; High: 645 feet.

BLAZES: White on the Main Trail, unmarked, blue, red, and white to return.

CLIMBING: There is a steep descent of about 50 feet over large boulders past a waterfall. Along the banks of the Black River, trails lead through roots, rocks, and some wet spots. The trail back from Rhinehart Brook is a long gradual climb of about 250 feet on wide roads.

PERMITTED USES: Hacklebarney State Park is a very popular family recreation, fishing, and hunting area. The park has about six miles of hiking trails, which can be combined for hikes ranging from easy level walking to moderately strenuous exercise. About two-thirds of the park lands are reserved for hunting and are kept separate from the public access portion. The Lamington Natural Area section of the park protects the gorge of the Black River and endangered plant species. Fishermen can find secluded fishing sites downstream from busy picnic areas.

OVERVIEW

The centerpiece of the park is the boulder-strewn gorge of the Black River, with its smaller tributary brooks. This hike is an easy walk through the gorge on wide woods roads and some footpaths through upland forest, with a descent past a waterfall over large angular boulders, and some clambering on roots and rocks along the riverbank. In May, the wildflowers along the trails are plentiful and lovely. The scenery along Trout Brook and the Black River is spectacular at any season, and benches are placed at picturesque outlooks. All stream crossings are on wide, secure wooden bridges. Stretches along the river will require some stepping over boulders; during high water, they may be wet and muddy, sometimes even impassable. However, just above the riverbank path, there is always a wide, dry woods road on which you can avoid the water. Although you are in attractive Highlands terrain, you are never very far from a picnic table or a bench. Be sure to stop at the park office for a trail map. There are some shorter walks you may want to take as well.

ACCESS: From NJ 10, turn south onto County 513 and drive 8.3 miles to the picturesque Morris County town of Chester. In Chester at a main intersection with US 206, continue straight ahead for 1.2 miles on County 513 and NJ 24 heading toward Long Valley. Immediately after passing the Cooper Mill County Park on your left and crossing over the Black River, turn left onto State Park Road. Continue on State Park Road for 2 miles, where there is a junction with Hacklebarney Road. Make a sharp right at this junction, driving 0.3 mile to the entrance to Hacklebarney State Park on your left. The entrance road goes uphill and to the left for 0.2 mile, to a large parking lot. On warm weekends and during school vacations, the parking lot may be full, and the many picnic facilities crowded and busy. However, we visited the park on a weekday in early June and found it practically deserted, with only three cars in the vast parking lot.

TERRAIN AND HISTORY

The topography of the park is characteristic of the Highlands. The bedrock is Highlands gneiss, visible in outcrops along the high ridges bordering the Black River gorge. Large boulders with very sharp angular edges lie strewn down the hillsides around the falls of Trout Brook and the banks of the Black River. The Wisconsin Glacier did not reach this terrain, so the boulders don't show any rounding from glacial abrasion and can't have been carried here by the ice. Some boulders are the size of trucks, and there are so many, it seems likely they were thrown down by the enormous force of an earthquake.

The park is near the southern end of the Jersey Highlands

formation; its highest elevation is 804 feet. During the nineteenth century, it was an active site of iron mining. The moist soils around the river have fostered a few groves of mature hemlocks, which somehow escaped nineteenth-century logging for their tannin, but are now dying from the attack of an Asian invader, the woolly adelgid. Because the soils near the streams are rich and moist, wildflowers are plentiful during early spring.

DETAILED DESCRIPTION

From among the several trails, we have chosen a loop hike that offers the most spectacular scenery in the park. It also goes off the wide park roads onto footpaths that present a few natural obstacles, such as large boulders and rainy season wet spots that may require some physical fitness to negotiate. The scenery along Trout Brook and the Black River is spectacular and provides an ample reward for your efforts.

The hike begins at the park office, where you can pick up a trail map and find the Main Trail. The Main Trail is a wide road, paved for much of its length and blazed with white rectangles. After about 50 yards on the Main Trail, you turn left down wide steps to a bridge across Trout Brook, a tributary of the Black River, and then turn gradually to the right beside picnic tables and grills. In May, the ground here is covered with spring beauties, a low plant, with a five-petaled white flower, with pink streaks in each petal. The trail is an unmarked wide paved road, and as you begin to climb past the picnic grounds at 0.2 mile, you turn off the road to the right onto a rock outcrop with a view from the top of a waterfall on Trout Brook. After viewing the falls from the top, continue steeply down, picking your way over large boulders to the brookside where you can look back up into the cascade. You are now following an unblazed trail, denoted by a dotted line on the park map, and identified as a rocky

Trout Brook as it tumbles into the Black River.

footpath. If you don't want to climb the boulders, return to the wide road, and, 20 yards further on the right find a long stone stairway down to the brookside.

Notice the hillsides covered with large, sharp-edged boulders, some of which have fallen into the brook. The rocks are all from the gneiss bedrock, with small crystals of milky quartz and feldspar and dark crystals of hornblende compressed into faint parallel bands. There are no rocks brought by glaciers, as this is south of the Wisconsin Glacier terminal moraine. Several flat rocks near the brook offer close views of the waterfall. From the waterfall, the trail continues along the brook over fractured boulders, and, at 0.4 mile, it is blocked by a huge downed tree, whose roots lie in the brook and whose trunk stretches across the trail. You will have to either climb over the root end or crawl under the trunk. At 0.5 mile, the trail arrives at a sturdy wooden bridge across Trout Brook where blue blazes begin, after which the trail bends left downhill. Just a little further on, the trail comes to a T-intersection with a gravel road, where you turn left onto a red-blazed trail, pass another wooden bridge, and come to a picnic area with a comfort station and a plank bridge leading to a tiny island in the river. At the south end of the picnic area nearest the river, find a red-blazed footpath heading west (right) along the riverbank.

The trail along the riverbank clambers over boulders and runs through wet spots where at high water, in order to stay dry, you might either have to climb a few feet up the steep bank or use the gravel road which parallels the footpath higher up. Whenever possible, stay close to the rush of the river where the scenery is delightful. Along the river the forest is a mixed oak and beech hardwood community, with occasional dying hemlocks. At 0.8 mile, the trail comes to a wide woods road that forks up to the right, but there is also a red-blazed narrow footpath very close to the water. The wide upper road meets the red-blazed riverbank footpath on higher ground in about 0.1 mile. The wide road, now blazed blue and called the Three Pools Trail, departs uphill to the right. You can cut your walk short by following the blue-blazed road uphill away from the river until it meets the white-blazed Main Trail, where you can turn right toward the parking lot. The red-blazed riverbank path you follow skirts a bench at a picturesque viewpoint looking upstream and passes two pools favored by fly-casting fishermen. At 0.9 mile, the trail comes to a wooden bridge over Rhinehart Brook, another tributary of the Black River. On the other side of the brook, the trail leads uphill on a wide dirt road and meets another woods road at a T-intersection at 1.0 mile. At this intersection, take the sharp right turn following red

Park visitors Blair Elzenbach and Jane Orf fishing in the Black River.

blazes heading uphill. Ignore an ambiguous red blaze that seems to indicate a left turn downhill. In this section of the walk, there are many tall tulip trees, and every once in a while you come across a picnic table alongside the trail. After a moderate climb, the red-blazed trail descends gently and recrosses Rhinehart Brook on a bridge at 1.1 miles.

On the other side of the bridge, where the trail meets the triple white blazes of the trailhead of the Main Trail, there is a wooden sign pointing to the parking lot. Follow the white blazes on a wide gravel road straight through an intersection, avoiding the yellow-blazed crossing trail. The Main Trail climbs briefly straight ahead, and then turns right, going gradually uphill through an upland forest of mixed oak and hardwoods, many with trunks close to two feet thick. Just off the trail to the left is a coppiced red maple tree, with three trunks, each about two feet thick, which have grown out of a wide stump that was at least five feet in diameter when it was cut. You could guess the original tree was at least two centuries old when it was felled a hundred years ago. Along the Main Trail in mid-May, we saw many uncommon woodland orchids called showy orchis, with wide, dark green basal leaves and spikes of several 1-inch magenta flowers each with a white lower lip. During a long moderate climb, the Main Trail (white blazes) is joined by a gravel road, called the Three Pools Trail on park maps, coming up from the right at 1.3 miles. This is the blue trail you passed while you were following the red-blazed trail along the river. At 1.5 miles, a paved road, called the Haki Trail, enters from the right from the picnic area at the mouth of Trout Brook, and the Main Trail itself has now become a paved road. It levels off and passes a playground on the left at 1.6 miles, then begins to descend. You complete the 2.2-mile walk by following the signs on the Main Trail to the parking lot where you left your car.

The Manor Loop

2.9 miles • 1½ hours

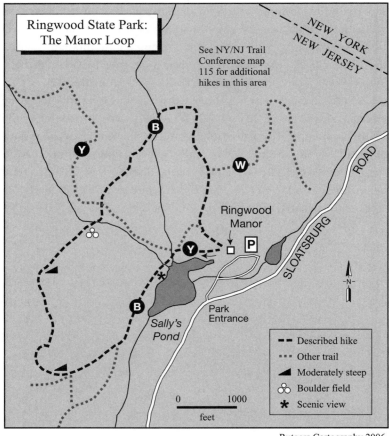

Ringwood State Park:
The Manor Loop

See NY/NJ Trail
Conference map
115 for additional
hikes in this area

NEW YORK
NEW JERSEY

Y

B

W

Ringwood
Manor

Y

P

B

*

Sally's
Pond

Park
Entrance

SLOATSBURG ROAD

-N-

0   1000
feet

- - Described hike
···· Other trail
◀ Moderately steep
⋇ Boulder field
✳ Scenic view

Rutgers Cartography 2006

ELEVATION: Low: 380 feet; High: 720 feet.

BLAZE: Blue.

CLIMBING: This easy walk has two gentle climbs; the first is 130 feet in 0.3 mile, and the second is 290 feet in 0.7 mile. There are two brook crossings on stepping stones, with small boulder fields near the streambeds. The trail mostly follows old woods roads where the footing is secure.

PERMITTED USES: Hiking only.

OVERVIEW

This walk takes you past the famous Ringwood Manor, home of iron makers from 1765 until 1936, when it was deeded to the state by the last of the owners, Erskine Hewitt. Some of the interior furnishings date as far back as the middle of the nineteenth century. The Manor is open to the public for tours, Wednesdays through Sundays, year-round. For information, contact Ringwood State Park, 1304 Sloatsburg Road, Ringwood, NJ 07456-1799, (973) 962-7031.

The hike begins on a gravel road heading south beside Sally's Pond. It climbs a knoll to the west on an eroded woods road, descends to cross a small stream, then climbs gently to the high point of the walk on a hill 0.5 mile northwest of the manor. It is a pleasant family woodland walk, with a sprinkling of wildflowers at all green seasons, and migrating birds on Sally's Pond and near brook and forest edges in spring and fall.

ACCESS: From I-287, take Exit 57 and continue on Skyline Drive north toward Ringwood until it ends at a T-intersection with County 511, Greenwood Lake Turnpike. Turn right onto Greenwood Lake Turnpike, continuing for 1.6 miles to a fork, where you bear right onto Sloatsburg Road. Follow Sloatsburg Road for 2.2 miles to the Ringwood State Park entrance on the left.

HISTORY

The manor site, and the mines and forests around it, were first operated from 1765 to 1767 by the German ironmaster Peter Hasenclever for an English syndicate. After disagreements with his London backers, he was replaced by the Swiss ironmaster Johann Faesch in 1769, and later by the Scotsman Robert Erskine, who put the iron furnaces at the disposal of the colonists during the American Revolution. Erskine died in 1780 and is buried in a concrete vault beside Sally's Pond. Martin Ryerson purchased the property in 1807 and operated it until 1853, when he sold it to Peter Cooper, the American engineer, inventor, and founder of New York City's technical college, the Cooper Union. On Cooper's death in 1884, the property descended to his son-in-law, Abram Hewitt, and it was Abram's son, Erskine Hewitt, who deeded the home and 95 acres to the state of New Jersey in 1936.

A view of Ringwood Manor, showing a Civil War mortar made from iron produced by the Ringwood iron mine and furnace.

A wrought-iron gate on the lawn in front of Ringwood Manor.

During more than 150 years of continuous iron manufacturing, the forests around the manor for many square miles were completely logged over at least three times. Few of the trees along the trail are more than two feet in diameter, suggesting that a hundred years ago the woodlands were open fields or clear-cut hillsides. The hills are crisscrossed by old woods roads once used for logging, farming, or hauling products to and from the furnaces.

DETAILED DESCRIPTION

The trailhead is on a gravel road behind a stone wall in back of the Ringwood Manor House. To find the blue blazes, follow the path from the west end of the parking lot and turn right through the garden to a set of stone steps leading to the road, where you turn left. A more attractive way to the trail is to follow the yellow blazes of the Hasenclever Iron Trail: walk west past the front of the Manor House, down onto the lawn and through the wrought-iron gate posts, passing a large beech tree, two enormous old maples, and a sycamore. Continue across a stream that runs into Sally's Pond on your left, until you find the gravel road with the Manor Trail's blue blazes on a telephone pole. Bear left (south) to the gravel road to begin the walk; at this point, the Hasenclever Iron Trail leaves to the right. You will also arrive at this junction if you follow the blue blazes behind the gardens.

The road crosses a bridge over a stream feeding Sally's Pond to the left of the trail, and shortly passes an Erskine-Morris-Hewitt family graveyard visible through a gate near the pond shoreline. At a gated Y-intersection at 0.3 mile, an unmarked trail turns left, but you will follow the blue blazes to the right, keeping to the gravel road. At this intersection, we saw an American kestrel, our smallest hawk, flying low overhead. To the left, there is a grove of dying hemlock trees infested by the woolly adelgid, and on the right, a slope of upland hardwoods. The largest hardwoods are not more than a foot thick, suggesting this hillside was a bare field 50 or 60 years ago. Along the roadside, clumps of daffodils and the domestic shrubs winged euonymous and barberry hedge indicate that this was a landscaped plot not long ago. At 0.4 mile, the trail passes a wide woods road on the left and continues to the right of an old, but recently inhabited, cottage with stucco sides and a hipped roof. The gravel surface of the road ends here, and the trail continues more steeply uphill on a wide, rocky eroded woods road. At 0.6 mile, blue blazes indicate a right turn (uphill) on a smaller woods road, which begins to level out at 0.7 mile.

Typical Highlands gneiss outcrops poke through the floor of the dry upland oak, beech, and hickory forest. Along this ridge in early March we caught glimpses of Monks Mountain to the southwest, Whaleback Mountain, due west, and Cupsaw Mountain to the east; however, these views are obscured during leafy seasons. The trail soon crosses another woods road and at 0.8 mile leaves the woods road it has been following, turning right into the woods on a foot-

Boulder field at a stream which feeds Sally's Pond.

path, and crossing a road associated with a buried AT&T cable. The trail shortly passes over the high point of the hike and heads down a moderate slope. It reaches a boulder field at 1.0 mile, where the going is uncertain and you will need to watch where you put your feet. This boulder field was probably produced by the tumbling into streambeds of either glacially carried or thaw-freeze weathered rocks, during or shortly after glacial melt. Emerging from the hollow, the trail turns right and, at 1.1 miles, reaches a ten-foot-wide stream, which it parallels for a while before crossing on boulders. This stream flows into Sally's Pond under the bridge at the start of the hike. At this crossing, we found a wide patch of spring-blooming trout lilies, with their dark spotted leaves and yellow drooping flowers. We also saw some rue anemone and hepatica near this hollow.

The trail first crosses a small tributary brook on easy boulders, and then crosses a wider stream, where a little more care is required. After fording the brook, the trail is fairly level, soon crossing a narrow old road, with several large glacial erratics beyond. At 1.3 miles, it passes a steep rock outcrop on the left, and shortly arrives at an intersection with the yellow-blazed Hasenclever Iron Trail, which crosses on a fairly well-trodden path. To the right, this yellow trail provides a shortcut back to Ringwood Manor. At 1.7 miles, the trail approaches another brook that runs into Sally's Pond; you follow the blue blazes across and to the left. At 1.8 miles, the trail passes a small water-filled quarry to the left where frogs will sing in the spring. The trail crosses the main stream and a smaller associated brook and, on the right, touches the curve of an unmarked woods road.

In this second half of the hike, the trees are evenly distributed in age, and some are two to three feet thick, perhaps 50 years older than the trees passed earlier in the hike. The trail meets and joins a woods road coming acutely in from the left at 2.2 miles. You now follow a wide road with a rock fence alongside and some domestic shrubs, indicating that this hillside was part of a farm perhaps 130 years ago, before the largest trees were seeded. The trail follows this woods road, bending right as it meets another woods road which is the terminus of the White Trail that heads uphill to the left. The blue-blazed trail now leads straight downhill until it meets the gravel road near the Manor, at 2.7 miles. Here you turn left and follow the blue blazes back to the trailhead in the manor garden at 2.9 miles and the path to the parking lot and your car.

Ringwood Manor. Photo by Daniel Chazin.

Pyramid Mountain Loop

2.8 miles • 1¾ hours

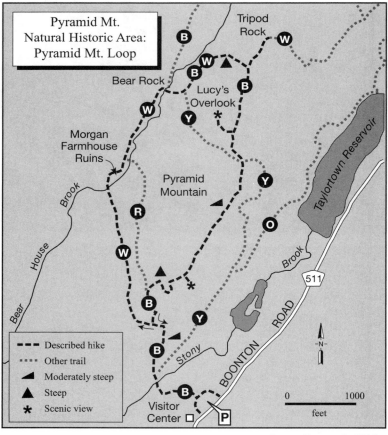

Pyramid Mt. Natural Historic Area: Pyramid Mt. Loop

Tripod Rock

Bear Rock

Lucy's Overlook

Morgan Farmhouse Ruins

Pyramid Mountain

Taylortown Reservoir

Bear House Brook

Stony Brook

BOONTON ROAD

511

Visitor Center

-N-

- - - Described hike
· · · Other trail
◀ Moderately steep
▲ Steep
✳ Scenic view

0   1000
feet

Rutgers Cartography 2006

ELEVATION: Low: 610 feet; High: 934 feet.

BLAZES: Blue, white, blue again.

CLIMBING: There are two climbs: the first, about 80 feet at an easy grade, and the second, about 100 feet at a steep grade of 40%. The rest of the hike is fairly level walking, with some seasonal wet spots near Bear House Brook.

PERMITTED USES: Hiking only. Deer hunting is allowed in specific areas of the park for periods during the fall/winter season by permit only. The specific area is posted with bright orange signs at these times. Check with the Morris County Park Commission, 53 East Hanover Avenue, P.O. Box 1295, Morristown, NJ 07962-1295, (973) 326-7600, www.morrisparks.net, for exact hunting dates.

OVERVIEW

This hike offers climbs for exercise, farmstead ruins for history, open ledges for long views, famous glacial erratic boulders for geology, and seasonal displays of birds and extraordinary wildflowers. Although shorter than Hike #5 (Ringwood State Park: The Manor Loop), this hike appears after it because of the steep climbs that make it more difficult. I have often led walks along the first mile of this hike as a wildflower guide for the New Jersey Audubon Society. Stop at the Visitor Center to see exhibits about local wildlife and plants, and to pick up a trail map, which will show you both shorter and longer hikes in this park.

ACCESS: Take Exit 44 (Boonton) from I-287 north or Exit 45 (Myrtle Avenue/Boonton) from I-287 south. Turn south from either exit toward a T-intersection with Main Street. Turn right uphill on Main Street past the post office to Boonton Avenue (County 511), where there is a traffic light. Turn right on Boonton Avenue and, at 2.4

miles, negotiate the slight jog to the right at the Taylortown Road intersection. Continue for 0.7 mile straight ahead on County 511 to arrive at the Pyramid Mountain Natural Historic Area Visitor Center and parking lot on your left.

DETAILED DESCRIPTION

Walk to the south end of the parking lot near the Directory and turn right onto a wide path, at 0.1 mile finding the blue-blazed trailhead of the Mennen Trail (formerly the Butler-Montville Trail). Follow the blue blazes straight ahead, winding slightly downhill to a wooden bridge over Stony Brook, the overflow from Taylortown Reservoir. Beside the bridge in early spring, you may see patches of woodland wildflowers, and in late summer, the white woodland aster blooms along the path. Just across the bridge at 0.2 mile, the trail arrives at a junction where the Yellow Trail leaves to the right on a footpath. You continue to follow the blue blazes, turning slightly right uphill across the contour of the ridge. At 0.5 mile, you reach an acute turn to the left, arriving shortly at a junction where the blue-blazed Mennen Trail continues ahead to the summit of Pyramid Mountain and the white trail begins to the left. You should now follow this white-blazed Kinnelon-Boonton Trail south under the power line. It soon turns right onto a wide woods road that enters the edge of the woods parallel to the power lines and then emerges into an open meadow. The power company periodically cuts back the vegetation to keep its wires clear, opening the fields to the sun and encouraging an entirely different set of summer meadow wildflowers. In May, the field is dotted with pink wild geraniums, pink gerardia blooms from July through September, a few blue monkey flowers open in August, and the spiral spikes of the white orchid called nodding lady's tresses come up in September. The power company's work also provides an edge environment for migrating and resident birds. In spring and early summer, we have seen and heard many of the most colorful songbirds of the Highlands at one time or another along this power line.

The trail next passes through some seasonal wet spots on buried stones and old logs. At 0.9 mile, it crosses Bear House Brook on a bridge near where in late August and early September you may see brilliant scarlet cardinal flowers blossom next to low-lying, deep blue bottle gentians. The trail now turns right, goes under the power lines, and enters the woods, still on a wide woods road. On your right at 1.0 mile, you pass the foundation of the abandoned Morgan farmhouse next to the brook. The trees here are less than two feet thick, so you can guess this land was an open field 100 years ago. The trail soon passes the trailhead of a red-blazed path heading across the brook and back toward the parking lot, a way to cut your walk short if necessary. At 1.3 miles, you come to Bear Rock, a cottage-sized glacial erratic. Because of the many flint arrowheads found here, local historians believe the overhang of this rock was used by Native Americans as a hunters' campsite.

The white trail is joined here by the blue-blazed Mennen Trail coming in from the north, and together they turn right, heading east across the brook on a wooden bridge. In a short distance, the Yellow Trail begins on the right, offering an easier and shorter path up and over the ridge of Pyramid Mountain. Continuing on the blue trail, at 1.4 miles you are at the base of the ridge, facing a steep climb of about 100 feet at a 40% grade. We may not bound up this cliff the way youngsters can, but we like to choose a pace, no matter how slow, that we can maintain steadily to the top, not stopping, but talking as we go and enjoying the rich draughts of oxygen deep in the lungs, the reassuring surges of an active life still thumping the breast. At the top at 1.5 miles, the white trail turns left, and you take the Mennen Trail (blue blazes) to the right. But before you turn, you should follow the white trail to the left for 0.1 mile to see the famous Tripod Rock, a huge glacial erratic set down by a melting glacier to rest on three

Tripod Rock, a famous glacial erratic, perched on three small boulders.

small boulders. There is a position from a space between stones where you can see the sun set at the summer solstice. This suggests to some observers that the rock was a sacred place for Native Americans, perhaps even moved there by them and not by a glacier.

Back at the junction and heading south on the blue trail, you walk slightly uphill through a thick laurel grove, passing at 1.8 miles a side trail to the right marked with blue-on-white blazes. This leads west through a laurel thicket for about 80 yards, then turns right up a short open ledge to Lucy's Overlook, named for Lucy Meyer who did so much to preserve this land, and Turkey Mountain to the east, as public open spaces. Back on the main trail after Lucy's Overlook, the Yellow Trail joins from the right and soon departs to the left downhill at 1.9 miles. The blue trail you follow turns right up toward the summit of Pyramid Mountain, reaching at 2.0 miles a short spur trail to the left, which leads to an east-facing overlook. Here you have views of Taylortown Reservoir and Turkey Mountain to the east, the

Essex County suburbs and Newark to the southeast, and New York City in the distance.

The original descent from the summit became so rocky and eroded that the park closed it and instead created a new path down the hill to the right. From the viewpoint, backtrack to the clearly marked newer trail section, which turns right off the summit over smooth bedrock and descends through rocky clefts, switching back and forth until the grade moderates. At the bottom of the descent, the blue trail passes the trailhead of the red trail. Follow the blue trail and eventually head slightly downhill to a junction with the trailhead of the white trail. Here at 2.1 miles, you continue on the blue trail to retrace your first 0.5 mile. The blue trail descends gradually south across the hill, turns left at the bottom of the incline, passes by the trailhead of the Yellow Trail on your left, and crosses the wooden bridge over Stony Brook. You retrace your steps past the trailhead of the blue trail and reach the parking lot and your car at 2.8 miles.

The east-facing overlook atop Pyramid Mountain.

Highlands Trail–Headley Overlook Through Hike

3.2 miles • 2¾ hours

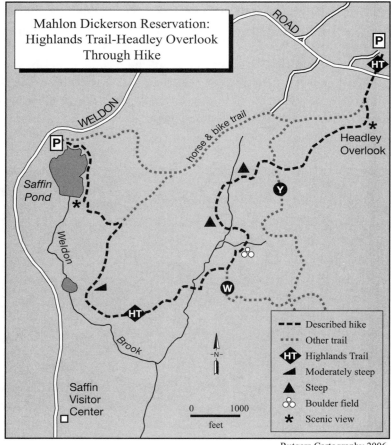

Mahlon Dickerson Reservation: Highlands Trail-Headley Overlook Through Hike

Saffin Pond

Headley Overlook

Saffin Visitor Center

-N-

0   1000
feet

Described hike
Other trail
Highlands Trail
Moderately steep
Steep
Boulder field
Scenic view

Rutgers Cartography 2006

ELEVATION: Low: 1,015 feet; High: 1,290 feet.

BLAZES: Highlands Trail teal diamond, teal diamond with black diamond center.

CLIMBING: Some short rock scrambles up and down, and a few boulder fields where footing is difficult.

This is a Highlands Trail hike.

PERMITTED USES: For the first 0.2 mile, horses and mountain bikes are permitted; thereafter, hiking only. In some years, deer hunting (by permit) is allowed in this park for short periods during November/December. At these times, the area is posted with bright orange signs. For hunting dates and information, check with the Morris County Park Commission, 53 East Hanover Avenue, P.O. Box 1295, Morristown, NJ 07962-1295, (973) 326-7600; www.morrisparks.net.

OVERVIEW

This walk follows the Highlands Trail through the southern section of the Mahlon Dickerson Reservation, one of the many open space preserves administered by the Morris County Park Commission. It is a straight through, easy-to-moderate hike, requiring two cars, one parked at each end of the trail. The hike presents several scrambles up and down through broken rock ledges and passes through two large boulder fields beside a mountain stream where the footing is difficult. The steep areas are not very long, however, and much of the trail follows wide woods roads. Common woodland wildflowers seen on this hike in mid-July included Indian pipe, yellow star grass, Indian tobacco, cow wheat, pale corydalis on the rock ledges, and meadow sweet at the edge of a parking lot. We also saw yellow swallowtail and spicebush butterflies, and heard a red-eyed vireo and an Eastern towhee. As we walked toward the trail crossing at Weldon Road at the start of the hike, a brown female harrier (marsh hawk) glided low across the road ahead of us, showing its white rump patch.

ACCESS: Take I-80 to Exit 34B (NJ 15), and continue north on NJ15 toward Jefferson and Sparta. After 6.0 miles on NJ 15, take the Weldon Road Exit north toward Milton and drive 2.9 miles to the Saffin Pond parking lot on the right. Leave the first car here, and continue 1.3 miles further, passing a trailer area on the left, and a camping and hiker parking area on the right, and finally reaching an entrance road on the left, 4.2 miles from NJ 15. Turn left into this parking area, leave the second car here, and walk over to the kiosk, where there is a trail map and information for hikers.

DETAILED DESCRIPTION

To begin the hike, find the Highlands Trail teal diamond blaze to the right of the kiosk. The trail heads south on an old woods road into a mixed upland hardwood forest, with a mountain laurel grove as its understory. At 0.1 mile, the trail crosses Weldon Road, heads right onto an old woods road, and soon turns left again through chestnut oaks and lowbush blueberries. At this left turn, the horse-and-bike trail leaves to the right, and your trail, the Highlands Trail marked with a teal diamond, is now for hiking only. At this junction, a wooden sign points toward Headley Overlook. The Highlands Trail next traverses a series of rock outcrop ledges. The view from the first ledge just off the trail is blocked by growth of trees, but the next one, at 0.3 mile, is Headley Overlook, open to the south-southwest with a fine view of Lake Hopatcong. From the overlook, the trail descends past a large glacial erratic through a steep rocky incline to an open grass-covered glade with rock outcrops on both sides. On one of these rock ledges, at 0.5 mile, there is again a nice view to the southeast; in leafless seasons, such views are available all along the ridge. Just beyond this spot in early summer, on a grassy opening, we encountered

A young buck with his first set of velvety antlers, on the trail near Headley Overlook.

a spindly young buck white-tailed deer; as we talked quietly to him, he approached to within eight feet, showing us his first set of fur-covered antlers.

At 0.6 mile, the trail begins a descent through moderately-sized boulders, probably plucked off this south-facing ridge by a glacier, and subsequently split by freeze-thaw weathering. At 0.7 mile, the trail crosses a woods road in a grassy clearing. Yellow blazes mark the road as a continuation of the equestrian trail indicated on the Mahlon Dickerson Reservation map. The Highlands Trail crosses straight ahead into the woods, blazed with a metal diamond tag imprinted with the Highlands Trail logo. The trail follows the contour of a ridge, descends past a boulder with the root of a sizable tree wrapped around it, and turns back beneath a rock face at 0.9 mile.

At 1.0 mile, the trail crosses the east branch of Weldon Brook and, on the other side, rises through a boulder field and passes two glacial erratics. At 1.2 miles, the trail enters an extensive boulder field between a rock ledge on the right and the stream on the left. The footing here is difficult; it's wise to slow down and step carefully. At 1.4 miles, the trail recrosses the brook on a split log bridge, soon passes through another boulder field and, at 1.5 miles, crosses a tributary stream. At 1.6 miles, the Beaver Brook Trail (white blazes) begins straight ahead, and you continue on the Highlands Trail to the right, now on a broad woods road. The trees in this part of the forest are not substantial; they are probably no more than 50 years old, suggesting this was open land in the mid-twentieth century. At 1.9 miles, the trail recrosses the east branch of Weldon Brook over a sturdy wooden bridge and begins to climb gently up a wide, rocky woods road.

At 2.2 miles, the trail turns right onto a woods road. At 2.3 miles, some of the blazes are faded teal-colored rectangles, not the newer teal diamonds we have seen. The trail bends left at 2.6 miles, becoming narrower and more overgrown, widening again at 2.8 miles, after merging with a woods road coming in from the right. At 2.9 miles, the trail turns sharply left onto another woods road. To the right at this intersection, an unmarked trail leads back to the horse-and-bike trail, which becomes the yellow-blazed trail that branched from the Highlands Trail near the beginning of the hike, just before Headley Overlook. Taking this unmarked trail to the right converts the hike to a loop of about 5.0 miles. Continuing on the marked Highlands Trail to the left, the trail descends to Saffin Pond, reaching the east

Looking southwest toward Lake Hopatcong from Headley Overlook.

shore at 3.1 miles, where there are picnic tables for a rest and a snack. From this junction the Highlands Trail departs to the left. A connecting trail blazed with a teal diamond with a black diamond center leads to the right along the shore of Saffin Pond toward the parking area and your first parked car, 3.2 miles from the start of the hike.

Cupsaw Mountain Loop

2.9 miles • 2½ hours

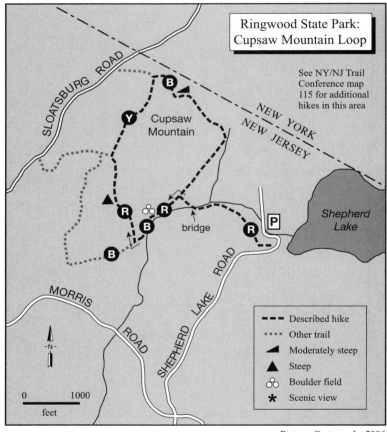

Ringwood State Park:
Cupsaw Mountain Loop

See NY/NJ Trail
Conference map
115 for additional
hikes in this area

Rutgers Cartography 2006

*The blaze circles marked in primary colors (e.g., "R" for red) may represent a color on
a white background (e.g., red triangle-on-white), as noted in the hike description.*

ELEVATION: Low: 450 feet; High: 739 feet.

BLAZES: Red-on-white, yellow, blue, red-on-white again.

CLIMBING: The climbs are moderate and do not include rock scrambles. Stream crossings through wetlands, involving boulder fields and blowdowns, can be difficult in wet seasons; however, a new bridge has made the worst of these crossings safe and dry.

PERMITTED USES: Mountain bikes and horses are permitted on the first 0.1 mile of this hike; thereafter, the trails are for hikers only.

OVERVIEW

This hike takes you through typical Highlands gneiss ridges and upland mixed oak forest over mostly easy footpaths and wide rocky woods roads. There are some small stream crossings through boulder fields that need care to negotiate during wet seasons. There is one limited view to the northwest. In spring, a good assortment of wildflowers blooms near, but not in, the moist areas.

ACCESS: From I-287, take Exit 55 and drive north on County 511 through the Towns of Wanaque and Ringwood. At 5.5 miles from Exit 55, you pass Skyline Drive coming from the right and after that junction, at 7.1 miles, take the second right turn onto Sloatsburg Road. On Sloatsburg Road, take the second right turn at 9.2 miles onto Morris Road. Continue for 1.2 miles to an intersection with Shepherd Lake Road, just before the entrance booth to the Skylands section of Ringwood State Park. Turn left at this intersection and follow the road to the large parking lot at Shepherd Lake. A parking fee is charged in season.

TERRAIN AND HISTORY

Cupsaw Mountain is a 600-foot-high Highlands hill in Ringwood State Park, bounded on the west by Sloatsburg Road and on the east by Cupsaw Brook, which flows out of Shepherd Lake. The mountain was part of the 1978 New Jersey State purchase of the Green Engineering Camp from Cooper Union, the New York City engineering college. In the 1920s and '30s, it was frequented by the Cooper Union Hiking Club, which built a shelter that still stands near the hilltop. Since Revolutionary times, the area has been logged over, perhaps three times, to supply fuel for the nearby Ringwood Ironworks. Today, very few trees on the mountain have reached two feet in diameter, indicating that these slopes were clear as late as the 1920s.

DETAILED DESCRIPTION

We placed this circuit hike among the starter hikes because its climbs and descents are moderate. However, at the crossings of small tributaries of Cupsaw Brook in spring and wet weather, it offers opportunities to experience the problems involved in fording freshets and wetlands through boulder fields. In such conditions, a hiker in sneakers will surely wind up with soaked feet.

Shepherd Lake is a popular public swimming and recreation site crowded on warm summer weekends, so it is best to try this hike either in cooler seasons or on a weekday during the summer. To begin the hike, you walk south (downhill) from the parking area. Find the red-on-white-blazed trailhead marker for the Ringwood–Ramapo Trail just before the entrance booth, where Cupsaw Brook flows under Shepherd Lake Road as it leaves the lake. Symbols on the roadside stake show that mountain bikes and horses are permitted at the beginning of this trail. Follow the red-on-white blazes westward

Crossing Cupsaw Brook on the new bridge.

into the woods (downhill) on a wide woods road beside Cupsaw Brook. The trail immediately crosses a small seasonal tributary brook and after 100 yards, leaves the road and enters the woods to the right on a footpath, while the horse-and-bike track continues straight ahead on the woods road.

The path is marked occasionally by brown posts with the trail blaze and hiker symbol at the top. At this point, the marker posts have no bike or horse symbols, indicating hiking only. At 0.1 mile, the trail passes through a boulder field washed by Cupsaw Brook. Near here, we saw some round-leaved hepatica, a lovely purple-blue early flower that often is the first blossom to poke through the ground leaves before the spring foliage comes out. In spring, when Shepherd Lake is full of water, Cupsaw Brook tumbles over a small cascade to the right of the trail; near the bottom of the descent, the trail turns right and crosses Cupsaw Brook on a wooden bridge. The red-on-white blazed Ringwood–Ramapo Trail is joined by the blue-

Shelter on Cupsaw Mountain built by the "Hiking, Eating, Arguing and Puzzle-Solving Club of the Cooper Union."

blazed Cupsaw Brook Trail, and together the trails continue left for 0.3 mile, crossing seasonal brooks on stepping stones before briefly turning right onto a woods road. Here, the Ringwood–Ramapo Trail (red-on-white blazes) you should follow turns off to the right, while the Cupsaw Brook Trail (blue blazes) leaves to the left.

Following the red-on-white blazes, the trail crosses a tributary stream coming down from the left. When we arrived here in high water, we had to go upstream a short way to find the easiest crossing, and then come back down to find the blazes again. The trail then heads northwest away from the stream, through a boulder-strewn lowland of beech, yellow and black birch, and tulip poplar. At 0.8 mile, the trail starts uphill toward Cupsaw Mountain. The trail turns briefly right toward the east to skirt a gneiss outcrop that seems to be the source of the boulders below. At 0.9 mile, the trail reaches the top of the ridge and starts down on the other side, in typical Highlands ups and downs through a maturing upland oak, hickory, and beech forest, whose thick canopy keeps the shaded understory mostly free of shrubs.

After a short climb, the trail reaches the Cooper Union Shelter at the top of Cupsaw Mountain at 1.0 mile, and 100 feet further to the north arrives at an intersection with the yellow-blazed Cooper Union Trail. Here the red-on-white blazes leave, joining the yellow blazes on a woods road to the left (west). You will now follow the yellow blazes of the Cooper Union Trail straight ahead northward on a woods road downhill toward Sloatsburg Road. During leafless seasons there is a good view toward the west from here. When you begin to hear traffic from Sloatsburg Road at 1.4 miles, you will find the blue-blazed trailhead of the Cupsaw Brook Trail on the right. Follow these blue blazes to the east to begin your return, climbing briefly part of the way back up the ridge that forms Cupsaw Mountain. On

This cascade of the branch of Cupsaw Brook coming from Shepherd Lake is just off the trail to the north.

the down side of the ridge at 1.8 miles you meet a woods road, which has been used as a horse-and-bike track. At 1.9 miles, Cupsaw Brook flows close to the trail on the left, and on the right a small almost rectangular hollow suggests the foundation of an old homestead.

Soon you will see the red-on-white-blazed Ringwood–Ramapo Trail coming in from the left to join the Cupsaw Brook Trail. Turn left onto the Ringwood–Ramapo Trail and again cross the wooden bridge over Cupsaw Brook; across on the other side, you parallel the brook on your left. In wet seasons, Cupsaw Brook tumbles down over boulders in a very attractive cascade, providing a pleasant place off the trail for a rest, a drink, and a photo opportunity. The trail climbs up to reach Shepherd Lake Road and the parking lot to complete the circuit of 2.9 miles.

Cupsaw Brook from the Cupsaw Brook Trail. Photo by Daniel Chazin.

SPARTA MOUNTAIN WILDLIFE
MANAGEMENT AREA

Ryker Lake Circle

2.3 miles • 2 hours

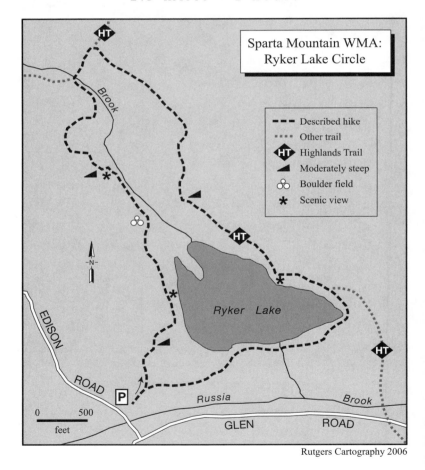

Sparta Mountain WMA:
Ryker Lake Circle

Legend:
- – – – Described hike
- ⋯⋯⋯ Other trail
- **HT** Highlands Trail
- ◢ Moderately steep
- ⚭ Boulder field
- ✳ Scenic view

Brook

Ryker Lake

EDISON ROAD

Russia Brook

GLEN ROAD

0   500
feet

Rutgers Cartography 2006

ELEVATION: Low: 1,050 feet; High: 1,215 feet.

BLAZES: NJ Audubon Society marsh hawk logo, Highlands Trail teal diamond, NJ Audubon marsh hawk logo.

CLIMBING: A moderate climb of 150 feet from the western shore of Ryker Lake to a ridge overlooking tributary brooks and swamps. Gentle, mostly level walking beside the lake on the return.

PERMITTED USES: Hiking only.

This is a Highlands Trail hike.

OVERVIEW

This is both a hike and a nature trail without signs and labels, offering easy walking for families and kids, with moderate climbs and descents through an area of pristine woodlands, brooks, swamps, and marshes. Early spring wildflowers are spectacular along the trail, and migrating songbirds are attracted to the plentiful water and great variety of woodland cover. Beavers are active in a swamp north of the lake. All this can be observed closely from rocky ledges and shoreline paths.

This is one of two connecting trails for hiking the Sparta Mountain Wildlife Management Area. A mile farther up Edison Road is a trailhead at the old Edison Mine property, where a monument with illustrations describes the extensive machinery and works whose remains surround the trail. That trail may be walked as a through hike or a turnaround, but does not form a loop. It leads to the Edison Bog, where birds and wildflowers are plentiful in all green seasons, and connects to the Ryker Lake Trail.

ACCESS: From I-80, take either Exit 34A or Exit 34B to NJ 15 north. Travel 2.1 miles to a slight right turn onto Berkshire Valley Road (County 699). Follow Berkshire Valley Road for 8.8 miles to a traffic light at Ridge Road. Turn left onto Ridge Road, which after 2.4 miles becomes Glen Road and continues for another 0.3 mile to a right turn onto Edison Road. Almost immediately, as Edison Road crosses Russia Brook, look for a small parking turnout on the right with a New Jersey Audubon Society kiosk visible from the road. This is the trailhead for the hike.

TERRAIN AND HISTORY

The 2,000 acres of this preserve were saved from development by the cooperative efforts of the Friends of Sparta Mountain, the New Jersey Green Acres program, the Victoria Foundation, and the New Jersey Audubon Society. The Friends, a local volunteer organization, aided by a water study prepared by Professor Douglas Williamson, persuaded the Sparta Planning Board to block extensive development on Sparta Mountain. Working with the New Jersey DEP Division of Fish and Wildlife and the New Jersey Audubon Society, volunteers from the Friends, and the New York-New Jersey Trail Conference constructed a trail system.

DETAILED DESCRIPTION

From the kiosk, where you can find a map of the trails, follow the Doug Williamson Memorial Trail, with the New Jersey Audubon Society's marsh hawk logo trail markers, north into the woods. The trail soon comes to a wide gravel road, where you turn right, pass under a power line, and continue, until at 0.2 mile you find the Audubon trail markers on the left leading across a parking area into the woods. The trail descends gradually to the western shore of Ryker Lake on a footpath, which in early May was lined with a profusion of common blue violets and the less-common downy yellow violets perched atop their short two-leaved stems.

Ryker Lake west shore from the Doug Williamson Memorial Trail.

The forest in this beginning section is the uplands mixed oak and other hardwoods type, with many yellow birches and no conifers. Half of the trees are little more than a foot in diameter, and none are larger, indicating this was a clear hillside some 70 years ago. Along the lakeshore, beginning at 0.3 mile and continuing to the marshes at the north end of the lake, we found not only violets but anemones, lousewort, wild oats, and marsh marigolds. In spots, the trail leads across boulder fields and very wet areas, which though quite level, provide uncertain footing. At the northwest end of the lake at 0.5 mile, the trail crosses a brook through boulder fields and begins to turn west, climbing away from the lake. At this turn we heard, but couldn't see, a rose-breasted grosbeak, one of the most beautiful songbirds of the northeast, whose numbers have been declining in recent years. As you pass by the north end of the lake, the forest includes red maples and some dying hemlocks, both moisture-loving species.

After a climb of about 150 feet, the trail reaches a rocky gneiss ledge from which there is a view back over the lake and its northern marshes. The trail descends off the ledge close to the wetland that surrounds the brooks feeding the lake, climbs briefly back up and down, and crosses a small tributary brook through a boulder field. You soon pass through another swampy area, where bright yellow clumps of marsh marigolds dot the wetland in early spring. The trail then climbs a small rise exiting the swamp, traverses short ups and downs, and meets another brook with associated boulders. On the next rise, there is a view across the swamp, where beavers have recently felled a few small trees near the water and were working on one with a trunk over a foot in diameter. Two beaver lodges can be seen in the swamp.

At 0.9 mile, the trail reaches a T-intersection at a woods road called Rock Lodge Road on maps. (This woods road goes off to the left toward the Edison Bog, about 2.5 miles to the northwest, and cir-

Canada geese in the marsh at the north end of Ryker Lake.

cles back to end at the Edison Mine works.) At the T-intersection you turn right, descend to cross the swamp on a ford of stones and logs, and climb gradually to the northeast on the wide, unpaved road.

At 1.0 mile, the trail reaches an intersection where the teal diamond-blazed Highlands Trail joins from the northeast and the two trails turn right together, heading southeast into the woods on a footpath. Most of the blazes here are the Audubon marsh hawk logo. You follow the combined trails to the right toward the east shore of Ryker Lake.

The level trail proceeds along the contour of the hillside, heading southeast, until at 1.2 miles it bends right and begins a slow descent to the shore of the lake, which it reaches at 1.4 miles. Early spring wildflowers are plentiful in this section, especially anemones, spring beauties, and yellow downy violets. At 1.7 miles, the Highlands Trail departs to the left down into a hollow, where it turns right, skirts a swamp, and heads away toward Russia Brook.

Following its marsh hawk blazes, you continue on the Audubon Trail, which hugs the shore and turns back sharply to the west at the south end of the lake, arriving at the dam at 1.9 miles. After crossing the dam, the trail joins a gravel road, going slightly uphill and to the left, until at 2.1 miles it turns left onto a rocky, eroded woods road. This leads back to the kiosk and parking area where you left your car, reached after a walk of 2.3 miles.

Ken Lockwood Gorge
Through Hike

3.3 miles • 2½ hours

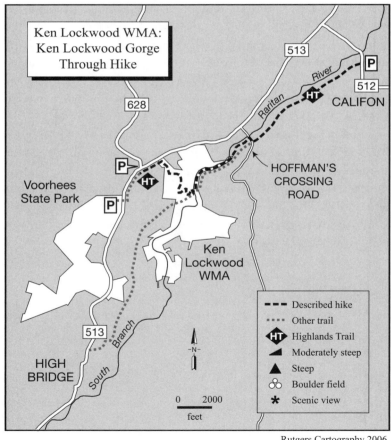

Ken Lockwood WMA:
Ken Lockwood Gorge
Through Hike

513

Raritan River

628

512

CALIFON

P

HT

P

HT

P

HOFFMAN'S
CROSSING
ROAD

Voorhees
State Park

Ken
Lockwood
WMA

513

South Branch

HIGH
BRIDGE

-N-

▪ ▪ ▪ Described hike
• • • • Other trail
HT Highlands Trail
◢ Moderately steep
▲ Steep
⚭ Boulder field
✱ Scenic view

0   2000
feet

Rutgers Cartography 2006

ELEVATION: Low: 330 feet; High: 760 feet.

BLAZES: Columbia Trail signage, Highlands Trail teal diamond.

CLIMBING: A climb of about 80 feet from the river bank to the railroad trestle, and a steep climb on switchbacks from the rail trail at 400 feet to the top of a knoll at 760 feet.

PERMITTED USES: For the first two miles, the trail is open to horses, bicycles, and joggers.

This is a Highlands Trail hike.

ACCESS: This straight through hike will require either two cars, or a car and a bicycle. The most direct route is to take I-78 to Exit 17, turning north toward Clinton and Washington. Merge onto NJ 31, and at 2.0 miles turn right onto West Main Street (County 513). Follow County 513 into High Bridge, after 1 mile turning right onto Bridge Street, then left onto Main Street (still County 513), right onto Church Street, and quickly left again uphill on Fairview Avenue (still County 513). From this turn it is 2.5 miles to Bunnvale Road (County 628), where Lebanon Township police suggest hikers park the first car in the parking lot of the Bunnvale Library, just 100 yards west (left) of County 513. Bunnvale Road (County 628) begins on County 513, 2.6 miles north of High Bridge, or 2.6 miles south of the County 513 intersection with County 512 (Academy Street) in Califon. If the Bunnvale Library lot is full, parking is always available opposite the ranger station in Voorhees State Park on County 513, 0.6 mile south (uphill) from Bunnvale Road on County 513.

You can accomplish this hike with just one car by leaving a bicycle in the Bunnvale Library parking lot, or chained near the dirt road where the Highlands Trail exits from the woods onto County 513 (look for the teal diamond blazes), 0.1 mile north of Bunnvale Road. The bicycle ride from this end of the hike to the starting trailhead where you will park your car is pleasantly almost entirely downhill.

After you have settled your first car or bicycle, drive 2.6 miles north on County 513 to the junction with County 512. Turn right onto County 512, which is Academy Street in Califon, cross a bridge over the South Branch of the Raritan River into the town, and park your car in the lot on the left opposite the old railroad station.

OVERVIEW

This hike takes you along one of the most picturesque stretches of wild river in New Jersey. It follows a section of the Highlands Trail, here co-aligned part of the way with the Columbia Trail, on the railbed of the old High Bridge Branch of the Central Railroad of New Jersey. After crossing Ken Lockwood Gorge on a refurbished steel bridge 80 feet above the river, the Highlands Trail leaves the rail trail, turning right and climbing 360 feet on moderate switchbacks through a young successional forest. The trail emerges from the woods on a dirt road, turns south onto County 513, and proceeds up-hill 0.6 mile to the Voorhees State Park parking lot. If you have found a place for a car or bicycle in the Bunnvale Library parking lot, you will not have to walk so far uphill on County 513.

HISTORY AND TERRAIN

Hunterdon and Morris counties acquired the surface rights to the railbed from the Columbia Gas Company, which built a gas pipeline under the abandoned railroad. The rail trail parallels the South Branch of the Raritan River for six miles of uninterrupted wide and level gravel road. From near Long Valley to High Bridge, it is open to walkers, joggers, bicycle riders, and horseback riders. Ken Lockwood Gorge is named for a trout fisherman who made the preservation of the area his lifetime project. The boulder-filled run has been cut through a Highlands ridge by hundreds of millions of years of river wash. The Gorge is steep because the underlying crystalline bedrock is hard; if the bedrock were softer, the gradients would be gentler. It is south of the terminal moraine of the Wisconsin Glacier, which didn't affect the Gorge directly, though water run-off from that glacier and many previous glaciations may have helped to form it. Because there is no great concentration of heavy industry in its watershed, the water of the South Branch here is unpolluted, and strains of native brook trout still survive, though they may have interbred with trout stocked by the state. It is one of the best trout habitats in New Jersey; fly fishermen try their skills daily from April through September.

DETAILED DESCRIPTION

From the parking lot opposite the old stone Califon railroad station, walk a few feet uphill to the railbed, turn right, and pass the station, built in 1876 when the High Bridge Branch of the Central Railroad of New Jersey was opened, with spurs to serve the iron mines further north in the Highlands. Although the Highlands Trail is co-aligned with the Columbia Trail here, there are no teal blazes along the railbed. A sign identifies the Columbia Trail, and at 0.2 mile there is a 2¼-mile post; these posts continue every quarter mile on the rail trail. In Califon, the trail passes near the yards of houses and a lot full of old cars and other decaying machinery, but better things are to come. In July, raspberries ripen along the trail and summer wildflowers bloom. At 0.4 mile, you enter a 60 to 70-year-old woodland, whose largest trees are no more than a foot in diameter. At 0.8 mile, the trail crosses a gravel road, and at 1.2 miles it arrives at Hoffman's Crossing Road, where, for the first time, the teal diamond blazes of the Highlands Trail are seen along the railbed.

The Columbia Trail continues on the railbed 80 to 100 feet above the river, with frequent glimpses of the wilder sections of the gorge. But you should follow a route that offers a more exciting experience

Fisherman Brent Coffin fly-casting for trout in Ken Lockwood Gorge.

by turning right on Hoffman's Crossing Road and walking down to River Road, a dirt track on the river bank, with parking turnouts for fishermen. The only blazes here are rectangles painted over with brown paint. It's hard to tell what the purpose of the paint-over was; there are no replacement blazes, so it would seem that the painter wanted no blazes at all.

Turn left on the dirt road at 1.3 miles and enter the deepest stretch of the gorge, where you can listen to the water washing over boulders and watch the fishermen. In spring at high water, cascades roar over the rocks, and spray sifts through the trees. The forest near the river includes hemlocks on the slopes to the left, and maples and yellow birches closer to the water; these are trees that thrive in moist environments. In early June, we watched a great blue heron fish the opposite shore. The slope up to the left away from the river is steep and littered with boulders whose sharp edges suggest they were blasted from bedrock above during construction of the railroad. At 2.2 miles, the trail passes an island in the river and comes to a bridge that takes the Columbia Trail across the river 80 feet overhead. Turn left beside the downstream wall of the bridge abutment and climb up a path to the railbed, turning left to cross the river. This bridge has been completely refurbished for recreational use, with a chain-link canopy arching over each side to keep people from falling into the gorge below.

On the other side of the bridge at 2.4 miles, near the 4½-mile post of the Columbia Trail, the Highlands Trail with its teal diamond blazes leaves the railbed and turns sharply right, angling uphill on the first of three switchbacks. (The Columbia Trail continues on the railbed into the Town of High Bridge.) As we climbed into the woods, we heard the eerie screech of two large tree branches rubbing together in the wind. Some of our Irish friends call this a banshee, the Irish word for a woodland spirit. Halfway up the first switchback, we came upon a small forest of Indian pipe, those low, ghostly white summer flowers that get nutri-

After a rain in January, the river rushes through the Ken Lockwood Gorge.

A cabin on the Highlands Trail near County 513. The white oak grown up in its doorway is more than 100 years old.

ents not from a chlorophyll cycle, but parasitically from fungi in the organic matter near its roots. The climb moderates at 2.5 miles, as the trail follows the contour of the hill slightly below the crest. After another switchback at 2.7 miles, the trail crosses a tumbled stone fence, probably originally built about four feet high to keep farm animals out of cropland. The woods here, of white oak, maple, beech, black birch, and tulip poplar, has few trees over a foot thick, suggesting this was farmland perhaps 70 years ago. The path near the top is pleasantly covered with soft duff without many rocks.

The trail levels off and, at 2.9 miles, goes left without a turn blaze, though a single blaze 15 feet to the left makes the direction clear. It soon meets a dirt road and turns right slightly downhill, passing on the left a log cabin old enough to have been built when this land was a farm. The big white oak in the doorway, with a diameter of 2½ feet, is surely more than 100 years old. The dirt road meets

County 513 at 3.2 miles, where you turn left uphill beside the paved road, with teal blazes on poles along the way. If you parked either your car or bicycle in the Bunnvale Library lot, you need to walk uphill only 0.1 mile to find it and complete a hike of 3.3 miles. However, the teal diamond blazes continue on telephone poles south uphill and lead, in another 0.6 mile, to the entrance of Voorhees State Park and the parking lot there at 3.9 miles.

This section of the Highlands Trail ends here.

(However, the Highlands Trail goes through Voorhees State Park and continues for 5.1 miles to the Spruce Run Recreation Area.)

Echo Lake West Turnaround

4.0 miles • 3 hours

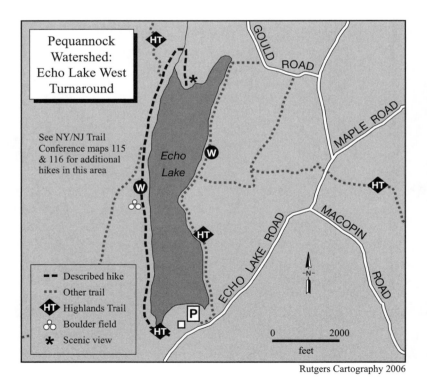

Pequannock
Watershed:
Echo Lake West
Turnaround

See NY/NJ Trail
Conference maps 115
& 116 for additional
hikes in this area

*Echo
Lake*

GOULD ROAD

MAPLE ROAD

ECHO LAKE ROAD

MACOPIN ROAD

-N-

Described hike
Other trail
HT Highlands Trail
Boulder field
✱ Scenic view

0   2000

feet

Rutgers Cartography 2006

ELEVATION: Low: 892 feet; High: 990 feet.

BLAZES: Highlands Trail teal diamond and white, white, reverse to return.

CLIMBING: Mostly level walking over lakeside paths, with small stream crossings and boulder fields.

PERMITTED USES: Hiking only.

This is a Highlands Trail hike.

OVERVIEW

A pleasant, easy walk along a glacial lake deepened by a dam, which was built to create a reservoir for the City of Newark. The trail follows the edge of the lake very closely, so there are continual beautiful lake views as you walk. Wildflowers bloom in green seasons, and migrating songbirds and waterfowl appear in spring. In the fall, trees around the lakeshore turn spectacular colors, particularly the tupelos, whose oval leaf clusters turn a deep scarlet early in the season. A peninsula at the north end of the lake is a good spot for lunch if you start out around 11 a.m.

ACCESS: From NJ 23, 4.3 miles west of Kinnelon Road in Butler, turn north onto Echo Lake Road. Drive 1.0 mile and turn left into the Newark Watershed Conservation and Development Corporation (NWCDC) office and parking lot. Hiking in the Pequannock Watershed is by permit only. An individual adult (over 18) must have an annual permit (Newark residents $4, non-residents $8), which is issued in person either at the Echo Lake Road office or at the Newark office at 40 Clinton Street. Permits for senior hikers are half price. Contact the NWCDC for information: (973) 697-2850, www.nwcdc.net.

DETAILED DESCRIPTION

From the southwest end of the parking lot, walk downhill on a wide driveway toward the lake. Either the teal diamond blazes or the blue/silver logo of the Highlands Trail and the white blazes of the Echo Lake West Trail are found on trees beside the driveway. The trail crosses the Echo Lake dam, where there is a carefully built stone shed housing the dam control equipment. Because the area around the dam is treeless, summer wildflowers thrive on both sides of the walkway.

The path hugs the lake's west shore at the base of Kanouse Mountain, offering continual water views. At about 0.5 mile, the trail crosses two small vernal streams with associated boulder fields, where the footing can be difficult during wet weather. The soil along the lake is rich and moist, producing wildflowers in all green seasons.

The dam and stone control shed at the south shore of Echo Lake.

Echo Lake with puddingstone boulders along the west shore.

At 0.8 mile, a small woods road comes down to the lakeshore. At 1.3 miles, a wide woods road coming in acutely from the left joins the path into a clearing. The Highlands Trail forks left (uphill) at 1.8 miles, but you continue to follow the Echo Lake West Trail, which bears to the right along the lakeshore.

This section of the Highlands Trail ends here.

This trail has been recently blazed and cleared. It is narrower than the Highlands Trail you have been following and, as it progresses into the woods, is somewhat enclosed by bushes.

A view of Echo Lake from the west shore on the white trail.

Nevertheless, press on, because the trail becomes wider and leads in the end to a very pretty setting. Along this section we saw a coppiced chestnut oak, a tree that had been cut as an old growth trunk about five feet across, from which five new sprouts grew into separate trees, each of which is now about a foot in diameter. The new trunks must be about 70 years old, and the original tree was at least 200 years old when cut 70 years ago. In late August, cardinal flowers thrust their brilliant red spikes up through the foliage around the brook to the right of the trail. At 1.9 miles, the trail turns right and crosses an Echo Lake source brook on stepping stones. Bending to the right, the trail becomes wider and joins a woods road as it approaches the lake's north shore. It arrives at 2.0 miles on a raised open point of land, with bedrock ledges and large boulders extending out into the lake, an ideal spot for a rest and some water, or lunch if you started by mid-morning. This lovely viewpoint provides the cover picture for this book.

It would seem logical to continue around the north shore and return along the east side of the lake, but logic doesn't work in this case. The property lines of private houses on the northeast shore come close to the water, and the narrow NWCDC-owned corridor along the edge is a wet marsh overgrown with impenetrable bramble thickets. Therefore, when you are ready to leave, retrace your steps back along the Echo Lake West Trail to the junction with the Highlands Trail. From this junction, follow the joint Echo Lake West and Highlands trails, with both white blazes and teal diamonds, 1.8 miles back to the parking lot and your car, to complete a hike of 4.0 miles.

Echo Lake East
Through Hike

4.3 miles • 3½ hours

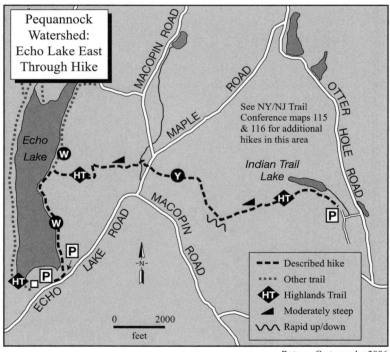

Pequannock
Watershed:
Echo Lake East
Through Hike

MACOPIN ROAD

MAPLE ROAD

OTTER HOLE ROAD

See NY/NJ Trail
Conference maps 115
& 116 for additional
hikes in this area

Echo Lake

Indian Trail Lake

W

HT

Y

HT

P

ECHO LAKE ROAD

MACOPIN ROAD

W

P

P

HT

-N-

0   2000

feet

- - - Described hike
····· Other trail
HT Highlands Trail
◄ Moderately steep
〰 Rapid up/down

Rutgers Cartography 2006

ELEVATION: LOW: 910 feet; High: 1,120 feet.

BLAZES: Highlands Trail teal diamond, HT teal diamond and white, HT teal diamond again.

CLIMBING: A few short, steep climbs up and down rocky ledges, and one longer gradual climb from 960 feet to 1,120 feet in 0.8 mile. Several very moist wetlands and stream crossings. In general, not much climbing.

PERMITTED USES: Hiking, hunting in season (see Caution below). **This is a Highlands Trail hike.**

OVERVIEW

This walk follows a section of the Highlands Trail from the western edge of the Wyanokie Plateau to Echo Lake in the Pequannock Watershed. It offers wildlife, wildflowers, and beautiful fall colors, particularly along Echo Lake. However, its principal interest is to illustrate the forest takeover of an abandoned farm area. The first 2.0 miles climb to a level plateau where tumbled stone fences indicate use as farmland a century ago. The trail descends from the plateau to a swampy area that was probably a water source for the farms. After crossing Macopin Road, the trail climbs to a summit where an early twentieth-century resort was built overlooking Echo Lake. The last section follows the shore of Echo Lake, with good water views to the west, a steep dramatic cliff along the east side of the trail, and wildflowers and birds in all green seasons.

CAUTION: From late September through December, on trails east of Macopin Road, hiking is permitted on Sundays only, to avoid conflict with hunters. (Hunting is never permitted on Sunday in New Jersey.) In the same area, from the middle of April to late May, to avoid conflict with spring turkey hunters, hiking is permitted daily only after 1 p.m., as well as all day on Sunday. Check with the Watershed office, by phone or at the website (see below), for exact hunting dates. From the end of May until late September, hiking is permitted on all Watershed hiking trails every day.

ACCESS: This is a straight through hike requiring two cars. From NJ 23, 4.3 miles west of Kinnelon Road in Butler, take the Echo Lake Road exit north 1.4 miles to a fisherman's parking turnout on the left at the bottom of a hill at the Echo Lake dam. You may leave your first car here. However, if there is not enough space, additional parking is available 0.3 mile back up the hill, at the office of the Newark Watershed Conservation and Development Corporation (NWCDC), which you passed on your way in. A permit is required for adults hiking in the Watershed. An individual (over 18) must have an annual permit (Newark residents $4, non-residents $8), which is issued in person either at the office on Echo Lake Road, or at the Newark office, 40 Clinton Street. (Permits for senior hikers are half price.) Call the NWCDC for information: (973) 697-2850, or check the website: www.nwcdc.net.

After leaving your first car, drive north on Echo Lake Road to a T-intersection, where you turn left onto Macopin Road. After 0.4 mile on Macopin Road, bear right onto Maple Road, continuing about 1.5 miles to its junction with Otter Hole Road. Turn right onto Otter Hole Road, and drive for 1.7 miles. As you approach a lake on your left, find Crescent Road on your right. Highlands Trail teal blazes are painted on telephone poles from this turn to the trailhead. Turn right onto Crescent Road, then at a T-intersection turn right onto Newton Road (no street sign when we were there) which, bearing left, becomes Algonquin Way. At 0.4 mile from Crescent Road, near the end of Algonquin Way as it bends sharply left, there is room for two or three cars where an old woods road enters the forest near a stone barrier. This is the trailhead for the hike.

DETAILED DESCRIPTION

The Highlands Trail section begins here.

The start of this hike is not a formal trailhead, but is a continuation of the Highlands Trail, whose teal diamond blazes you may have seen on telephone poles on roads leading to the parking area. A single Highlands Trail blaze is clearly visible on a tree on the left about fifteen steps from the road. Through the trees to the right beyond houses, you can see Indian Trail Lake. The road is wide and much eroded, leading slightly downhill toward a muddy spot where a seasonal stream comes out of the woods into the road. At this point, about 300 feet from the first blaze, you will find a second blaze on a tree to the left of the road. The trail bears left into the woods on a footpath. This turn is easily missed, so go slow and be alert to find it. A third teal diamond blaze a little further in the woods will confirm the left turn.

The trail climbs easily for 100 feet through small boulders and a bedrock outcrop. The forest at the outset consists of relatively young hardwoods, with an understory of many saplings, and a sparse floor of ferns and blueberry shrubs. The trail crosses a woods road at 0.2 mile and goes very slightly uphill. Many trees along this part of the trail have multiple trunks nearly a foot thick growing out of a cut stump originally more than two feet thick. These coppiced trees suggest that a grove of hardwoods was logged here about 50 or more years ago. At 0.5 mile, the trail crosses a wet spot and passes through an area where the trees are larger. The coppiced tree trunks here are over a foot thick, and the cut stumps are about three feet across, indicating they were 130 to 150 years old when they were felled. The trail soon climbs a short ridge and passes through an eroded and broken stone wall, probably built more than a century ago to contain cattle. The walking is basically level here; more than one broken stone wall can be seen from the trail, with the several woods roads providing evidence that this flat part of the ridge was a once a farm.

Field of puddingstone boulders broken by glaciers and weathering from the ridge above.

At 0.7 mile, the trail turns right onto a well-used woods road that shows signs of being used by ATV's and full-size four-wheel-drive vehicles. To the left, the trail passes some large old trees with trunks more than three feet wide, indicating that they had probably been left standing for some domestic purpose, perhaps to provide shade for nearby buildings or animals. At 0.8 mile, the trail crosses another old stone fence almost flattened by weathering. At 1.0 mile, it turns left off the woods road, crosses a grass-covered road, heads into the woods on a footpath and climbs very gently to a level ridge. The elevation at the top of this ridge is 1,110 feet, not quite the highest point of the hike, but very close to it.

The trail now begins to descend a series of three steep ledges, 20, 30, and 30 feet high, between and through broken boulders with bedrock outcrops on both sides. The trail next passes through a long laurel grove, reaching the bottom of a hollow at 1.2 miles, with level walking between swamps in a boulder field. To the left, about 15 feet from the trail, you may notice an abandoned utility trailer, last licensed in 1971, but whose bulbous fenders look more like 1950s style. In this damp lowland, the trees are thicker. At a T-intersection at 1.3 miles, the trail turns right onto a woods road, passing a swamp to the right. In 200 feet, it turns left, leaves the road and follows a footpath into the woods. The trail soon crosses a muddy spot on stepping stones over drainage from the swamp to the right. This damp area can be expected to produce good wildflowers in early spring. Nearby, the trail passes a heart-shaped depression full of water surrounded by stones that could have been a spring long ago. This wetland, like many such in the Highlands, is formed over hard bedrock, where the water cannot seep through the substrate, but is held as if in a basin until it finds a way to run off. At 1.5 miles, the trail passes a square excavation about the size of a cellar and foundation for a small dwelling.

Leaving the wetland, the trail climbs to a smooth rock outcrop and descends into a hollow. The trail follows a switchback around a sheer 20-foot-high rock ledge, bears right, and, at 1.7 miles, reaches a T-intersection with a woods road. It follows the road to the right and, in 20 yards, crosses another woods road and enters the woods on a footpath, soon crossing a stone fence completely flattened by age. The walking is level here since the trail descended that last ledge. At 1.8 miles, be alert for a double blaze, where the trail leaves the wide footpath it has been following. The trail turns left across another stone fence and into a fern field on a narrower track. At 1.9 miles, you run into some crudely painted orange blazes, typical of ATV tracks. The trail has become a woods road here. It turns right off the woods road (which continues straight ahead), leads over a rock outcrop, and then, after a short distance, quickly returns to the woods road. The trail now goes through a hemlock grove dying from infestation with the woolly adelgid, an Asian insect accidentally brought into the United States. Yellow blazes have replaced the orange ones used by ATV's, and the trail next zigs left and zags right, arriving at Macopin Road at 2.1 miles.

To find the trail on the other side of Macopin Road, walk about 30 feet to the right (north) and look for a teal blaze on a wooden post in tall weeds on the roadside. The hemlocks in these woods are all dead, but some white pines survive; the soft, fine needles you find on the path are white pine needles. At 2.2 miles, the trail turns left off the eroded track into an open grassy area and reaches a 12-foot-wide running brook to be crossed on stones. This stream can be very difficult to cross during high water. The trail next passes through a grassy meadow and a small rivulet, coming to an area where ATV's have torn up the trail. In a swamp to the right, a great blue heron flapped away as we passed. The trail turns right onto a woods road at 2.4 miles and begins to climb the ridge forming the eastern boundary of Echo Lake. The wide woods road is rocky and deeply eroded. At this point, in November, you will find the straggly fragrant yellow flowers of native witch hazel blooming well after the trees have lost their leaves. The trail levels out to a more gradual incline at 2.5 miles. We heard a pileated woodpecker sound off here.

To the right on top of this ridge, some 80 years ago, was a large resort hotel, to which this road provided access. Along the way you see many barberry hedges, an escaped garden shrub that is a sure sign of human cultivation, and a group of tall red spruce, not a common species in the area, which were surely planted at about that time. The trail turns left onto a smaller woods road, and turns left again off the road into the woods on a footpath through brambles. It returns to the woods road and comes to a T-intersection with a wide gravel road where the trail turns left again, paralleling a stone fence. At 2.7 miles, the trail turns right off the wide road onto a smaller, less traveled, grassed-over road heading slightly uphill, through hemlocks, white pines, a few hardwoods, and more introduced red spruce trees. The trail reaches the crest of the ridge, the high point of the hike (1,120 feet), and starts down to the shore of Echo Lake on an overgrown woods road surrounded by blowdowns and dotted with boulders. A hemlock cut here by trail maintainers, is 15 inches thick with about 125 rings.

Within sight of the lake 100 yards away, the trail turns right off the woods road, meeting the Echo Lake East Trail (white blazes) at 3.0 miles, about 40 feet from the shoreline. Turn left here, following both teal diamonds and white blazes, walking gradually closer to the shore. The trail follows the shoreline, offering pleasant level walking on a mossy path with continual views across the lake, and wildflow-

At the top of the ridge overlooking Echo Lake, a hemlock stump, 15 inches thick with about 125 rings.

ers growing along the trail at all green seasons. To the left of the trail are many dying hemlocks and, at 3.6 miles, a high steep ridge curves close to the shoreline, with dramatic cascades of large broken boulders split off from the cliff by weathering or glaciers. Some have tumbled down close to the trail and some across the trail to the shore. The trail reaches the dam of Echo Lake at 4.0 miles and parallels a channeled inlet stream out to Echo Lake Road. Here the white trail ends, and if you parked your car in the fisherman's turnout, you will find it just off the road a few yards away waiting for you. The teal blazes of the Highlands Trail continue to the right up the hill to the Watershed office parking lot at 4.3 miles.

This section of the Highlands Trail ends here.

Spillway at Echo Lake dam, with the lake in the background.

View of the shoreline of Echo Lake, from the Echo Lake East Trail. Photo by Daniel Chazin.

TURNING POINT

Deep into unfamiliar mountains
I take a map, pack full of gear,
and try to see how far I can go
without using any of it,
choose trails I think I've seen before,
that seem to lead to viewpoints, pleasing
my climbing heart, though the aged body
balks, stumbles on slick roots and cobbles,
gasps on the steeps, trembles on scarps,
and I'm so far into the woods
I can't recall the names of flowers
or recognize the trees.
That's when I sit on a cold rock,
shed my pack in the calm forest
softly busy with seeds, saplings and death,
and think about not going back.

Of course I soon get up,
shoulder the pack, take out my compass,
and find my way back into memory.
But on each return some part of me
stays behind on that crucial rock,
searching up slope for distant light,
toward the highest, longest lookout,
where body's quiet, heart satisfied,
and compass swings in gentle circles.

—George Petty

LONGER HIKES, CLIMBS, AND SCRAMBLES

Up to 6.1 miles, 4 hours

13. NORVIN GREEN STATE FOREST:

Wyanokie Torne Loop

1.5 miles • 1¼ hours

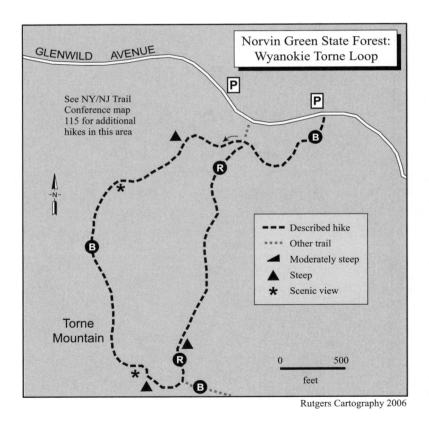

Rutgers Cartography 2006

ELEVATION: Low: 840 feet; High: 1,160 feet.

BLAZES: Blue, red, then blue again

CLIMBING: A steep climb of 200 feet in 0.2 mile near the start, a rock scramble down off the ridge, and a climb back up to a saddle between two ledges.

PERMITTED USES: Hiking only.

OVERVIEW

Although this hike is short in terms of distance, it is included in "Longer Hikes, Climbs, and Scrambles" because it is not an easy walk. It offers steep climbs, rock scrambles up and down, and an ankle-twisting boulder field. After a rain, these rocks can be slippery, and in snow or ice, the average hiker would do well to avoid these trails. However, in return for the difficulties, you get a sequence of excellent open lookouts to the west, south, and east; from the last of which the New York City skyline is visible on a clear day. The hike also provides plenty of exercise for your cardio-vascular system and for the muscle groups involved in bending, stretching, and lifting your body over the rocks. We took some young friends, a couple in their twenties, on this walk; at the end they were ready to agree it was a better workout than an hour session at the gym. You will be introduced to features typical of the Jersey Highlands, including glacially scoured bare bedrock outcrops, sudden steep downs and ups over solid rock faces and loose boulders, and upland and ridgetop plant communities, with understory wildflowers and flowering shrubs in season. This hike produces more rewards per unit of energy expended than most other hikes on trails in New Jersey.

ACCESS: Approaching Butler heading west on NJ 23, turn right (north) at the Boonton Avenue exit (County 511) into the center of town. Boonton Avenue heads downhill, makes a small circuit near the bottom of the hill, turns right onto Park Place and, at 1.0 mile, crosses railroad tracks, ending at a T-intersection with Main Street.

Approaching on NJ 23 heading east, take the Kinnelon Road/Kiel Avenue exit north into Butler. The street ends at a T-intersection with Park Place, where you turn left to cross railroad tracks to a T-intersection with Main Street.

In both cases, turn right onto Main Street and, at another T-intersection where Main Street ends, turn left onto Hamburg Turnpike. In 50 yards, take the next right turn (uphill) onto Glenwild Avenue. Continue on Glenwild Avenue for 3.2 miles to the Otter Hole parking area on the right, at the top of the hill. If this area is full, there is another, 0.2 mile farther ahead on the right.

DETAILED   DESCRIPTION

Begin the hike from the east (downhill) end of the Otter Hole parking area. Cross Glenwild Avenue and find the blue blaze of the Hewitt-Butler Trail on a marker post across a small ditch. This footpath starts steeply uphill through a notch in a small rock outcrop of weathered Highlands gneiss, heading southwest parallel to, but slightly away from the road. The trail reaches the crest of the rise, runs level for a while, and then climbs down into a hollow and back up the next ridge. The forest is a Highlands dry upland collection of hardwood trees, including chestnut oak and red oak, black birch, hickory, beech, and an occasional white pine, with an understory of lowbush blueberry and mountain laurel.

At 0.2 mile, at the bottom of a small hollow, the trail passes a triangle of three red blazes on a tree to the left, indicating the north terminus of the Torne Trail. You will return to this junction after climbing and circling Torne Mountain. If you parked in the second area, you can reach this intersection by walking 100 yards left (southeast) to find an unmarked footpath across the road heading into the

View to the east over South Torne from the south ridge of Wyanokie Torne.

woods over a ditch. In a short distance to the west, that footpath reaches this same intersection of the red and blue trails; in fact, the blazes at the intersection are nearly visible from the road.

In either case, leave the red trail to your left, and continue by following the blue blazes as the trail heads steeply uphill, passing over glacially smoothed gneiss outcrops near the top, for a climb of about 200 feet in 0.2 mile. The curved rock surfaces will be slippery in wet weather. Following blue blazes over the rocks, the trail stays on the outcrops as it heads west. The Wisconsin Glacier of 15,000 years ago came from the northwest, rubbed soil and vegetation off the Highlands bedrock, and smoothed the north-facing edge and top of the ridge. You may see some of the grooves made by rocks that were caught in the bottom of the moving ice. On the south end of the ridge, the glacier clawed at crevices and plucked off large chunks of the rock, leaving behind cracks in the rock face and broken rocks as it retreated. You will notice this different effect when you arrive at

The red trail begins with a steep scramble up a rocky gorge.

the south end of the mountain.

Continuing on the blue trail, you reach the first overlook toward the west and north at 0.4 mile. In late May, we have seen the lovely woodland orchid called pink lady's slipper along the trail near here. The trail now levels out, following the contour of the ridge southward just below the crest of the hill, and passing three bare rock viewpoints along the way. When the leaves are down, you will have good views at every step along this part of the trail. At 0.7 mile, the trail bends left eastward and reaches the south end of the Torne, where the final viewpoint looks southeast toward South Torne with Osio Rock perched on its south end, and east toward High Mountain and the New York City skyline.

After this viewpoint, the trail descends steeply over bare rock, where in one spot we were not embarrassed to abandon walking and shimmy down on our backsides. In this location, you can see how the glacial pull pried rocks apart and roughened the cliff face, opening the way for fractures from freeze-thaw cycles and other weathering. Also on this ledge, there are sheet fractures, places where the rock peels off in layers like the skin of an onion, which are caused by the unloading from the bedrock of the weight of high mountains worn away by ages of erosion. At the bottom of this descent, at 0.9 mile, you find a triangle of three red blazes on a tree marking the south end of the Torne Trail, which you now follow north toward your starting point. The blue-blazed Hewitt-Butler Trail leaves to the right, southward toward South Torne and Osio Rock on its summit. If you have a little extra time and energy, Osio Rock provides a spectacular 360-degree view of the Wyanokie Plateau and the Pequannock Watershed. The 0.3-mile climb on the blue trail is steep and rocky, but well worth the half-hour you spend going up and back.

Turning left on the red trail at 0.9 mile, you face a rock scramble up a small gorge choked with boulders broken off from local bedrock and rounded by erosion and weathering. We have sometimes found ourselves stymied here by a tall rock with no toeholds, but a little searching can usually locate a somewhat easier path. At the top of this climb at 1.1 miles, the trail becomes level again between the two ridges of the Torne. After the leaves fall in November, mature native witch hazel shrubs bloom on both sides of the trail, presenting their distinctive straggly yellow blossoms on fragrant twigs. In early June, a little farther along the trail, the mountain laurel is beautiful, especially because some of these blossoms are a pink color that is deeper than usual. At 1.3 miles, the red trail ends at a T-intersection with the blue trail in the hollow where you began the first climb to the top of the Torne. Turn right on the blue trail and retrace your steps back through the woods to the Otter Hole parking area, at 1.5 miles. If you parked in the north area, follow the unmarked path directly to Glenwild Avenue, turn left (west) on the road, and walk back to your car.

Buckabear Pond Loop

2.5 miles • 1¾ hours

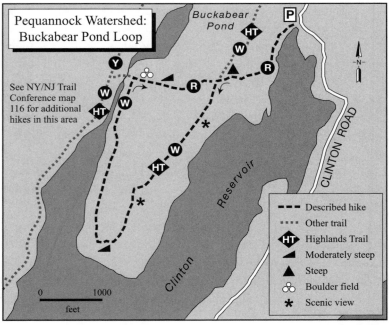

Rutgers Cartography 2006

ELEVATION: Low: 980 feet; High: 1,224 feet.

BLAZES: Red, white and Highlands Trail teal diamonds, and red again.

CLIMBING: The first climb is 180 feet at a moderate to steep grade on a woods road. The summit of the ridge, at 1,224 feet, is reached after an easy ascent at the south end of the trail where there is a view of the reservoir. On the west side of the ridge, the trail has been rerouted around a boulder field partly immersed in water raised by beaver activity at the edge of Buckabear Pond.

PERMITTED USES: Hiking only.

This is in part a Highlands Trail hike.

OVERVIEW

This is a loop hike over the southern tip of Bearfort Mountain, which juts into Clinton Reservoir. Two viewpoints along the ridge overlook the east arm of the reservoir. No long steep climbing is required. The southwest tip of the loop goes through an extensive laurel grove and descends to the water's edge. The return from Buckabear Pond skirts a boulder field partly submerged by beaver activity. Caution: From late September through December, hiking on these trails is permitted only on Sundays to avoid conflict with hunters. From the middle of April to the end of May, hiking is permitted on weekdays and Saturdays, but only after 1 p.m., to avoid conflict with spring turkey hunters. Sunday hunting is never permitted in New Jersey. Check with the Watershed office (see contact information following) for exact hunting dates of the year.

ACCESS: From NJ 23, 6.5 miles west of Kinnelon Road in Butler, take the Clinton Road exit north. Drive on Clinton Road for 3.9 miles to parking area P3, next to a bridge over a stream feeding Clinton Reservoir. Adults hiking in the Pequannock Watershed require an annual permit, issued at the office of the Newark Watershed Conservation and Development Corporation at 223 Echo Lake Road, Newfoundland, NJ 07435, (973) 697-2850, www.nwcdc.net. An annual permit for a family of two adults with children under 18 years is currently $8; a senior permit is half price. To get to the office, head west from Butler on NJ 23 to Echo Lake Road, 4.3 miles from the Kinnelon Road exit in Butler. The office is 1.1 miles north of NJ 23.

DETAILED DESCRIPTION

The trail begins on a woods road leading south from the parking area. Three red blazes in a triangle on a tree to the right mark the trailhead. Along the water, a few hemlocks fight a losing battle against the woolly adelgid. The red blazes lead slightly away from the water's edge until the road turns sharply right uphill past a boulder at 0.2 mile. The road is wide and rocky, and for a short distance climbs at a 30% grade beside a rocky ridge, with associated boulders fractured from the bedrock by glaciers and weathering. The top of the ridge is reached in 0.4 mile, at an intersection with the co-aligned white-blazed Clinton West Trail and the teal diamond-blazed Highlands Trail. Here you leave the red blazes and follow the white blazes to the left (south) along the ridgetop.

The Highlands Trail section begins here.

The Highlands Trail is co-aligned here, but its teal diamond blazes are less frequent than the white blazes of the Clinton West Trail. The forest is the dry ridgetop combination of chestnut and red oak, hickory, black birch, and beech, with a blueberry and mountain laurel understory. The trees are neither tall nor wide in diameter, not only because this area was logged mercilessly to feed nearby iron furnaces in the nineteenth century, but also because the bedrock is close to the surface and the thin soil will not retain moisture or support in-

A view from the first overlook on the Clinton West Trail southeast over the Clinton Reservoir, frozen in November.

tense growth. Trees in moist uplands may reach a diameter of two feet in a century, but on dry ridgetops, a one-foot diameter may represent a century's growth. There are many blowdowns on the ridge, victims of drought, gypsy moths, limited root structure, and exposure to winds and weather. In winter among the fallen leaves along this path, you will see the low wintergreen, a tiny plant with three heart-shaped, dark red and green leaves and bright red berries. When rubbed against your finger, the wintergreen leaves are very fragrant. At 0.8 mile, a rock outcrop about 40 yards to the left of the trail provides a year-round view of the east arm of Clinton Reservoir. There is no marked trail to this overlook.

Soon the trail passes a garage-sized glacial erratic on the right and begins a slow climb toward the summit of the ridge. At 1.0 mile, it reaches the top at 1,224 feet, where there is a view of the reservoir off to the left. The trail continues straight ahead along the edge of the

Buckabear Pond in November, seen from near the dam at the west trailhead of the Buckabear Pond Trail.

ridge, reaching the southern tip, where again a rock outcrop to the left of the trail offers a good view of the reservoir. The trail immediately descends through a short rocky ledge and bends right, heading diagonally down toward the point where Bearfort Ridge juts into the reservoir. The trail circles the point, staying about 50 feet above the water on a narrow footpath, climbing and then descending through a long grove of mountain laurel at 1.4 miles. The trees are a little taller and the vegetation a little denser on this southwest slope of the ridge. The trail descends all the way to the water's edge at 1.6 miles, and reaches a dam across the outlet of Buckabear Pond and the trailhead of the Buckabear Pond Trail at 1.8 miles. Here you leave the white-blazed Clinton West Trail and the teal diamonds of the Highlands Trail, which together cross the dam. You will now follow the red blazes of the Buckabear Pond Trail, which leaves at a sharp right angle along the edge of the pond near the dam.

This section of the Highlands Trail ends here.

In past years, beavers built up the level of this dam with thickets of branches, making the crossing difficult and submerging parts of the Buckabear Pond Trail along the shore of the pond. What used to be a swamp became a body of water. On the other side, the yellow-blazed Bearfort Waters-Clinton Trail, which provides a loop opportunity back to the north end of the Clinton West Trail, was deeply under water for at least a half mile along the shore. The beavers seem to have abandoned this pond now, and the water level is decreasing. A new bridge across the pond was installed as a project for National Trails Day in 2005, and the Buckabear Pond Trail has been rerouted to avoid the water. It is now possible to continue on the Highlands Trail across Buckabear Pond in positive comfort.

The red-blazed Buckabear Pond Trail, on which you return, crosses a boulder field on the east shore of the pond before turning uphill. The footpath climbs on a long, moderate grade toward the top of the ridge, reached at 2.1 miles, where it turns right to run jointly with the Clinton West Trail (white blazes) for just a few yards. The red trail you are following then turns left, away from the white-blazed trail, down the slope, retracing your steps toward the parking area where you left your car, reached at 2.5 miles.

Wawayanda Mountain Turnaround

2.5 miles • 2 hours

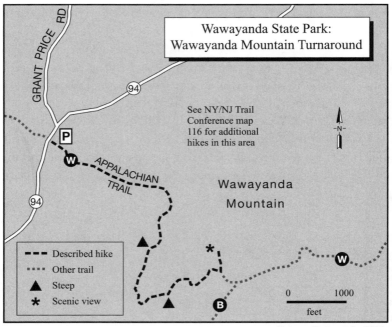

Wawayanda State Park:
Wawayanda Mountain Turnaround

GRANT PRICE RD

94

See NY/NJ Trail
Conference map
116 for additional
hikes in this area

–N–

P

W

APPALACHIAN TRAIL

Wawayanda
Mountain

94

- - -	Described hike
· · ·	Other trail
▲	Steep
✳	Scenic view

W

B

0   1000

feet

Rutgers Cartography 2006

ELEVATION: Low: 480 feet; High: 1,300 feet.

BLAZES: Appalachian Trail (AT) white vertical rectangle, blue, and white again, returning.

CLIMBING: A steep climb up switchbacks and rock steps, gaining 700 feet in a little over 0.8 mile, an average grade of 18%. Some ledges need hands as well as feet, and you follow the same steep trail coming down.

PERMITTED USES: Hiking only.

OVERVIEW

This is an up-and-back hike on a section of the Appalachian Trail (AT). It begins with an easy, almost level walk beside fields recently abandoned from cultivation, and then becomes a steep climb with switchbacks, rock steps, and some rock scrambles up a gneiss escarpment forming the face of Wawayanda Mountain at the western edge of the Highlands. A short spur trail north of the AT, at the top of the ridge, leads to Pinwheel's Vista, a long viewpoint over the Pochuck Creek Valley toward Pochuck Mountain and the Kittatinny Ridge, with the High Point Monument visible to the north. Interesting wildflowers and shrubs grow along the trail. Trail maps show that, farther east on the AT, a spur trail to the right (south) leads in 0.5 mile to another viewpoint over the Pochuck Valley. During leafy seasons, we have found that view obscured, not worth the added mile you must invest in it. The hike described here stops at Pinwheel's Vista and returns.

ACCESS: Take NJ 23 north to the intersection with County 515 (Stockholm/Highland Lakes Road). Turn right (north) onto County 515 and travel 8.5 miles to the center of the Town of Vernon, where County 515 meets NJ 94 at a traffic light. Continue straight ahead on NJ 94 for 2.2 miles to a small parking turnout for the AT on the right, just past Grant Price Road. Approaching from the north through the Town of Warwick, drive south on NJ 94, continuing until you pass the Heaven Hill Garden Center on your right, about 5.8 miles from Warwick. After passing the garden center, look for the AT turnout immediately on your left.

Approaching from Greenwood Lake on Warwick Turnpike, turn left at the T-intersection with NJ 94, drive for 3.7 miles, and look for the AT parking turnout on the left just past the garden center.

HISTORY AND TOPOGRAPHY

Wawayanda Mountain is the western edge of the Highlands geological province; its steep escarpment is Highlands crystalline gneiss. In the valley below to the west, the underlying rocks are softer sedimentary rocks, including limestone in and around Vernon and McAfee. In the second half of the nineteenth century, when railroads and anthracite coal made it cheaper to produce iron in Pennsylvania, a limestone quarry in McAfee became the principal supplier of that raw material to the Lehigh Valley foundries. On the trail, along the level valley floor, you will notice cobbles and boulders of smooth-surfaced nearly white limestone among the gneissic rocks on the path. The Pochuck Valley below the mountain is part of the Great Valley of the Appalachians that extends from Maine to Alabama. The softer and chemically sweeter bedrock of the valley provides good soils for farming; this area was settled early by farmers and was productively worked until the middle of the twentieth century. A drawing by Robert Dickinson in the first edition (1923) of the New York-New Jersey Trail Conference's *New York Walk Book* shows most of the lower hillsides on this mountain and the ridge across the valley clear of trees and either under cultivation or used as pasturage. On top of Wawayanda Mountain, the old Barrett Farm, active for several generations through the nineteenth and twentieth centuries, has been preserved as a National Historic District. A living history museum, it provides an example of how New Jersey earned the nickname "the Garden State." Road access to this farm is through the Wawayanda State Park office off Warwick Turnpike.

DETAILED DESCRIPTION

The hike begins at an AT kiosk at the parking turnout. Following posts painted with the vertical white rectangle blaze of the AT, walk east on a straight path with a very gradual ascent past formerly culti-vated fields. In May, open field wildflowers such as cy-press spurge, moth mullein, and hawkweed bloom along the trail here. At 0.4 mile, the trail enters the woods on a wide woods road through a young successional forest at the base of the mountain. The trail passes a large boul-der and, at 0.5 mile, begins to climb to the right (south) on a rocky footpath through immense boulders split from the cliff above by the

A section of the Appalachian Trail leads to Wawayanda Mountain at the western margin of the Highlands.

Wisconsin Glacier or subsequent freeze-thaw weathering. The soil, though thin and rocky, is moist and supports some conifers, as well as hardwoods and interesting wildflowers and shrubs. In May, we saw the five-petalled pink flowers of Herb Robert, a species of wild geranium which, though not officially endangered, is no longer common in the Highlands.

The trail begins the steep ascent of the mountain at 0.6 mile, climbing gradually to the south across the contour of the slope. In the frequent steep pitches, the hiker can mount stone steps built by Appalachian Trail Conservancy crews and New York-New Jersey Trail Conference volunteers in the late 1980s, when the AT was relocated to this track. From valley to ridgetop, there are nearly 300 stone steps. The trail continues to climb in this direction on a rocky footpath through boulders with an occasional few yards of level walking, at 0.8 mile reaching a small rock outcrop on the right, with a view of the Pochuck Valley through trees. In another 0.1 mile, the long southbound climb ends and the trail turns sharply left to a northbound switchback, still climbing on a rocky footpath. The trail passes a bedrock outcrop on the right and, at 1.0 mile, comes to a right turn blaze on a 3-foot-thick red oak, where the trail turns more directly up the slope for a few yards, and then resumes its diagonal climb. At 1.1 miles, a set of steep stone steps leads straight up the slope, and the trail bends left again for about 40 yards of level walking. At the end of the level stretch, the trail climbs steeply again on rock steps, turns north under a cliff, and bends up around the edge of the cliff.

At 1.2 miles, the AT reaches the dark blue trailhead blaze of the short spur trail to Pinwheel's Vista. Follow these blue blazes fifty yards to the left (north) past a large glacial erratic to the wide open Pinwheel's Vista on a rock outcrop overlooking the Pochuck Valley to the west, the Kittatinny Ridge in the background, and the High Point Monument, the Shawangunks, and the southern Catskills to the north. Several open rock outcrops provide viewpoints and protected spots for rest, a drink of water, and a snack. In May, we saw many anemones and Dutchman's breeches blooming on this spur trail.

Returning to the AT (white rectangle blazes), you may continue to the left (east) to the top of Wawayanda Mountain to find another blue-blazed spur trail leading to the right (south) for 0.5 mile toward what some maps indicate is a viewpoint over the valley. However, when we walked that path, we found the view obscured by maturing trees and not worth the extra mile. We suggest you turn back after Pinwheel's Vista and retrace your steps down the cliff.

Stone steps ease the climb up the west face of Wawayanda Mountain.

As you may have discovered, climbing down steep ledges tests your balance and your knees even more than climbing up, so be cautious as you descend, and make sure your foot is steady before putting weight on it. On the way down, a hiking stick (or two) is useful. Though you have been on this trail before, there is still good reason to keep your eyes and ears alert. Often on a return trip over the same trail, the light and angles are different, and you may notice plants, animals, birds, and even rocks you missed on the way up. After the steep descent, you arrive at the AT parking turnout, having completed a hike of 2.5 miles in about 2 hours.

The view west over the Great Valley, from Pinwheel's Vista on Wawayanda Mountain.

Point Mountain Loop

3.1 miles • 2½ hours

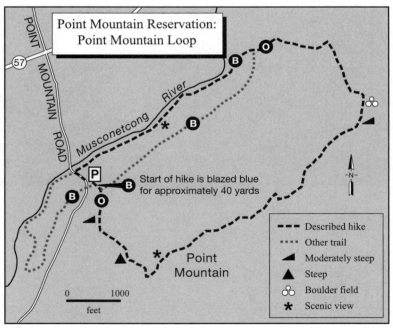

Point Mountain Reservation:
Point Mountain Loop

Start of hike is blazed blue
for approximately 40 yards

Point
Mountain

0   1000

feet

- - - - Described hike
· · · · · Other trail
◄   Moderately steep
▲   Steep
⚇   Boulder field
✴   Scenic view

Rutgers Cartography 2006

ELEVATION: Low: 395 feet; High: 935 feet.

BLAZES: Blue, orange, then blue again.

CLIMBING: The walk begins with a steep 400-foot climb through boulders and rocky outcrops. On the top of the ridge, walking is fairly level. On the descent, the trail passes through wetlands and, at its lowest point, follows the bank of the picturesque Musconetcong River.

PERMITTED USES: Hiking only.

OVERVIEW

Point Mountain, at 935 feet, is one of the last high hills at the southwestern end of the gradually diminishing chain of exposed ridges of crystalline rock that make up the Highlands geological formation. More than 1,000 acres around the mountain are preserved as the Point Mountain Section of the Musconetcong River Reservation (a Hunterdon County Park). The peak stands out amidst this area of gently rolling farmland. After the first climb, an excellent viewpoint looks northwest over farmland still in cultivation. The trail follows footpaths and woods roads over the mountain, through typical rocky Highlands steeps, ridgetop forest, and stream-fed wetlands, and returns along the edges of cultivated grain fields and the banks of the trout-filled Musconetcong River.

ACCESS: From I-78 west, take Exit 17, and turn north on NJ 31 to the Town of Washington. Turn right (east) on NJ 57 and drive for 4 miles to a traffic light at Point Mountain Road.

Approaching from the north on I-80, use Exit 26 to US 46 toward Hackettstown, and after crossing the Musconetcong River, turn left at the next intersection onto NJ 182. After 1.0 mile, turn right onto NJ 57 and drive west 6.5 miles to the traffic light at Point Mountain Road.

At the traffic light on Point Mountain Road, turn south slightly downhill, through open fields. Just after crossing a bridge over the Musconetcong River, as you start uphill, there is a small parking turnout for fishermen on the right, and 0.1 mile farther up on the left, at the trailhead, a gravel parking area for hikers.

DETAILED DESCRIPTION

The trailhead is on the uphill (south) side of the parking area near the road, at a kiosk displaying a trail map. You will find a double blue blaze on a tree to the left of the trail. About 40 yards from the trailhead, you reach an intersection with a woods road. Here the blue trail goes off to the left, and the orange-blazed trail you are to follow leads to the right at an easy, almost level track through the woods, with one left turn to the base of the mountain.

Like many Highlands hikes, this one now begins a steep climb up a rocky footpath. The orange-blazed trail winds through a field of boulders, probably produced by a rockslide from the gneiss bedrock above, then scattered by gravity down the slope. Point Mountain is south of the edge of the Wisconsin Glacier, so its rocks have not been ground smooth as have the Highlands summits further north. I hiked this trail with my daughter Susan, a geologist, who found evidence of a geological fault at the western end of the ridge, and suggested the rockslide had been caused by tremors associated with the fault.

The forest on this mountainside is the moist upland mixed hardwood combination of oak, maple, black birch, hickory, and beech. The largest trunks are about a foot in diameter, suggesting that these slopes were still open fields 60 to 70 years ago. The many understory dogwood trees produce beautiful blooms in the spring. Along this stretch of trail in August, we found several wildflowers, including white snakeroot, enchanter's nightshade, and white baneberry with its small black-dotted white toxic fruit called "doll's eyes."

As you near the top of the climb, there are helpful wood and rock steps. At 0.3 mile, the steep climb begins to moderate. The trail passes a short unmarked path to the right that leads to a private dwelling. Keep your head up and follow the orange blazes straight up through the boulders. The trail markers on this part of the trail are three-inch plastic squares nailed on end as a diamond-shape. At 0.4 mile, the trail opens onto a rock outcrop providing a wide view of the valley, with farmlands and wooded hills to the north and northwest.

As you leave the lookout, avoid the unmarked trail to the left down through a cleft in the rocks; instead, stay on the orange trail, which leads off to the right. A few yards from the lookout, a yellow-blazed trail comes in from the right, from a trailhead near homes on Point Mountain Road, about half a mile away. But stay on the orange

A view over rolling farmland to the west, from the overlook on Point Mountain.

trail, and at 0.5 mile, you come to another uphill rock scramble, with large boulders split from the bedrock to the left of the trail. At the top of these rocks, at 0.6 mile, the trail levels out on the drier crest of the mountain, where chestnut oak, red oak, and black cherry dominate. At 1.0 mile, there is an area where the prolific alien invasive plant called garlic mustard has taken over and squeezed out native species. At 1.4 miles, the trail passes the remains of an old stone fence, probably intended to enclose cattle; when first built, this fence would have most likely been at least four feet high. Along the ridgetop, many trees, weakened by gypsy moth infestation and recent years of drought in this thin soil, have been blown down. At 1.7 miles, the trail turns right and soon begins to descend slightly as you approach the northeast end of the ridge.

The trail turns left below the ridgetop and descends westward toward the Musconetcong River. At 1.9 miles, the trail crosses a brook through a boulder field and a mountain wetland. In spring, the drier slopes along the trail near this location will produce low-lying wildflowers. The trees here are 20 or more feet taller than those on top, though the trunks are not much thicker. There are different species in this moist and deeper soil, including tulip trees, beech, ash, dogwood, and maple, trees not found high on ridgetops. At 2.0 miles, a woods road joins the trail from the right, and the trail follows that road downhill, crossing another small brook. This section will be muddy in spring, as well as during wet weather at other seasons. At 2.3 miles, the trail emerges from the woods and skirts the south side of a field of grain. At the end of the field, the trail turns left back into the woods and in 20 feet emerges onto another grain field.

At the beginning of the second field, the orange trail ends; three blue blazes on a post mark the trailhead of the blue trail, which you now follow back along the river. The blue trail runs beside the left (south) edge of the field, until at the end of the field it turns left into the woods. At 2.7 miles, as the trail becomes broad and open, the Musconetcong River comes into view on the right. The blue trail splits into two sections here. The left branch heads straight back to the parking area on a woods road if you need a quicker exit, while the more interesting right branch descends toward the river. Soon you are on the riverbank, passing benches where visitors can sit and watch fly fishermen angle for trout. Along this section, you might slow down and look for wildflowers, birds, and excellent river views. At 3.1 miles, the trail enters a thicket of tall brambles, emerging onto Point Mountain Road. A short distance uphill to the left, you will find the parking area and your car.

However, if you have the time and inclination, this hike can be extended. The blue trail crosses Point Mountain Road here and continues along the river for 0.5 mile. From this point, at 3.6 miles it circles back, returning after 4.1 miles to Point Mountain Road and the parking area where you left your car.

A quiet pool on the Musconetcong River at the foot of Point Mountain.

Otter Hole–Wyanokie Crest Loop

3.0 miles • 3 hours

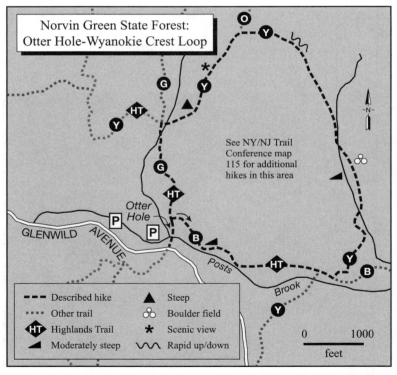

Rutgers Cartography 2006

ELEVATION: Low: 670 feet; High: 1,030 feet.

BLAZES: Blue, yellow, green and Highlands Trail teal diamond, and blue again.

CLIMBING: Posts Brook must be crossed both going and coming on large boulders, which can be difficult at high water. There are two seasonal muddy spots along Posts Brook, then a long ascent through a boulder field, a crossing of a perched wetland, and three ups and downs over Highlands ridges.

PERMITTED USES: Hiking only.

OVERVIEW

Crossing Posts Brook at Otter Hole requires jumping from one large boulder to another across the stream. Usually this is simply fun, but at high water or in icy conditions it can be too difficult to attempt. There are seasonal muddy spots on the descent along Posts Brook. After a long, moderate but ankle-twisting climb through a tightly packed boulder field, the trail crosses a swamp near the top of the hike. Three ups and downs over 30-foot gneiss ledges guard the top of the ridge. On the return leg, two excellent rock-ledge lookouts face Buck Mountain to the west. After the viewpoints, a brief rocky descent leads from the last ridge to the hollow of a small tributary of Posts Brook. The final 0.5 mile descends easily on a woods road to the return crossing at Otter Hole.

ACCESS: Approaching Butler heading west on NJ 23, turn right (north) at the Boonton Avenue (County 511) Exit into the center of town. Boonton Avenue heads downhill, makes a small circuit near at the bottom of the hill, turns right onto Park Place, and at 1.0 mile crosses a railroad track, ending at a T-intersection with Main Street.

Approaching Butler on NJ 23 east, take the Kinnelon Road/Kiel Avenue exit north into Butler. The street ends at a T-intersection with Park Place, where you turn left to cross railroad tracks to a T-intersection at Main Street.

In either case, turn right onto Main Street and at another T-intersection where Main Street ends, turn left onto Hamburg Turnpike. In about 50 yards, take the next right turn (uphill) onto Glenwild Avenue. Continue on Glenwild Avenue for 3.2 miles to the Otter Hole parking lot on the right. If this one is full, there is another lot 0.2 mile farther ahead on the right.

DETAILED DESCRIPTION

At the east (downhill) end of the first parking lot, find the footpath of the blue-blazed Hewitt-Butler Trail heading north into the woods toward the Otter Hole cascade of Posts Brook. Otter Hole is notable for its wildflowers in all green seasons. Among its specialties, in late May, there are pink lady's slippers; in August, bright spikes of the cardinal flower wave from the water's edge above and below the falls. But don't be eager to step off the entrance trail; dense mats of poison ivy patrol its borders. The trail crosses Posts Brook above the falls, where the brook is about 20 feet wide. You must leap from boulder to boulder, with blazes indicating the easier steps. In dry weather, the best path is marked by boot scuffs on the tops of the stones, but in high water or icy conditions, the crossing may be too difficult to attempt. A safer crossing can usually be found further upstream. However, if you are thinking it's more than you can handle, try the rewarding Wyanokie Torne hike across the road, which has no stream crossings (Hike #13).

Once across Posts Brook, the trail comes to a Y-intersection, with both the south trailhead of the green-blazed Otter Hole Trail and the teal diamond-blazed Highlands Trail on the left branch, and the Highlands and Hewitt-Butler trails on the right branch. Take the right fork, and follow the blue blazes of the Hewitt-Butler Trail and the teal diamonds of the Highlands Trail uphill on a rocky, eroded woods road. In 25 yards, you reach a fork where the dual blazes indicate a bend to the right. The trail climbs easily to the top of this rise at 0.2 mile, and begins a gradual descent through a maturing oak-beech-hickory forest. The trail parallels Posts Brook, which you may hear through the trees to the right. At 0.4 mile, the trail turns left off the woods road onto a footpath, which soon becomes a woods road. The largest trees here have trunks up to two feet thick, indicating these hills were cleared and left to reforest about a century ago. Most of the area had been logged over at least twice by the end of the nineteenth century to fuel the Ringwood and Long Pond iron furnaces. The forest has come back, however, as it has all over the Highlands since the abandonment of the iron industry at the beginning of the twentieth century.

Along Posts Brook, we have seen and heard some of the loveliest woodland songbirds: orioles, scarlet tanagers, hermit thrushes, wood thrushes, and migrating warblers, including redstarts and black and white warblers. Woodland spring wildflowers have returned along the trail, among them several varieties of blue and yellow violets, spring beauties, anemones, and a startling patch of the tiny orchid-like fringed polygala, popularly called gaywings.

The Hewitt-Butler Trail is joined from the right at 0.7 mile by the yellow-blazed Wyanokie Crest Trail, which heads almost immediately to the left. Here you turn left onto the yellow-blazed Wyanokie Crest Trail, while the Hewitt-Butler Trail departs straight ahead. The yellow trail follows the contour of the slope on a slightly descending woods path, until at 1.0 miles it meets a tributary of Posts Brook, which it follows left, upstream. The trail turns right to cross the stream, which seems to disappear into a large hill of boulders. As you cross, you can hear the water gurgling deep under the rocks. The trail now begins a steady ankle-turning climb through an extensive boulder field, formed by rocks split from the ridges by glaciers, erosion, or weathering, and tumbled down into the streambed, where

The author, with trail maintenance gear, descending from lookout ridges on the Wyanokie Crest Trail. The rounded boulders include puddingstone and gneiss, probably carried here by a glacier.

they were rounded and heaped by torrents of rushing meltwater. At high water, the brook cascades over the rocks but in dry seasons, it runs unseen beneath them. The trail climbs for 0.5 mile, crossing the water twice, until at 1.5 miles it reaches a swamp at the stream head-waters, where you tramp through slow-running rivulets at all seasons. On the other side of the swamp, the trail climbs a steep ridge, glacially smoothed at the top, where thin soil and years of drought have killed most of the mature trees. The snags blow down randomly over the ridgetop, often directly across the trail, providing the trail maintainer, who, incidentally, is the author of this trail guide, with plenty of exercise cutting and clearing them.

At the end of this open rock clearing at 1.7 miles, the trail turns sharply right around a large bedrock slab and climbs down a short, steep slope. Here, trail blazes are located on rocks and small saplings, for lack of anything else on which to paint them. The trail climbs and descends another ridge, then climbs once more to the highest point of the hike, a treeless rock outcrop at 1,030 feet, from which the views are obscured by the surrounding forest. At the end of this clearing, at 1.9 miles, the trail passes the trailhead of the Outlaw Trail, blazed in orange on a boulder to the right of the path. The yellow blazes you

A winter view of Buck Mountain from an overlook on the Wyanokie Crest Trail. The hiker is Bob Whitney, photographer and Montclair State University professor, one of three companions who hiked the trails for this book.

continue to follow now enter the woods, descend quickly, and then climb gently back up to a rock outcrop facing west. Here, at 2.2 miles, two ledges offer excellent views of the Buck Mountain ridge.

The trail tunnels through a thick laurel grove and climbs down a rocky incline to cross a tributary of Posts Brook on rounded stones. The trail then rises out of the hollow and descends to an intersection at 2.4 miles, where the green-blazed Otter Hole Trail crosses. The Highlands Trail comes from the left and turns onto the yellow-blazed Wyanokie Crest Trail, both continuing straight ahead. At this crossing, you leave the yellow-blazed footpath and turn left onto the Otter Hole-Highlands Trail (green rectangles, teal diamond blazes), heading south on a wide woods road. This road crosses the tributary brook at 2.5 miles, crosses another smaller brook at 2.7 miles, and finally descends to meet, at 2.9 miles, the blue-blazed Hewitt-Butler Trail at the Y-intersection within sight of Otter Hole. You turn right onto the blue-blazed trail and cross Posts Brook at Otter Hole, retracing your steps up to the Glenwild Avenue parking lot after a hike of 3.0 miles.

The trailhead cairn and blaze for the Outlaw Trail. Photo by Daniel Chazin.

High Point–Iron Mines Loop

3.3 miles • 3 hours

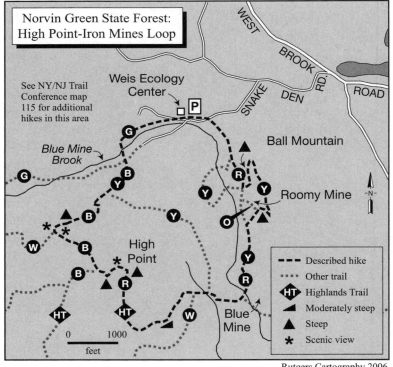

Rutgers Cartography 2006

The blaze circles marked in primary colors (e.g., "R" for red) may represent a color on a white background (e.g., red triangle-on-white), as noted in the hike description.

ELEVATION: Low: 420 feet; High: 960 feet.

BLAZES: Green, blue, red-on-white, yellow-on-white, yellow-on-white and red-on-white to the end.

CLIMBING: The beginning climb, from the kiosk at the blue-blazed Hewitt-Butler trailhead to the first crest of the Wyanokie High Point ridge, is steep and rocky, gaining about 300 feet in 0.3 mile, at an average grade of 20%. In wet or icy weather, some of the smooth rock outcrops near the top can be slippery. A brief rock scramble leads to the High Point summit. On the descent from High Point, a stream crossing can be difficult at high water. There is also a rocky climb past the shafts of the Roomy Mine.

PERMITTED USES: Hiking only.

OVERVIEW

The 360-degree views at the summit of Wyanokie High Point are spectacular. The trail passes the remains of two nineteenth-century iron mines. Wildflowers on moist slopes and in hollows and migrating birds on the ridges are colorful in the spring. The hike goes through several Highlands habitats, from stream banks to rich, moist uplands, dry rocky ridges, and bare rock outcrops.

ACCESS: From I-287, use Exit 55 and take NJ 511 north. Follow signs to Wanaque. Drive north through the towns of Wanaque and Midvale to find the Skyline Diner on your right, at 3.3 miles. About 25 yards past the diner, turn left onto West Brook Road, heading west across the Wanaque Reservoir. In 1.5 miles, West Brook Road meets Stonetown Road at a T-intersection, where you turn left. Follow West Brook Road 0.5 mile to the second left turn, Snake Den Road, with a sign for the Weis Ecology Center. Turn left (uphill) on Snake Den Road, bear left at a fork, and continue on Snake Den Road to a large open parking lot on the right.

DETAILED DESCRIPTION

At the west end of the parking lot, find the trailhead of the green-blazed Otter Hole Trail at the gated entrance road to the Weis Ecology Center. Follow the green blazes on a gravel driveway along Blue Mine Brook under a row of spruces. Hikers who are interested in local fauna and flora should follow the driveway to the right, leaving the Otter Hole Trail and heading toward the large brick building which houses the offices of New Jersey Audubon's Weis Ecology Center. The Center offers exhibits of animals and plants typical of the area, and a variety of guided hikes, programs on birding and wildlife for children and adults, and wildflower hikes led by the author of this book. The North Jersey Trails map set, as well as other maps and guidebooks published by the New York-New Jersey Trail Conference, are available for sale in the gift shop. Returning to the green-blazed Otter Hole Trail, continue along Blue Mine Brook past a brick pump house to reach the base of a hill. Here, the Otter Hole Trail joins the green-on-white-blazed "W" Trail and the orange L-blazed Loop Trail, and heads up a rocky rise near the Highlands Natural Pool.

As you start to climb beside the pool, you will notice a 20-foot-wide swath through the forest, uphill to the right. This is the remnant of a ski tow and parallel ski trail built in the 1930s by Nature Friends, the original occupants of this camp. The Loop Trail leaves to the right up that path, and you continue to the left with green and W blazes. At the crest of the rise on your left, you will see a concrete weir that diverts some of the brook's water to fill the pool below. The trail next turns left to cross a metal bridge over the brook, where the Loop Trail rejoins at 0.3 mile. From the bridge, continue straight ahead on the green-blazed Otter Hole Trail, as the L-blazed trail leaves to the left, and the "W" Trail leaves to the right. The Otter Hole Trail reaches a broad woods road at 0.4 mile, at the trailheads of the Hewitt-Butler Trail (blue blazes) and the Mine Trail (yellow

Hiker Richard Duemmer with his son, Brian, 6, and daughter, Megan, 4, at the first overlook on High Point.

dot-on-white blazes). At this junction, a kiosk erected as an Eagle Scout project displays a trail map and a placard listing New Jersey State Forest Regulations for the Norvin Green State Forest you have entered.

Follow both the blue and the yellow-dot blazes to the left of the kiosk and uphill, leaving the Otter Hole Trail, which turns right here on the woods road. The trails climb a rocky hillside with crude stone steps, cross a rocky outcrop, and descend through a grove of mountain laurel. In a short distance, the Mine Trail (yellow dot-on-white blazes) leaves to the left (southeast), and you follow the Hewitt-Butler Trail (blue blazes) over a patch of exposed bedrock. You follow the blue-blazed trail as it turns sharply left, drops down around another rock outcrop, squeezes through a narrow defile between two massive rock exposures, and continues (uphill) into the woods. The trail climbs steeply until it reaches the top of the ridge, where a rock outcrop to the right of the trail offers a view of Assiniwikam Mountain to the northwest. Shortly after the viewpoint, a triangle of three white blazes marks the trailhead of the Macopin Trail, which heads off to the right.

Proceeding straight ahead on the blue-blazed trail, at 0.6 mile you come to a ten-foot face of weather-fractured bedrock that requires a tall step, or hands and knees to climb. A large glacial erratic is perched on the top of this outcrop. During leafy seasons, the view here is to the south and east, but in winter it is clear in every direction. Coming off this overlook, the trail levels out along the crest of the ridge, where exposure to wind, cold, recent drought, gypsy moth infestations, and poor, thin soil prevents most trees from achieving tall growth. The largest trees, whose trunks, though gnarled and stunted, have reached 8 to12 inches in thickness, could very well be over 100 years of age. In spring, during bird migration, we have seen bluebirds, indigo buntings, thrushes, and a variety of warblers on this ridge.

At 0.8 mile, at the foot of High Point summit, the blue-blazed trail meets the red-dot-on-white Wyanokie Circular Trail (WCI), which joins from the right. At this intersection, the blue trail leaves to the right, heading west along with the red-dot trail and the Highlands Trail (teal diamond blazes).

Trail Conference maintainers have added Highlands Trail blazes to the section of the Wyanokie Circular Trail from this intersection, over High Point, and down to the Blue Mine as described below. These blazes connect to the new section of the Highlands Trail being constructed from Windbeam Mountain to the Blue Mine in order to avoid having extensive road walking on the HT.

Directed to High Point by a wooden sign and an arrow painted on the bedrock, you now follow the red-dot-on-white trail (co-aligned with the HT) to the left up a short, steep rock scramble to the summit at 960 feet. The 360-degree view from High Point of the

Wyanokie Plateau and the Ramapo Ridge is one of the most spectacular in the Highlands. Wanaque Reservoir lies to the east, with the New York City skyline visible beyond on a clear day. Windbeam Mountain rises in the northeast, Assiniwikam and Buck mountains to the west, and Carris Hill to the south.

After a long pause to appreciate the view and have a snack, follow the red-dot-on-white Wyanokie Circular Trail and the HT over the crest of High Point and down the northeast side of the summit. The exposed bedrock here is Highlands gneiss, a pinkish-gray rock made hard by tiny, interlocking crystals, formed as the rock cooled after being baked, squeezed, and folded by the collision of continental plates at least 20 miles deep in the earth. The tall mountains that heaved up during that collision have eroded away over thousands of millions of years, leaving their roots exposed for us to have lunch on. The rock outcrops on this summit seem to be peeling off in sheets like an onion. The process is known as "exfoliation," brought on by the unloading of pressure from the deep overlays of rock now carried away by the chemistry of time, and the physics of glaciers and weathering.

As you leave the summit, you enter an area of snags and blowdowns, another consequence of prolonged drought, shallow soil, gypsy moth infestation, and exposure to heavy weather from the north. About 200 yards from the summit, a double blaze on an exposed tree points the way to the right for the red-dot-on-white trail (WCI) you are following. As the trail enters the woods, it begins a series of turns that ease the grade of the hill. The trail now continues in a moderate descent (east) through a field of boulders broken from the bedrock outcrop above by glacial fractures, subsequent thaw-freeze, and other weathering action over thousands of years.

The trail soon comes to a muddy, level stretch at 1.3 miles, where the water flow is trapped close to the surface by an underlying layer of clay left by outwash from melting glaciers 15,000 years ago. Because the soil is deeper and moister, the trees in this area are taller and thicker than those on the ridgetop. The trail follows the contour of the hill, making the descent very easy here. At 1.7 miles, the trail crosses a brook about four feet wide and, at 1.9 miles, the white-blazed Lower Trail begins to the right. The red-dot-on-white trail you are following almost immediately comes to a larger stream, which you can usually ford on rock steps. In spring during heavy rains, this brook can become an impassable torrent near the trail; sometimes we have had to seek a better crossing further upstream. The yellow-dot-on-white-blazed Mine Trail joins the red-dot-on-white trail from the left at 2.0 miles, and along with the HT, the trails continue together on a narrow woods road for about 100 yards. The three co-aligned trails then turn left off the road onto a rocky foot-path, wide enough to have been a mining road 150 years ago. The trails cross a small brook that seems to travel under the pathway rocks. Local historians say this was a sluiceway from a dam across Blue Mine Brook which provided water power for operations at the mine. At 2.1 miles, still following the red-dot, HT teal diamond, and yellow-dot blazes, you come to a clearing at the top of a small rise, where to the left of the trail there is a dilapidated shelter built 70 years ago by the Green Mountain Club. Today, under regulations of both the state of New Jersey and the North Jersey Water Supply District Commission, camping is not permitted in this area.

A hundred feet further down a short slope, the trail crosses Blue Mine Brook on a sturdy bridge built in 2002 as an Eagle Scout proj-ect and turns left (uphill) in front of the entrance to the Blue Mine. This mine, named for the dark blue color of its ore, was the site of one of the first iron deposits found in New Jersey. Discovered by Peter Hasenclever in 1765, it was worked steadily until 1855, almost a century of continuous operation testifying to the richness and extent of the ore. Thereafter, it was operated intermittently. Its principal shaft was vertical and extended well below the water table, requiring continual dewatering. When, finally the mine was permanently abandoned in 1905, the shaft filled with water, forming the pool you

The author and his daughter, Susan, a geological engineer, examining quartz veins in the crystalline gneiss bedrock on High Point summit. Wanaque Reservoir and the Ramapo Ridge are in the distance.

see at the entrance. For more information on this and other iron mines, see Edward Lenik's *Iron Mine Trails*, published by the New York-New Jersey Trail Conference. In the woods near the mine, trout lilies bloom by the brook in April, Mayapples a few weeks later, as do early saxifrage and pussytoes, which cover the rocks over the mine entrance. At 420 feet elevation, this is the low point of the hike.

Turning north here at a sign directing you to the Weis Ecology Center, the red-dot-on-white trail climbs up a deeply eroded old mine road. (Trail Conference maintainers have plans to reroute this trail onto a parallel track.)

In about 100 yards up the hill, where an unmarked woods road forks to the right, you take the left fork, again following both the red-dot and yellow-dot blazes, and cross a small seasonal brook. At 2.2 miles, you leave the red-dot trail to follow the yellow-dot Mine Trail,

The entrance to the Roomy Mine, which produced iron ore from 1840 to 1857.

which turns right (up-hill) toward the Roomy Mine. After a short climb, you face the mine entrance and can look into some of its shafts. Although its opening is quite large, the mine was named not for its size, but rather for Benjamin Roome, a nineteenth-century surveyor. It was operated from 1840 to 1857. A short orange-blazed crossover trail, that was once a road for hauling ore, leads from the mine to the left (downhill) to join the red-dot Wyanokie Circular Trail on the way back to the Weis Ecology Center. Taking this orange trail and turning right onto the red-dot trail will shorten your hike by about 0.5 mile and will skip the steep rock scramble beside the Roomy Mine.

To continue the hike, follow the yellow-dot trail sharply to the right and up a steep, rocky footpath to the ridge at the top of the mine, reached at 2.4 miles. In about 100 yards, the yellow-dot trail crosses a clearing from which you can look up to the south at the summit of High Point where you rested about an hour ago. At 2.5 miles, the trail skirts a cliff below on the left where, in May, a large colorful patch of bright red and yellow columbine blooms among the rocks. After a climb past mine tailings and what might have been an ore test pit, the trail turns left up to a bare rock outcrop. The ball-shaped, glacially-rounded rocks found here gave the name "Ball Mountain" to this ridge. After passing these rocks, the trail doubles back and heads steeply downhill.

At 2.8 miles, the Mine Trail crosses the Wyanokie Circular Trail, where you leave the yellow dots and turn right for a steady, moderate climb uphill as you follow the red dots. At 2.9 miles, the yellow-dot Mine Trail rejoins from the left and is co-aligned with the red-dot Wyanokie Circular Trail to the end of the hike. At 3.0 miles, the red-dot trail reaches the top of a ridge, beside a cliff of Highlands gneiss off to the right, with many large boulders split off by glacial fracturing and subsequent weathering. The trail levels off into a boulder-filled wetland, where in wet weather the water is sometimes too deep to walk through, requiring a detour. It then passes through private property along a fence and rises at 3.2 miles to meet Snake Den Road (East). Turn left and walk on the road to reach, at 3.3 miles, the parking lot where you left your car.

Split Rock Loop South

3.7 miles • 3¼ hours

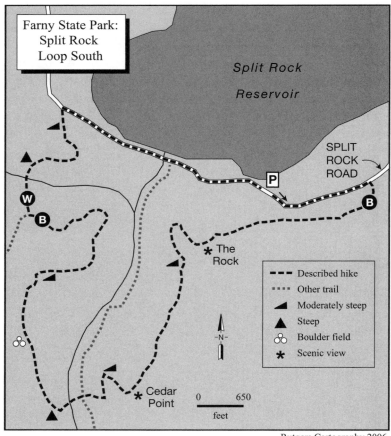

Farny State Park:
Split Rock
Loop South

Split Rock
Reservoir

SPLIT
ROCK
ROAD

P

W

B

B

* The
Rock

- - - Described hike
····· Other trail
◀ Moderately steep
▲ Steep
⚭ Boulder field
* Scenic view

-N-

* Cedar
Point

0   650
feet

Rutgers Cartography 2006

ELEVATION: Low: 680 feet; High: 980 feet.

BLAZES: Blue, white.

CLIMBING: One stream crossing on large boulders, difficult at high water. After the stream crossing, one long ascent of 160 feet in 0.5 mile. Frequent 20-foot-high rough, rocky ledges.

PERMITTED USES: Hiking only.

OVERVIEW

This is a moderate-to-strenuous hike, with frequent ups and downs over rocky ledges. There are two long views south over the Farny Highlands from open bedrock, and a wide crossing of Split Rock Brook, a rushing stream from the spillway of Split Rock Reservoir. The marked trail leads over large rounded boulders, on which you must leap from top to top. In high water, you may have to search for an easier crossing upstream over fallen trees and across small islands in the torrent. There is one long, steady climb at a moderate grade, 160 feet in 0.5 mile. The viewpoint called "Cedar Point," a nice place to eat lunch, is about an hour from the eastern trailhead and two hours from the western end.

ACCESS: From I-80 west, take Exit 37 (Rockaway/Hibernia) and turn right at the traffic light at the end of the exit ramp. In 20 yards, you come to another traffic light, where you turn left onto Morris Avenue.

From I-80 east, take Exit 37 (Rockaway/Hibernia) and at the traffic light at the end of the ramp, turn left under the highway. In 30 yards, you come to a traffic light, where you turn right onto Morris Avenue.

From the Morris Avenue traffic light drive 0.9 mile, passing Morris Catholic High School on your left, and coming to an intersection where you pass Kitchell Road, which turns acutely left uphill.

Make the immediate next left onto the continuation of Morris Avenue. From this turn, drive 0.8 mile to a T-intersection. Turn left onto Diamond Spring Road (called Rockaway Valley Road in Boonton Township), and drive 3.5 miles, passing the beautiful early nineteenth-century Dixon Farm with its historic home and pond on your left. Take the next left (uphill) on Split Rock Road. Follow Split Rock Road, bearing right at a fork with Decker Road at 0.8 mile. Continue on Split Rock Road, bearing left past Charlottesburg Road, where it soon becomes a dirt road, and arriving at a gravel parking area on your right at 2.6 miles.

DETAILED DESCRIPTION

From the parking area, walk east (uphill) about 0.3 mile to the second crossing under the power lines. On the right side of the road, find a rock with the blue blaze of the Split Rock Loop Trail, and follow the footpath leading uphill under the wires. Before the crest of the hill, on the right side of the trail, find another rock with a double blue blaze for a right turn and take the footpath heading into the woods. A blue blaze on a tree should be visible to the right from the open field under the wires.

The trail heads south on a gentle uphill grade through dry upland oak-hickory forest, with a blueberry understory. The largest trees are not much over a foot in diameter and the canopy is sparse because the thin ridgetop soil, long-term drought, and attacks by gypsy moths have diminished the forest. After 0.4 mile of level walking, the trail crosses a rock outcrop and begins a two-stage rocky descent into a hollow, soon rising on the other side. At 0.6 mile, the trail crosses open bedrock and bends to the right (west) along the top of a ledge. At 0.7 mile, the trail turns right to descend sharply from the ledge, turning left again in front of the rocks. It descends into a hollow and climbs to the right towards a ridge on the other side.

A trail marker of piled rocks (a cairn) on the rock outcrop at Cedar Point, a south-facing viewpoint overlooking the Split Rock Brook valley.

Here you can see southward down into the valley of Split Rock Brook. From this ledge, the trail descends again into a hollow and climbs briefly on the other side. At 1.0 mile, the trail crosses an old logging road. After a level grassy stretch, the trail reaches a rock outcrop with a cairn marking the high point of the hike at 980 feet.

A few yards past the cairn at 1.2 miles, the trail comes to an open ledge called "The Rock," with a view south down the Split Rock Brook valley. From "The Rock," the trail descends sharply down a cleft in the rocks and turns left down a steep incline, losing 100 feet in 0.1 mile. At the bottom of the descent, the trail turns left again, climbing south to another viewpoint called "Cedar Point," at 1.6 miles. From "Cedar Point," the trail turns sharply right, then left (downhill), passing to the right of the path a square hole in the forest floor that might have been an iron ore test pit. After turning right again at the test pit, the trail descends to an old woods road that leads to the iron furnace near Split Rock Reservoir. At 1.7 miles, the trail arrives at a ford over Split Rock Brook. The blue blazes lead you across the brook on large rounded boulders, with a step or two on mossy tufts of soil on the way. This path is available in all but the highest water, but in very wet seasons, when the boulders are submerged in deep splashes and waves, you may have to look upstream

A woods road beside Split Rock Brook, leading to the nineteenth-century iron furnace at Split Rock Reservoir.

for an easier track on fallen trees and larger "islands."

Across the brook, the trail climbs at first to the left, then turns right, passing through several rough, rocky ledges and crossing an old logging road at 1.8 miles. When leaving the ledges, you head gently down into a large, ankle-twisting boulder field called "The Maze," crossing a small seasonal tributary half-way through, and emerging from the rocks at 2.1 miles, at the base of a steep incline. The trail turns right to moderate the climb, and then turns left (north) to take the hill more steeply, leveling off on a crest at 2.3 miles. The trail turns left here, making a broad U-turn to head south again, climbing up onto an open bedrock ledge at 2.4 miles. The trail follows the left edge of this rock outcrop, where blazes are painted either on the bedrock or on small saplings. There are no mature trees with blazes because trees reaching any girth in this thin soil have died and fallen during the severe drought years. At the end of the outcrop, the trail enters the woods on a straight and level course, ending at 2.6 miles at a T-intersection with the white-blazed Four Birds Trail.

At this intersection, you turn right to follow the white blazes which descend steeply over rocks to a streambed with associated boulders. The trail emerges at 2.8 miles on the other side at the base of a cliff whose top is 100 feet above you. The trail turns right to take the cliff obliquely, climbing gradually through rocky clefts, until at 3.0 miles it reaches a crest and levels off. After descending briefly under a power line where there is a small brook, the trail slowly climbs a 40-foot ledge, turns right, and heads downhill to meet Split Rock Road at 3.2 miles. You turn right here and walk 0.5 mile east on the road as it crosses over a dam with long views of Split Rock Reservoir. At the eastern end of the dam, stop and peer over the downstream side; through the trees you will see the ruins of an iron ore furnace that dates back to pre-Civil War days. Continue on the road, which climbs up to the parking area where you left your car, having completed a hike of 3.7 miles.

The author and Bob Whitney at the Split Rock Brook crossing. In spring, during high water, most of these rocks are covered with rushing water.

Boundary Loop

6.1 miles • 4 hours

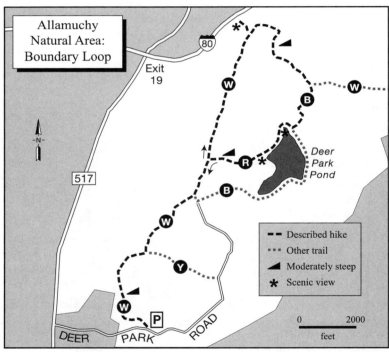

Rutgers Cartography 2006

ELEVATION: Low: 930 feet; High: 1,060 feet.

BLAZES: White, red, blue, and white again.

CLIMBING: The climbs are all less than 100 feet, on easy trails or woods roads. There are several muddy spots on this trail.

PERMITTED USES: Hiking, biking, horses, snowshoeing and x-country skiing in winter.

OVERVIEW

Although this hike is longer than others in this section, it is not a very strenuous hike because the terrain is relatively level. However, there are some short ups and downs on rocky paths and woods roads. There is one long view and a circuit of a picturesque lake where migrating waterfowl congregate and where beavers have built three lodges. The trails cross several moist areas where spring wildflowers appear.

The park is a popular recreation area for residents of nearby housing developments. All of its trails are designated multi-use, which includes mountain bikes and horses. In winter, they are used by cross-country skiers and people on snowshoes. The trails are suitable for families with young, active children, but in wet seasons many damp spots cannot be passed comfortably in sneakers. Hikes shorter than the one described here, are available. A trail map is posted at a kiosk at the main parking lot, and printed maps may be found in a box there. However, the trails have been reblazed, and a new map brochure is in preparation. The following trail description and corresponding map are based on the new blazes. (These trails are maintained by the Chain Gang Mountain Biking Club.)

ACCESS: Take Exit 19 from I-80, and turn south toward Hackettstown on County 517. Drive for 2.2 miles (passing the Panther Valley development on your right), until you come to a small brick house on the left. Turn left here onto the clearly signed Deer Park Road, a partly paved, partly gravel road beside the small brick house, and drive 0.7 mile to the grassy main parking area and the kiosk with a posted trail map.

TERRAIN AND HISTORY

Allamuchy Natural Area is a section of Allamuchy Mountain State Park, south of Route I-80. As late as 80 years ago, the park was a working farm, with several natural streams running into and out of Deer Park Pond, a shallow lake of about one square mile that is the central topographical feature of the tract. Most of the formerly cultivated fields have been allowed to return to forest, though there are still some open fields that have been tilled more recently. Around the ridges with rock outcrops and steep rocky slopes, where cultivation was impossible, some stands of tall, mature second- or third-growth trees have been preserved. Beautiful views across Deer Park Pond can be found on the red-blazed and white-blazed trails that circle its shore. In spring and fall, migrating songbirds and waterfowl take advantage of this refuge of abundant water and variety of cover, in the midst of surrounding farms and villages. The various habitats, from wetlands to rocky slopes to field edges, produce attractive patches of wildflowers from April through October.

The hills in the park are not very high; the maximum elevation gain on any of the trails is not more than 100 feet. However, the northern limit of the hike gives access to a rest area on the eastbound side of Route I-80, where there is an excellent view of the Great Valley, Kittatinny Mountain, and the Delaware Water Gap. The area provides fishing opportunities in trout-stocked water, as well as spring and fall seasonal hunting. Contact the Stephens State Park office, 800 Willow Grove St., Hackettstown, NJ 07840: (908) 852-3790; www.njparksandforests.org, for information and schedules.

DETAILED DESCRIPTION

The walk winds through all the varieties of terrain found in the park, including some short, rocky climbs and a few patches of wetland. Although longer than other hikes in this section, it is included here because there are no steep climbs or rock scrambles to negotiate. An easier, shorter, and very attractive walk begins at a second parking lot farther into the park; it follows a gravel road and woodland footpaths around Deer Park Pond. Though easier, it, too, has seasonal wet spots that may soak through sneakers. Consult the trail map for trail blazes and intersections for this shorter walk.

To begin the hike, find a sign for the Deer Path Trail at the west end of a grassy clearing on the side of the parking area opposite the

The hike begins by crossing a dam, which in wet weather spills water onto the trail, making a sizable mud puddle.

kiosk. Head west on this white-blazed trail, crossing a concrete bridge over the outlet from a pond on the right. During high water, spillover from cracks in the dam that forms the pond can turn the path into a puddle. This trail section is marked with white metal blazes, but you may also see old yellow blazes, some of them metal, which should be ignored.

After the bridge, the trail heads easily uphill on a narrow footpath through a grove of young gray birch trees and some oaks, mostly saplings and shrubs; the small size of the trees indicates that this land was open field not long ago. About 50 feet to the right of the trail, behind some underbrush, you pass a red oak with five trunks, each almost two feet thick, growing out of its five-foot wide base. This is a coppiced tree, one whose wide old-growth trunk was cut long ago, but then produced these new trunks from its old root struc-

Bikers pile logs and stones beside a blowdown to provide a jump across the white trail.

ture. Using a rough estimate of two and a half feet thickness of trunk for a hundred years of age, we can guess the tree was cut a century ago, and at that time was perhaps 200 years old. You will notice other coppiced trees on this hike, though none as large as this one (see photograph on page 50 in "Highlands Habitats: Typical Plants and Trees," in the introductory section of the book).

The trail passes under two power lines at 0.3 mile. Along the trail here are thickets of barberry hedge, an alien plant imported by nineteenth-century settlers and householders for domestic gardens; it has now become a fast-spreading menace, crowding out indigenous species. You will come across many such thickets in this park, evidence of the former use of the land as farmsteads. As you walk gradually uphill, the trees beside the trail are much more mature, perhaps a hundred feet tall with trunks from one to two feet thick, indicating this knoll was allowed to return to forest almost a century ago. The trail crosses a large old stone fence, a structure built by early farmers, usually to a height of about four feet, to keep animals away from cultivated fields; this one is now tumbled and dispersed by weathering to no more than a foot or two. The trail comes to the crest of the rise at 0.5 mile, and passes a spur trail (signed "patrolled and closed to all public use"). It leads to the left (uphill) over a clearing under two large oak trees and down into private fields. Along that path, an automatic security camera is positioned to photograph passersby, so it is clear that trespassing should be avoided.

As the white trail descends easily from the crest, you can see a mowed field through the trees to the left. This section is overgrown with impassable barberry hedge on both sides of the trail. A short path to the left, also marked as "leased land" and signed "area closed," leads to the open field and a fence. The trail bends gradually to the right around a low hill and, at 0.7 mile, levels off in a damp spot. Along this stretch, mountain bikers have piled thick logs across the trail beside a blowdown to create a jump. You will see more of these jumps in other parts of the hike.

At 0.8 mile, the trail forks; to the right is the trailhead of the yellow trail (the Birch Trail), heading off to the east. You follow the white trail, taking the left fork. This section has been reblazed as a white trail, but some of the previous red blazes are still visible. The new blazes you follow are all white metal rectangles. The white trail passes through another damp area in a moist upland forest of oak and beech, with many yellow birch trees near a seasonal swamp. At 0.9 mile, the trail passes a 30-foot-high rock outcrop with associated loose boulders on the right. The trail widens, passes a group of ironwood trees (American hornbeam), and, in the next 0.3 mile, crosses three small brooks flowing from the right. It parallels a stone fence on the left for about 80 yards. At 1.2 miles, the trail passes an unmarked trail to the left (some old painted blazes may be visible), which you should ignore. The white trail reaches a T-intersection with a woods road at 1.3 miles. To the right, the road leads to another road and the trailhead of the blue-blazed Lakeview Trail, with a parking area beyond. You should turn left at this intersection, following the white blazes along the woods road, with several ups and downs.

At 1.6 miles, a newly blazed red trail, labeled the Barberry Trail, leaves to the right, and you now follow the white trail, with white blazes only, to the left. The trail skirts a 50-foot-high rock outcrop on the right at 1.9 miles, with an open field behind it on a knoll that is the highest point in this southern part of Allamuchy Mountain State Park. You should resist the temptation to forge up the ledge to the top of the rise for a view; impenetrable thickets of brambles cover the open crest, and there is no view at the top. The white trail follows the old woods road over two rocky ridges and down through a damp area skirting I-80, which you can hear in the background. At 2.4 miles, a path off the trail to the left leads, in about 200 yards, through a break in a wire fence to the overlook and picnic area on eastbound I-80, where there is a good view of the Great Valley, the Kittatinny Ridge, and the Delaware Water Gap.

A view of Deer Park Pond through a Norway spruce, from the shore nearest the intersection of the Barberry and the Lakeview trails.

Continuing on the white trail, at 2.8 miles the trail comes to a T-intersection with an old woods road where you follow the white turn blaze to the right and soon begin a moderate descent. The track turns into a road of sand and small gravel, as happens often in this park, suggesting the area was covered with outwash from the edge of the retreating glacier just to the north. The path crosses a running brook and comes to a Y-intersection at 3.3 miles, where the white trail turns off to the left, and you now follow the blue-blazed Lakeview Trail, which begins to the right. At 3.6 miles, you get your first glimpse of Deer Park Pond through the trees. Near the margin of the pond, the trail comes to a T-intersection where you leave the blue blazes, which continue left to circle the east shore of the pond, and you now follow the red trail (Barberry Trail) to the right around the west shore. A path just to the left of the intersection leads to the shore of the pond, a pretty spot for rest and a drink.

The red trail soon comes to a running stream with a little pond behind it, which you cross easily on stones. Circling the west shore, the red trail alternates between narrow footpath and wide woods road, and is crossed in muddy spots by several seasonal brooks feeding the pond. All along this shore, you have good views of the pond. In early spring, you might see migrating ducks on the water. On a short unmarked path to the left at the west end of the pond, where beavers have built two lodges, there is a pleasant cleared space to stop for a drink and a snack. At 4.2 miles, the trail turns away from the pond and heads uphill on a woods road that in wet seasons is the bed of a running freshet. At 4.5 miles, you reach a Y-intersection, where you leave the red trail and turn left onto the white trail, which enters from the right. You are now returning on the path you took on the way out, and you will continue to retrace your steps on the white trail all the way back to where the hike began. At an intersection reached at 4.8 miles, your white trail makes a sharp turn to the right, and the wide woods road straight ahead leads to the trailhead of the blue trail, a gate, and a parking area. At 5.3 miles, the yellow trail begins to the left, but you continue ahead, following the white trail you started out on. This completes the 6.1-mile circuit by taking you to the parking area where you left your car.

The beaver lodge on frozen Deer Park Pond. Photo by Daniel Chazin.

Big Beech Mountain Turnaround

4.4 miles • 3½ hours

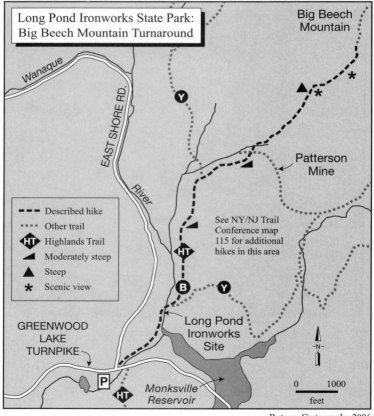

Long Pond Ironworks State Park:
Big Beech Mountain Turnaround

Big Beech
Mountain

Wanaque

EAST SHORE RD

River

Patterson
Mine

- **- -** Described hike
- **· · · ·** Other trail
- **HT** Highlands Trail
- ◀ Moderately steep
- ▲ Steep
- ***** Scenic view

See NY/NJ Trail
Conference map
115 for additional
hikes in this area

GREENWOOD
LAKE
TURNPIKE

Long Pond
Ironworks
Site

–N–

Monksville
Reservoir

0   1000
feet

Rutgers Cartography 2006

The blaze circles marked in primary colors (e.g., "R" for red) may represent a color on
a white background (e.g., red triangle-on-white), as noted in the hike description.

ELEVATION: Low: 510 feet; High: 1,210 feet.

BLAZES: Blue-on-white and Highlands Trail teal diamond. Reverse to return.

CLIMBING: At 1.5 miles, there are two streams to be crossed, which in wet seasons can be very muddy. The last 0.8 mile of the inbound walk is a rocky climb up a succession of four typical 100-foot Highlands ridges of glacially scoured bedrock and associated boulders, with short level stretches between ridges.

PERMITTED USES: Hiking only.

This is a Highlands Trail hike.

OVERVIEW

This hike follows the co-aligned Sterling Ridge and Highlands trails from the Long Pond Ironworks to Big Beech Mountain, and returns the same way. It travels along woods roads built in the nineteenth century to carry ore from the Patterson Mine to the Long Pond Ironworks, and to transport logs to the mines or to charcoal pits making fuel for the furnaces. The summit of Big Beech Mountain is just over 1,200 feet high, the tallest peak in the Sterling Forest tract, and one of the highest spots on the Highlands Trail in New Jersey. The rock outcrop at the summit is surrounded by upland oak-hickory-beech forest, allowing views from that point only when leaves are down. However, open ledges at the south end of the Big Beech ridge offer year-round views. Starting at mid-morning, you will reach these viewpoints in time for a picnic lunch. In spring and during wet weather, there will be muddy stretches on this hike, and waterproof boots would be useful. In planning your walk, allow some time to read signs and examine the remains of the Long Pond Ironworks.

ACCESS: From the south and east, take I-287 to Exit 55, continuing north through Wanaque on Ringwood Avenue (County 511). In 3.9

miles, at the Wanaque/Ringwood boundary, the name of the road changes to Greenwood Lake Turnpike (it remains County 511). In another 3.2 miles, near the northern end of the Wanaque Reservoir, you will reach a fork where Sloatsburg Road begins to the right. Continue on Greenwood Lake Turnpike for 3.6 miles past Sloatsburg Road, crossing a causeway over the Monksville Reservoir and passing buildings preserved as part of the Long Pond Ironworks site. Parking is available on the south side of Greenwood Lake Turnpike at the junction with East Shore Road.

From the north, take I-87 to Exit 15A (NY 17 North). Proceed north on NY 17 for 1.2 miles to the exit for Ringwood/Sterling Forest/West Milford. Follow the exit ramp onto Sterling Mine Road (County 72) and continue straight ahead for 4.8 miles to Margaret King Avenue (after 3.3 miles, at the New York-New Jersey state line, Sterling Mine Road becomes Sloatsburg Road). Turn right onto Margaret King Avenue and continue for 2.3 miles to the end of Margaret King Avenue at Greenwood Lake Turnpike. Turn right onto Greenwood Lake Turnpike and drive for 1.3 miles to trailhead parking on the left side of the road oposite the intersection with East Shore Road.

If using public transportaion, take New Jersey Transit Bus #197 from the Port Authority Terminal on 42nd Street in Manhattan. This bus will stop at East Shore Road.

DETAILED DESCRIPTION

To begin the hike, walk across Greenwood Lake Turnpike to the north side and find the Highlands Trail marker on a telephone pole behind a guardrail along East Shore Road. The trail follows a wide, level woods road (the remains of the railbed leading to the furnaces) heading north by northeast into the woods. In late April on both sides of this road, large patches of trout lilies, rue anemone, and bloodroot will bloom. Notice that the trail is marked with both Sterling Ridge Trail blue-on-white blazes and Highlands Trail teal diamonds, and sometimes with a metal white diamond printed with a small blue HT logo. You will follow this combination all the way up and back.

In about 0.2 mile, you pass the ruins of a mid-nineteenth-century stone building and reach a fork with another woods road. Here the trail bends right to begin a short, rocky descent toward the Wanaque River. At the bottom of the descent, a woods road joins the trail from the right. On the left side of the trail at 0.4 mile, you find the remains of a blast furnace built in 1766 by ironmaster Peter Hasenclever, and two Civil War era furnaces. Signs explain the ruins and their history. The Long Pond Ironworks used the waterpower of the Wanaque River which parallels the trail just to the east. The river was dammed east of here in 1987 to form the Monksville Reservoir,

View of the northwest shore of Monksville Reservoir from near the Long Pond Ironworks.

burying the town of Monksville and creating a shoreline of tall snags. Both the Wanaque River and the reservoir are stocked with fish by the New Jersey DEP Division of Fish and Wildlife, and are popular with fishermen. This is a good area, too, for migrating woods warblers.

Leaving the ironworks ruins, the trail turns east over a bridge and follows the rocky woods road north uphill through a long grove of hemlocks. The yellow-blazed Hasenclever Iron Trail begins at the bridge and is co-aligned with the other two trails for about 100 yards before it departs to the right. At 0.5 mile, an overgrown woods road joins the trail from the right. We heard a pileated woodpecker banging heavily on a dead tree trunk along here. The trail emerges from the hemlocks at 0.6 mile and levels off briefly before resuming a long,

The ruins of a Revolutionary War iron furnace and two larger Civil War furnaces on the Highlands Trail toward Big Beech Mountain.

moderate climb. At 1.1 miles, the trail reaches a fork. The left fork is the trailhead of the Jennings Hollow Trail; you will notice the triangle of three yellow blazes on a tree on the west side of the trail. The right fork is the Sterling Ridge-Highlands Trail you are following. Bearing right at this fork, the trail begins a steeper climb, until leveling at 1.3 miles and reaching another fork where the Sterling Ridge-Highlands Trail heads left. The unmarked woods road which leads right (uphill) goes to the Patterson Mine, which was opened in about 1870 and worked until 1903. After passing this woods road, the Highlands Trail climbs briefly, then levels and crosses a small brook. In spring or extended wet weather, this section is muddy, and crossing the brook will require careful stepping.

After crossing the brook, the trail skirts an eroded bedrock ridge to the west and, at 1.5 miles, reaches another smaller seasonal rivulet. A hundred yards farther on, the trail bends left and begins to climb. As is typical of Highlands ledges, the south end of the ridge has many boulders broken off the bedrock by the immense power of glaciers, while along the bare tops and northern sides, the exposed rock is usually smooth and unbroken. Here in late April, early saxifrage, Dutchman's breeches, and field pussytoes bloom in the rocks along the trail. The trail levels at the top of this first ridge, then at 1.8 miles begins to climb steeply through a rock ledge, reaching an open rock outcrop on the second ridge. This lookout has a view south toward Monksville Reservoir, with Horse Pond Mountain to the right, Harrison Mountain in the center, and Board Mountain in the left distance. Past this viewpoint there is a short level stretch; the trail then climbs steeply through a cleft beside a red cedar, reaching an open ledge on the third ridge with a southern view at 1.9 miles. The trail levels briefly, then climbs again; halfway up this ledge there is a sharp left turn. At this location in spring, an uncommon wildflower, yellow corydalis, can be found blooming among the rocks. At the top of this fourth ridge at 2.0 miles, there is an open view to the southeast. At a spot 0.2 mile farther on the same ridge, is another open lookout with

A view of the Wanaque River from a spot about 50 feet west of the trail.

a year-round view to the west. After this viewpoint, the trail veers slightly to the west away from the edge of the ridge. In early spring along this section, deep purple sharp-lobed hepaticas bloom. The summit of Big Beech Mountain at 2.4 miles is a rock outcrop just east of the trail, but it is surrounded by trees and has no views at any season. The New Jersey-New York border is at 2.6 miles, but for most hikers, the last point of interest is the west facing overlook at 2.2 miles. That is a good spot to rest, have some water and lunch if it's time, and then turn around to retrace your steps.

The north end of the New Jersey section of the Highlands Trail starts here at the state line.

On the way down, go slowly on the rocky steeps; descending is always a little trickier, and harder on the knees. You are following the Highlands Trail, co-aligned with the Sterling Ridge Trail from its first entry into New Jersey.

Though you are following the same trail on which you hiked up, on the return trip the views often seem different. Sunlight crosses through the forest at changed angles, and you see other flowers, rocks, and trees, hear other birds, and may even find drier ways to cross water. Landmarks on the way back are the moist areas near seasonal streams, the woods road leaving the trail east (uphill) to the Patterson Mine, the trailhead of the yellow-blazed Jennings Hollow Trail turning off acutely to the west at the halfway point, and a long grove of hemlocks as you approach the Wanaque River.

When you have found your way again past the furnace ruins of the Long Pond Ironworks, notice that the trail comes to a fork of two wide woods roads. The Sterling Ridge and Highlands trails take the right fork (uphill), though the blazes are set back from the fork and may not be easy to see. After a short climb and a brief level walk, you will come to the Greenwood Lake Turnpike and your car in the parking area across the highway, completing a hike of 4.4 miles.

This section of the Highlands Trail ends here.

Carris Hill Circuit

4.1 miles • 3½ hours

Norvin Green State Forest:
Carris Hill Circuit

Carris
Hill

See NY/NJ Trail
Conference map
115 for additional
hikes in this area

Otter
Hole

Chikahoki
Falls

GLENWILD AVENUE

Posts Brook

	Described hike
	Other trail
HT	Highlands Trail
	Moderately steep
	Steep
	Boulder field
*	Scenic view

Osio
Rock

0   1000
feet

Rutgers Cartography 2006

ELEVATION: Low: 600 feet; High: 1,050 feet.

BLAZES: Blue, blue and Highlands Trail teal diamond, yellow, white, white (different trail, same blaze), blue and HT teal diamond, blue.

CLIMBING: Posts Brook must be crossed going and coming at Otter Hole on large rounded boulders. A steep, rocky climb up a rocky ledge gains over 200 feet in 0.2 mile, an average grade of 20%, with one section at 30% grade. The descent from Carris Hill is more gradual over five ledges. The last 0.5 mile is a moderate climb of 200 feet on a rocky woods road.

PERMITTED USES: Hiking only.

O V E R V I E W

This moderately strenuous lollipop loop offers tramping through varied terrain, a rushing stream crossed from boulder to boulder, pleasant woods walking through a maturing hardwood forest, a steep rocky climb, a beautiful long view from a mountaintop, and some brief clambering down rocky ledges. If you begin the hike in mid-morning, you should be at the summit of Carris Hill for lunch. This is good habitat for resident and migrating woodland birds and displays of wildflowers through the growing season.

ACCESS: Approaching Butler heading west on NJ 23, turn right (north) at the Boonton Avenue Exit (County 511) into the center of town. Boonton Avenue heads downhill, makes a small circuit at the bottom of the hill, turns right onto Park Place, and at 1.0 mile crosses railroad tracks, to end at a T-intersection with Main Street.

If approaching on NJ 23 east, take the Kinnelon Road/Kiel Avenue Exit north (left) into Butler. The street ends at a T-intersection with Park Place, where you turn left to cross railroad tracks to a T-intersection at Main Street.

In either case, turn right onto Main Street and, at another T-intersection where Main Street ends, turn left onto Hamburg Turnpike. In 50 yards, take the next right turn uphill onto Glenwild Avenue. Continue on Glenwild Avenue for 3.2 miles to the Otter Hole parking area on the right. If this area is full, there is another at 0.2 mile farther ahead on the right.

DETAILED DESCRIPTION

From the southeast end of the parking area, find the blue-blazed Hewitt-Butler Trail entering the woods from the northeast and leading toward Posts Brook and Otter Hole. Wildflowers bloom along here in all green seasons, but near Glenwild Avenue stay on the path to avoid dense patches of poison ivy. The trail soon crosses Posts Brook, where you must jump from top to top on large rounded boulders. Most of the time this is simply fun; in dry seasons, the best path is marked by boot scuffs on the rocks, but in high water or icy conditions, the crossing can be very difficult. Experienced Wyanokie hikers have been stopped here at least once or twice in their hiking careers by such conditions. If you think the crossing might be more than you can handle, try the rewarding Wyanokie Torne Loop hike that begins on the other side of the road (Hike #13).

After crossing Posts Brook, the trail reaches an intersection with a woods road, where the green-blazed Otter Hole Trail ends, and the Highlands Trail enters from the left. The teal diamond blazes of the Highlands Trail join the blue blazes of the Hewitt-Butler Trail as you head (uphill) to the right on a rocky, eroded woods road. In about 25 yards, you reach a fork where you follow the dual blazes to the right. The trail climbs easily to the top of this rise at 0.2 mile and begins a gradual descent through a maturing oak-beech-hickory upland hardwood forest. You are walking parallel to Posts Brook, which you may hear and occasionally see through the trees to the right. At 0.4 mile, the trail turns left off the woods road onto a footpath, which once again becomes a woods road where the trail descends. In wet seasons, there are very muddy spots where logs were thrown across the track years ago to form a "corduroy" road over this soggy terrain. At 0.5 mile, an unmarked woods road forks to the right and, at 0.7 mile, the yellow-blazed Wyanokie Crest Trail joins from the right but in 20 yards leaves to the left.

Along the joint trail (Hewitt-Butler blue blazes, HT teal diamonds) here, in early spring, there is a patch of the low orchid-like fuchsia-colored blossoms of the fringed polygala, a plant not officially endangered, but becoming scarce in the Highlands. The mature trees, understory blueberry shrubs, and the presence of water make this good habitat for woodland songbirds, both migrant and resident species. In mid-spring in these woods, we have seen and heard ori-

The Otter Hole Falls of Posts Brook at the start of the Carris Hill Circuit.

oles, scarlet tanagers, rose-breasted grosbeaks, hermit and wood thrushes, and woodland warblers, such as the redstart and the black-and-white warbler, not all at one time, of course, but two or three on each walk.

After the yellow trail departs, you continue following the teal and blue blazes, with glimpses of Posts Brook through the trees to your right. Near the banks of Posts Brook, the trail crosses a tributary on a log bridge at 1.0 mile. Beyond this crossing, in about 40 yards, you arrive at a junction where the white-blazed Posts Brook Trail begins and continues straight ahead; this junction, at an elevation of 600 feet, is the lowest point of the hike. The blue-and-teal-blazed trail you should follow turns left onto a woods road and begins the climb up Carris Hill.

For a short distance, you walk gradually uphill, as the trail becomes a footpath. At 1.1 miles, the trail bears left and begins to ascend through a boulder field associated with a seasonal stream. Emerging from the boulders, the trail turns left onto what seems to be a woods road, but is actually the remains of the world's first oil pipeline, built in 1880, which extended 315 miles from Olean, New York, to Bayonne, New Jersey. Ahead you can see a rocky cliff rising to the right. The trail shortly turns right to face the cliff and, at 1.2 miles, it begins a steep climb through broken, weathered boulders and rock outcrops, gaining 200 feet in 0.2 mile. About two-thirds of the way up, the trail turns right and continues to climb.

The ascent becomes more gradual at the top of the first ridge; the trees are smaller and further apart in the dry, thin soil, and the understory is thick with blueberries. Ascending slowly but constantly, the trail soon bends around to the right into a grove of laurel and climbs a small ledge. You continue up a series of such ledges, at first small bedrock outcrops, and then over two smooth, glaciated rock outcrops edged with ridgetop pitch pines and scrub oaks. This section is similar to an elongated stairway leading to the summit. There are two limited views along the way. At 1.7 miles, you reach the

Rebecca Hunninghake, Paul Tedesco, Ruth Selle, and Gloria Syphern call themselves the Lone Wolf Hikers. Here they are having lunch on the summit of Carris Hill.

smooth rock outcrop at the summit of Carris Hill, with dramatic views of the Wyanokie Plateau, High Point to the northeast, Assiniwikam Mountain to the north, and Buck Mountain to the west. If you began this hike at mid-morning, you should now be ready for lunch at this prime location.

On the bedrock at the summit, you will find the trailhead of the Carris Hill Trail, with yellow blazes arrowed to show the way east off the ridge. Follow this trail to the right over a rock outcrop, as it descends over a series of four ledges. From the first ledge, the view is to the south and west, with South Torne to the south, and the Torne and Buck Mountain to the west. The views from subsequent outlooks are more to the south and east, over the Wanaque Reservoir toward New York City. The first viewpoint is reached at 1.9 miles, and the best view is from the third ledge, at 2.1 miles. From that overlook, the trail turns left down behind a tall rock face and descends over two

A view to the south past a glacial erratic boulder at the first overlook on the descent from Carris Hill summit.

more rock outcrops. The trail leaves the last viewpoint at 2.3 miles, descending through taller trees, including sturdy straight-trunked tulip poplars with a more open understory, and then bends left across a seasonal stream with its boulders. At 2.6 miles, the yellow-blazed Carris Hill Trail ends at a junction with the white-blazed Lower Trail, where you turn to the right beside a fence which marks the boundary of the Wanaque Reservoir property.

The Lower Trail ends in 0.1 mile, at a junction with the white-blazed Posts Brook Trail entering from the left. You turn right here, following white blazes now belonging to the Posts Brook Trail. The trail bends right, keeping to the north side of Posts Brook, then makes a short climb through and around a rock outcrop, and drops down to lowlands bordering Posts Brook. In May, we saw interesting wildflowers along this stretch. After crossing a small tributary of Posts Brook, the trail bears left, climbs a rocky ridge, levels out, and descends almost to the bank of Posts Brook, where you have an angled view of Chikahoki Falls. To see the falls straight on, you must leave the trail and cross Posts Brook to its south side on one of the blowdowns fallen over the water. Whether this is worthwhile or not depends on how much confidence you have in your balance. The straight-on view of the falls over the pond at its base is very pretty.

From the viewpoint on the drier north side of the stream, the white-blazed Posts Brook Trail climbs away on a narrow footpath, with displays of a few pink lady's slippers in spring and interesting summer wildflowers. At 3.1 miles, the Posts Brook Trail ends at a junction with the Hewitt-Butler Trail (blue rectangles) and the Highlands Trail (teal diamonds) coming in from the right on a woods road. Here again you are at the hike's lowest point, the junc-

Chikahoki Falls seen head on from a vantage point on the south bank, across Posts Brook from the trail. The north bank, where the trail meets the brook, provides an angled view of the falls.

tion where you began the climb to the Carris Hill summit. In another 40 yards, you cross the tributary on the log bridge, and follow both the blue and teal blazes straight ahead on a woods road, retracing the steps of the first section of your hike. The trail next offers a few ups and downs, at 3.5 miles passing the yellow-blazed Wyanokie Crest Trail entering from the right and leaving quickly to the left. You then climb steadily with some moderate rises for 0.4 mile, reaching a crest above Otter Hole at 3.9 miles. Descending from the crest, you pass the junction where the Highlands Trail leaves with the Otter Hole Trail to the right, and you continue straight ahead to cross Posts Brook for the last time. At 4.1 miles, you arrive at Glenwild Avenue and the parking area where you left your car.

Glacial erratic at viewpoint along the Carris Hill Trail. Photo by Daniel Chazin.

Ghost Lake Loop

4.6 miles • 3¾ hours

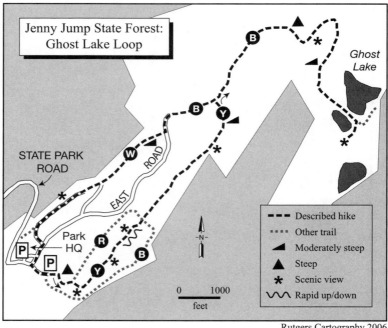

Jenny Jump State Forest:
Ghost Lake Loop

Ghost
Lake

STATE PARK
ROAD

EAST ROAD

Park
HQ

P

P

R

Y

B

W

B

Y

B

-N-

0   1000
feet

Described hike
Other trail
Moderately steep
Steep
Scenic view
Rapid up/down

Rutgers Cartography 2006

ELEVATION: Low: 590 feet; High: 1,108 feet.

BLAZES: Yellow, turquoise, yellow and blue, white.

CLIMBING: A 100-foot rocky climb from the parking area begins the hike. A descent of 300 feet in 0.3 mile leads to Ghost Lake. This must be climbed up on the way back.

PERMITTED USES: Hiking only.

OVERVIEW

A moderate walk through Highlands ridges and hollows to Ghost Lake, with a series of long views toward the Great Meadows to the east and the Delaware Water Gap to the west. A return through woodlands, and along the edges of cultivated fields. Interesting wildflowers and birds at all green seasons.

ACCESS: From I-80, take Exit 12 (Hope/Blairstown). At the end of the exit ramp, turn south on County 521 toward the village of Hope. At the crossroad blinker in the middle of Hope, turn left (east) onto Johnsonburg Road (County 519). Proceed 1 mile to Shiloh Road, the third right turn. After 1.2 miles on Shiloh Road, turn right on State Park Road and follow it to a junction with a sign pointing to the park office. Turn left toward the office, then take the next fork (uphill) to the right to reach a parking area opposite a building with bathrooms for campers and hikers.

TERRAIN AND HISTORY

Jenny Jump State Forest is a 4,244-acre forested Highlands preserve in the middle of rolling countryside and farmland. Elevation in the park ranges from 399 to 1,108 feet, with Highlands gneiss rock outcrops on the summits scraped and gouged by glaciers 15,000 to 20,000 years ago. Some of these ledges open onto long views of the Delaware Water Gap to the west and fertile farmland to the east. The trails in the park can be combined into loops of varying terrain and difficulty. We have chosen a combination leading to Ghost Lake at the north end of the park and returning by another route past farmlands along its western edge. Check the park trail map for other walks. Trail maps and information are available at the park office downhill from the parking area or from Jenny Jump State Forest, P.O. Box 150, Hope, NJ 07844; (908) 459-4366; www.njparksandforests.org.

DETAILED   DESCRIPTION

From the parking area, walk straight uphill past a sign directing you to the Summit and Swamp trails. The path is wide, eroded, and rocky. It leads steeply up and to the right past campsites to the dual trailhead of the yellow-blazed Summit Trail and the red-blazed Swamp Trail at 0.1 mile. From this trailhead, follow the Summit Trail (yellow blazes) up to the right, in about 50 yards reaching a gneiss outcrop and a spur path on the right. This spur path leads to excellent east and south views over the Great Meadows and the cone-shaped mountain called the Pinnacle, at 1,106 feet, the second highest point in the park. The Summit Trail continues uphill and bears left along the top of the ridge, passing another spur to an eastward overlook at 0.2 mile. The path across the ridge is basically level, with occasional rocky ups and downs. The exposed bedrock is Highlands gneiss, scratched and gouged by the Wisconsin Glacier 15,000 years ago. At 0.3 mile, the trail passes between two glacial erratics; the left one is a quartzite rock with calcareous layers that have been dissolved by water and deeply eroded. At 0.4 mile, there is another view to the east on a rock outcrop, and, at 0.5 mile, a mossy spur path down to the left (west) leads to an excellent view of Kittatinny Mountain and the Delaware Water Gap. The yellow-blazed Summit Trail you are

View of the Great Meadow from the first overlook on the Summit Trail.

following reaches an intersection with the blue-blazed Spring Trail at 0.6 mile, but you continue straight ahead with the yellow blazes.

Fifty yards past this intersection, a short path on the right puts you atop a bedrock outcrop with a nice view to the east. The Summit Trail continues along the rocky ridge, at 1.0 mile, climbing gradually and reaching a forested knoll on the right at 1.2 miles. At the top of this knoll, about 30 feet above the trail, a tall rock cairn on a rock outcrop marks the highest point in the park at 1,108 feet; however there is no path to this summit. To reach the cairn, you must make your way through dense undergrowth, but what must once have been a good view is now completely obscured by tall trees. However, if you want to be able to say you reached the highest point of the park, this is the place to do it.

As the Summit Trail comes off the top of the ridge at 1.3 miles, there is a thick grove of mountain laurel on the left. At the bottom of a moderate descent at 1.4 miles, the Summit Trail meets the

View of the Delaware Water Gap looking west from the Summit Trail.

turquoise-blazed Ghost Lake Trail, where you turn right. This part of the Ghost Lake Trail begins on a level stretch, and at 1.9 miles bends to the right, running into a series of ups and mostly downs over 20-foot rocky ridges. The trail then merges with a wide woods road in a long descent, at 2.2 miles passing a large rock outcrop on the right and some sharp-edged boulders on the left that look as if they might have been blasted out of bedrock to make the road. Farther along, both sides of the trail are covered with periwinkle, a ground cover common in household gardens, suggesting that at one time this spot was an extensive homestead. The trail (turquoise blazes) soon passes a seasonal brook and reaches its end at Ghost Lake, at 2.5 miles. There is a pleasant place to rest and have lunch across the lake on a small peninsula, where in late May we heard an oriole and a wood thrush, and saw wild iris, wood betony, pussytoes, striped wintergreen, and partridgeberry, all in bloom. During dry summers, the western part of Ghost Lake becomes shallow and algae-covered, but the borders of this peninsula on the lake's deeper east section remain open and pleasant. Late summer wildflowers around Ghost Lake are attractive.

The return on the Ghost Lake Trail begins with a long climb on the woods road through a shady hardwood forest. Off to the left of the trail, at 0.5 mile from the lake, a wide woods road leads to the site of a dismantled cabin, where there is a good view to the east. Past this viewpoint, the climb back to the top of the ridge goes through two short, steep stony ledges. You reach the intersection of the Ghost Lake Trail with the yellow-blazed Summit Trail at 1.1 miles from the lake and 3.6 miles from the start of the hike. Here you avoid the return via the yellow-blazed Summit Trail on the left, and instead, for a different way back, continue on the Ghost Lake Trail to a woods road straight ahead. This woods road is marked with both yellow blazes and blue blazes, and at 3.8 miles ends at the paved East Road, with a picnic ground and restrooms to the right.

Follow East Road to the left (southwest) for 0.1 mile to the trailhead of the Orchard Trail, marked by a triangle of three white blazes

The peninsula at the north end of Ghost Lake.

on a tree opposite a bench. The Orchard Trail starts out on a moderate descent and shortly crosses a seasonal stream, which was running strong when we were here in spring and, for 25 feet, thoroughly soaked the downhill side of the trail. In late summer, however, the path was bone dry. The trail bears left at the bottom of the hill beside an open grassy meadow at 4.0 miles, with a view of the Great Valley and the Delaware Water Gap. From here, the walking is mostly level on a rocky woods road, until at 4.2 miles the Orchard Trail meets a gravel road. Avoid the fork up to the left and instead follow the white blazes straight ahead. At 4.5 miles, the road reaches another fork, where you leave the white-blazed Orchard Trail and turn left (uphill) on the gravel road. Follow this road to the left until it again reaches paved East Road, where you turn right to pass the park office and return to the upper parking area and your car at 4.6 miles.

This outcrop of Highlands gneiss bedrock shows the scratches and gouging of the Wisconsin Glacier 15,000 years ago. Photo by Daniel Chazin.

BOULDER FIELD

At night in a spring thaw I hear
loose boulders crack and tumble,
small lives crushed, made into mud,
washed away by seasonal streams;
at dawn the equivocal sun
steams the hill like morning coffee.
Through the window I watch the deer
find new paths across broken rocks,
fawns follow in line, sniff and twitch
like flags in a stiff breeze.

Down from a ridge in late November
I head home through rainsoaked boulders,
shouldered by earth-shifts against me.
I skid and teeter, hope my boots stick.
In this slippery world I'm alien,
like men in space, tethered to fears
called safety, fingers curled with cold.

For wild creatures fear is like fur;
they live in it, slip through sharp cracks,
sleep among snakes like saints. In autumn
target deer dodge from rock to rock,
light as windblown leaves, sniff old bones
at brookside, drink by neighbor death
the way shrews mate in an owl's shadow.

—George Petty

Title poem from *Boulder Field*
Finishing Line Press, 2004

CHALLENGES

Up to 11.1 miles, 8 hours

24. ABRAM S. HEWITT STATE FOREST:

Surprise Lake Loop

4.1 miles • 3½ hours

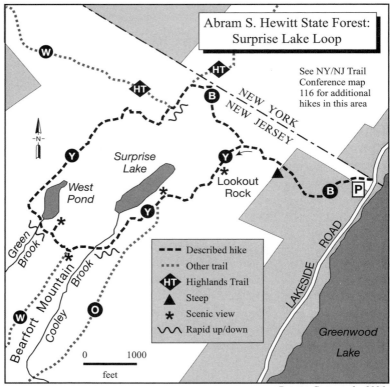

Abram S. Hewitt State Forest:
Surprise Lake Loop

See NY/NJ Trail
Conference map
116 for additional
hikes in this area

NEW YORK
NEW JERSEY

Surprise
Lake

West
Pond

Lookout
Rock

Green
Brook

Bearfort Mountain

Cooley
Brook

LAKESIDE ROAD

Greenwood
Lake

- - - Described hike
••••• Other trail
HT Highlands Trail
▲ Steep
* Scenic view
∿∿ Rapid up/down

0   1000

feet

Rutgers Cartography 2006

The blaze circles marked in primary colors (e.g., "R" for red) may stand for a combination of a color on a white background (e.g., red triangle on white) as noted in the hike description.

ELEVATION: Low: 680 feet; High: 1,410 feet

BLAZES: Blue-on-white, yellow, Appalachian Trail vertical white rectangle, blue-on-white again.

CLIMBING: At the start, a long, steep climb of 550 feet in 0.8 mile up the east face of Bearfort Mountain to a lookout at 1,220 feet; then ups and downs of 20 to 30 feet to Surprise Lake at 1,260 feet; a gradual climb with ridges and hollows to a ledge west of West Pond at 1,410 feet, and a return down the steep slope to the trailhead at 680 feet.

PERMITTED USES: Hiking only.

OVERVIEW

This hike is a strenuous workout with a reward of great natural scenery. The views from Bearfort Mountain east over Greenwood Lake are spectacular. Surprise Lake and West Pond are beautiful spots for lunch or rest. The Bearfort Mountain puddingstone bedrock is striking and geologically unusual, and in addition to the steep start, there are enough 25-foot ridge and hollow ups and downs with a scramble or two, to stress-test your body from beginning to end. The half-mile of ridgewalk on the west side of West Pond is relatively level with a slight grade up to the high point of the hike. Taken at your own easiest speed, with time out for views, this hike is one of the most memorable in the Highlands.

ACCESS: From I-287, take Exit 55, and turn north on County 511, following signs to Wanaque. Drive 12.5 miles around Wanaque and Monksville reservoirs, where County 511 becomes Greenwood Lake Turnpike, passes the lower end of Greenwood Lake, arriving at a traffic light intersection opposite the Hewitt Post Office. At this intersection, turn right following County 511, which becomes Lakeside Road. On Lakeside Road, drive for 3.6 miles to a marina with a parking area on the left (uphill) side of the road. Park in this turnout, but leave room for boats and other cars to maneuver. Do not park in the parking area on the right; it is only for patrons of the marina.

Using public transportation, take New Jersey Transit Bus Route #197 which goes by the marina at the trailhead.

DETAILED DESCRIPTION

On the southwest side of the parking lot opposite the marina, about 50 yards from the road and just south of the state line, look for the blue-on-white blazes of the State Line Trail. The path heads down into a ditch, climbs to the southwest within sight of houses, and crosses a small stream. The loose cobbles and boulders on the path are pieces of puddingstone, the metamorphosed purple sedimentary sandstone with quartz pebble inclusions that forms the bedrock of Bearfort Mountain. Throughout the nineteenth century, the forest on this mountain was clear-cut at least twice to supply fuel for nearby iron works. The terrain is too steep and rocky for farming, so there will be no old stone fences or other signs of husbandry near the trail. At 0.2 mile, the path parallels another brook, then crosses it and passes an unmarked woods road leading to a back yard. At 0.3 mile, the trail meets a woods road coming in from the left, and turns right to climb more steeply up the side of Bearfort Mountain. The path is rocky and severely eroded, and, though wide enough, it probably is not a woods road. It has been widened and deepened by hikers for at least a century. The first edition of the *New York Walk Book*, published by the Trail Conference in 1923, calls the Surprise Lake walk "easy of access" and "quite a resort of climbers in the district." The route has been changed slightly in some places to avoid over-hiking, but the old eroded path is still visible and inviting. Hikers can help trail maintainers by following blazes carefully and staying on the trail.

Lookout Rock, with a view east over Greenwood Lake, is a famous Highlands viewpoint.

Because the soil is thin and dry from rapid water run-off, there are not many wildflowers near the trail on the way up. But nature is irrepressible; in early May, we did see a starflower, some pussytoes and early lowbush blueberry in bloom. At 0.5 mile, the trail steepens through rock outcrops and ridges, and turns left to begin a switchback put in place to moderate the slope. The old trail goes steeply straight ahead, but be sure to follow the new path. The trail continues to switchback, turning left under a small cliff and crossing a small seasonal stream. At 0.7 mile, the State Line Trail meets the trailhead of the Ernest Walter Trail, marked by yellow blazes on a rock, and nearby on a tree. Turn left here onto the yellow-blazed trail, which heads steeply up rocky ledges, and may require some hand scrambling. At 0.9 mile, the yellow trail emerges onto a glacially smoothed puddingstone rock outcrop, with wide views over Greenwood Lake. This viewpoint was called Lookout Rock in 1923, indicating that it

A group of hikers takes a break at lunch time beside Surprise Lake.

was already a popular hikers' destination. Sterling Mountain is seen to the north, Horse Pond Mountain to the south, and Little Bear Mountain directly across the lake with Big Beech Mountain behind it.

The yellow trail leaves Lookout Rock to the right (west), climbs down a short steep ledge into a hollow and crosses a small stream on fallen logs and submerged stones, at 1.0 mile. Tectonic forces heaved these puddingstone ridges up on edge, and time exposed their layers to differential erosion, creating a series of narrow ledges and hollows along the northeast-to-southwest folds. For the hiker, this makes walking along the ridges fairly level and easy, but going across the ridges leads to rugged 20- to 50-foot up-and-down climbs. On the exposed dry and thin-soiled ridgetops, only pitch pine, stunted chestnut oak, and scrub oak will survive, but the moist protected hollows can support a mixed hardwood community of maple, beech, black birch, some tall chestnut oak, red oak, and often hemlock and occasional

white pine. At 1.2 miles, the trail reaches Surprise Lake, a deep glacial pond almost a half-mile long that you would hardly expect to
find on top of a mountain. This is a great place to rest, have a bite to
eat, and take in the scenery. Although wildflowers are not abundant
around these open rocks, in late May, along an unmarked path into
the woods north of the overlook, we have seen pink lady's slippers
blooming. Migrating songbirds will stop on this ridge, as they do on
other Highlands heights, for berries and water.

As the yellow trail leaves Surprise Lake to the right, it immediately passes the trailhead of the Quail Trail (orange blazes), which angles off to the left toward Warwick Turnpike. After passing the
Quail Trail, the yellow trail crosses a wetland with a small stream
running out of Surprise Lake, begins a gradual climb. At 1.4 miles,
passes through an impressive tunnel of rhododendron that in a good
year produces spectacular blooms in June. At 1.6 miles, the trail crosses Cooley's Brook, the major stream outlet from Surprise Lake, and
on the other side of the brook climbs a steep two-level rock ledge
where hands and knees may be required. At the top of this rise at 1.7
miles, you can see back through trees to Surprise Lake, Windbeam
Mountain to the east, a bit of Monksville Reservoir, some of the
Wyanokie Plateau and on a clear day a few Manhattan towers.
Coming off the last rock of this viewpoint, the Ernest Walter Trail
passes the trailhead of the white-blazed Bearfort Ridge Trail and
turns right (west), across low ridges, to reach at 1.8 miles a junction
with a view trail (unmarked) heading right to the West Pond overlook. A short side trip to pristine West Pond, 0.1 mile north, is well
worth taking the time. There is no easy access to the shore of West
Pond.

Returning to the Ernest Walter Trail, continue to the right
(west), climbing down a steep ledge to cross Green Brook, the outlet
from West Pond, on stepping stones. Over hundreds of millions of
years, this watercourse and its predecessors have eroded the gap between the north and south sections of Bearfort Mountain, through

Pristine West Pond seen from an overlook at the end of a short spur trail off the Ernest Walter Trail.

which Native Americans, colonists, and now motorists on Warwick Turnpike, have traveled.

After crossing the brook, the trail climbs a ledge on the other side, and, at 2.1 miles, turns right (north) to follow the ridgeline north along West Pond, seen occasionally through trees. The path ascends easily along glacially smoothed open puddingstone outcrops, with occasional jumps across eroded joints. The path continues straight ahead over the smooth rocks, and yellow blazes appear often enough. At about 2.5 miles, the trail reaches the highest elevation of the hike at 1,410 feet, and at 2.6 miles the Ernest Walter Trail climbs off the ridge to the right, ending at a T-junction with the Appalachian Trail (AT), and its tall rectangular white blazes. Turn right onto the AT and follow it north across several 20-foot ridges until it meets the western trailhead of the blue-on-white-blazed State Line Trail at 2.9 miles. The AT departs to the left at this junction, and you follow the

State Line Trail to the right (east), again over rock outcrops, until at 3.2 miles it begins its descent off Bearfort Ridge. The trail soon passes a substantial rock cairn. Cairns like this one usually indicate an important turn or junction, but at this spot the meaning is obscure and probably obsolete. At 3.4 miles, the State Line Trail passes the yellow-blazed trailhead of the Ernest Walter Trail you took uphill to the right to Lookout Rock. You can now retrace your steps on the blue-on-white-blazed State Line Trail, down the slope of Bearfort Mountain and past the cliff face. Follow the switchbacks to the steep, eroded, rocky footpath, coming in sight of houses, crossing the two lower streams, and arriving at the marina parking area at 4.1 miles.

Windbeam Mountain Through Hike

4.4 miles • 3¾ hours

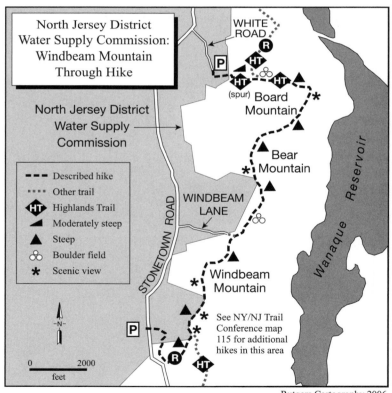

North Jersey District
Water Supply Commission:
Windbeam Mountain
Through Hike

WHITE ROAD

North Jersey District
Water Supply
Commission

(spur) Board Mountain

Bear Mountain

WINDBEAM LANE

STONETOWN ROAD

Windbeam Mountain

See NY/NJ Trail Conference map 115 for additional hikes in this area

Wanaque Reservoir

Legend:
- **- - -** Described hike
- **· · · ·** Other trail
- **HT** Highlands Trail
- ◢ Moderately steep
- ▲ Steep
- ⚬⚬ Boulder field
- ✳ Scenic view

-N-

0   2000
feet

Rutgers Cartography 2006

The blaze circles marked in primary colors (e.g., "R" for red) may represent a color on a white background (e.g., red triangle-on-white), as noted in the hike description.

ELEVATION: Low: 510 feet; High: 1,065 feet.

BLAZES: Black diamond-on-teal diamond, red triangle-on-white rectangle, teal diamond.

CLIMBING: This is a strenuous hike, with three mountains to climb: Board (from 520 to 870 feet in 0.3 mile), Bear (from 610 to 910 feet in 0.7 mile), and Windbeam (from 520 to 1,065 feet in 1.0 mile). The last 0.3 mile up Board is steep, at nearly 25% average grade. Bear is a little easier, though steep in short pitches, and Windbeam is a long, steady climb, with some steep sections. There are rock scrambles at the top of each climb, with wide views as a reward. Windbeam has a long, flat summit with a woods road to follow part of the way across. The wetlands in the hollows between summits should be passable even in wet seasons.

PERMITTED USES: Hiking only.

This is a Highlands Trail hike.

OVERVIEW

The Stonetown Circular Trail is often hiked as a strenuous 10-mile loop beginning on Stonetown Road at Mary Roth Drive, which is the entrance to the Stonetown recreation complex. The eastern half of that loop, described here, provides steep climbs that offer many excellent views to the west, south, and east from rock outcrops at or near the summits. For most of this hike, the Highlands Trail (HT) runs jointly with the Stonetown Circular Trail. The terrain includes wetlands and associated boulder fields with moist hemlock and hardwood forest, steep rocky uplands with mixed hardwoods, and ridgetop open forest with chestnut, red, and scarlet oaks, black cherry, hickory, and pitch pine.

ACCESS: This through hike will require two cars. From I-287, take Exit 55 to Wanaque and County 511. Turn north toward Wanaque, passing through Wanaque and Midvale, until, 3.3 miles from I-287, you will find the Skyline Diner on your right a few yards before the junction with West Brook Road on your left. Turn left here, crossing the Wanaque Reservoir and arriving at a T-intersection, where you turn right onto Stonetown Road. Drive 0.5 mile to Mary Roth Drive on your left. Turn left here into the large parking lot at the Stonetown recreation area. Leave one car here and proceed north on Stonetown Road for 2.4 miles to find White Road on your right. Turn right onto White Road and follow it until the pavement ends, where there is room for one or two cars to the left. On a tree to the right, you will find the black diamond-on-teal diamond blaze of the Ricker Hill/Highlands Trail Connector Trail. This is the trailhead for the hike.

DETAILED DESCRIPTION

Follow the blazes (black diamond-on-teal diamond) into the woods along a wide woods road, descending gradually eastward past houses on both sides and a rocky bluff on the right. In about 50 yards, the trail turns right off the woods road onto a rocky footpath leading uphill. At 0.1 mile, the trail opens onto a lookout from which there is a restricted view to the northeast. Off the trail below, the rock angles down like a children's slide. Glacial action has smoothed this rock and left an erratic boulder perched on its top. From the lookout, the trail continues to the right (south) on a mossy footpath. After only 30 yards, the trail leaves that path and turns left (downhill) on a moderately steep pitch. The trail climbs down into moist terrain where the tree trunks are noticeably thicker, some larger than two feet in diameter. At the bottom of this hollow at 0.3 mile, the trail winds through a boulder field and crosses a small seasonal stream and a woods road. On the other side of the brook, the trail bends right on an old woods road, then descends to the left and turns right again

The dam at Monksville Reservoir seen from an outlook just below the summit of Board Mountain.

onto another woods road. Here, the walking is mostly level, and the trail often crosses or joins woods roads winding through the hollow. The black diamond-on-teal diamond blazes turn right on a footpath and descend again into another wetland with a running stream. Leaving the wetland on a newly cleared footpath, the trail first turns right, then left, and at 0.5 mile arrives at an intersection with the red triangle-on-white-blazed Stonetown Circular Trail, co-aligned with the Highlands Trail.

The Highlands Trail section starts here.

At the intersection, you turn right, following the co-aligned trails south, and descending into a third hollow, at 510 feet the low point of the hike. After crossing a stream and passing a square depression (probably the foundation of a nineteenth-century dwelling), on the right, the trail crosses a woods road and begins to climb the northwest slope of Board Mountain, gradually at first, then steeply straight up the hill. The path is alternately grass-covered and rocky, and presses on straight ahead; there is neither subtlety nor respite to this climb. Near the summit, the trail bends left, still climbing, but now across the contour of the slope. At 0.8 mile, it reaches a rock outcrop where there is a view to the north and east. To the north, the Monksville Reservoir dam is visible, to the near northeast is Governor Mountain, and behind and to the right of it is Mount Defiance, with the ridge of Ramapo Mountain directly to the east across the reservoir and the Wanaque Valley. The trail leaves the outlook bearing right (south) and climbs gradually to the nearby summit at 865 feet, where there is no long view. On these rocky ridgetops, the few trees do not form a closed canopy, so on bright days the hiker is often exposed to open sunlight.

The trail leaves the summit angling across the contour on the southwestern slope through snags, the remains of trees killed by drought, gypsy moths, or hard weather. At 1.0 mile, the trail descends steeply through rock ledges and fractured boulders. It reaches a level shoulder of the mountain at 1.2 miles, crosses a wide eroded woods road, and starts to climb Bear Mountain. The trail follows a woods road for a short distance and, at 1.4 miles, becomes steeper. At the top of the rise, the trail skirts a rock outcrop on the right, and heads across the slope toward the summit. A short off-trail walk here to the top of the ridge to the right will lead to a worthwhile wide view to the west. However, an even better one is available just ahead at the summit of Bear Mountain. The trail proceeds through a laurel grove and emerges from the woods onto a rock outcrop near the summit marked by a cairn at 1.7 miles. A few steps off the trail to the right, there is a lookout to the near northwest toward Monks Mountain; Big Beech Mountain, where the Highlands Trail enters New Jersey, is behind it to the north. Tory Rocks is in the middle distance due west, Horse Pond Mountain is further away to the north of Tory Rocks. Along the western horizon is the long ridge of Bearfort Mountain, which is divided by a gap through which the Warwick Turnpike passes. The view to the southwest is restricted by trees and

Looking west from a vantage point near the summit of Bear Mountain, toward Saddle Mountain and the long ridge of Bearfort Mountain behind it.

marred by the Braen rock quarry, but West Brook Mountain, Saddle Mountain, and some of the other Wyanokies can be seen. A few yards farther on, a climb up a 15-foot knob leads to the true summit at 910 feet elevation; the views to the south and west are obstructed by pines, but those to the north and east over the Wanaque Reservoir are clear.

From the top of Bear Mountain, the trail (with the co-aligned blazes of the HT and the Stonetown Circular Trail) turns left toward the southeast, at 1.8 miles arriving at a south-facing viewpoint. From this spot, the curve of the Wyanokies can be seen from West Brook Mountain to the right (west) through Saddle Mountain and Assiniwikam to High Point, which overlooks the Wanaque Reservoir. A short distance farther ahead there is an even better view, ranging from southwest over the Wyanokies, to south with Windbeam Mountain right in your eyes, and from southeast to northeast over the whole of the reservoir, and finally east over the

The south end of Wanaque Reservoir from the second peak of Windbeam Mountain.

reservoir to the Ramapos. From this viewpoint, the trail descends the southeast face of Bear Mountain on an open grassy path through some loose boulders. Here in August, a display of wildflowers might include white snakeroot, pearly everlasting, mountain mint, dittany, and, of course, a few varieties of goldenrod. The trail descends, alternating between steep and level along the contour of the mountain, and entering a mixed oak-hardwood forest with a shady canopy. At 2.1 miles, the trail crosses a stream with two associated rivulets and descends gradually to the bottom of the hollow between Bear and Windbeam mountains.

At 2.3 miles, the trail crosses a wide gravel road, which if followed to the right becomes paved Windbeam Lane and in 0.4 mile reaches Stonetown Road about 0.7 mile north of your first car. After crossing this road, the trail heads southwest into the woods on a footpath and fords a seasonal stream at 2.4 miles. From this spot looking west, you can see the back of a house on Windbeam Lane. The trail passes through a grove of dying hemlocks at 2.5 miles, where there are also some hardwoods well over a hundred years old, and soon turns right, climbing the north end of Windbeam Mountain. As the trail climbs, there are many snags along the way. Here, sun filters through the canopy and, stimulated by the sunlight, brambles and thick underbrush grow across the trail. At 2.7 miles, the trail crosses a woods road and enters a shady stretch where the forest has not been so damaged. The trail then crosses another woods road, and, at 2.8 miles, begins to encounter rock outcrops nearer to the summit. At 2.9 miles, the trail leads right over the concrete foundations of an old tower and, turning left, it begins to level out on the flat ridge of Windbeam Mountain where it joins a woods road coming in from the right.

Here, to the right of the trail, open areas appear through the woods where a lookout to the west can be found. At 3.1 miles, you can walk a short way off to the right to reach west- and south-facing viewpoints opposite the Sam Braen quarry, with West Brook Mountain, Saddle Mountain, Assiniwikam, and Wyanokie High Point all visible. These viewpoints are slightly obscured by trees, but there are better ones ahead. The forest at this section of the Windbeam Ridge is thick enough to have a dense, shady canopy, with trees about 80 feet high. The trail is level and grassy here, on an old woods road that could only have been used for logging. The trail leaves the woods road and descends briefly to the right over some rock outcrops, then climbs a steep ridge to where a cairn, at 3.4 miles, marks the summit of the mountain. This is the highest point of the hike, at 1,065 feet elevation. From this spot, there are wide, dramatic views to the west, south, and east. To the west and south, the highest summits of the Wyanokies are visible, and, to the east, the view overlooks the Wanaque Reservoir and the long Ramapo Mountain beyond. There are many snags on this mountaintop, but the views are pretty much unobstructed.

Leaving the summit, the trail climbs down a steep ledge to a hollow and climbs up another ridge at 3.7 miles to the lower south summit (985 feet), where there are even more dramatic views, particularly to the southeast over Wanaque Reservoir, and east and northeast to the Ramapo Ridge. Descending steeply from this knoll through open rock outcrops, the trail passes other lookouts with interesting views over the reservoir to the north, east, and south. The trail continues to descend steeply on a rocky footpath with occasional rock steps, and enters the shady mature upland mixed oak-hardwood forest on the southwest slope at 3.8 miles.

This section of the Highlands Trail ends here.

A new section of the Highlands Trail has been constructed from this point. It leaves the Stonetown Circular Trail here, descends the south face of Windbeam Mountain, crosses West Brook Road, and climbs Ball Mountain to join the Wyanokie Circular Trail at the Blue Mine. By spring 2007, two parts of this new section of the HT were finished, but the last third, from Townsend Road to the Blue Mine, is still to be built.

The red triangle-on-white-blazed trail you are following continues to descend steeply on a rocky footpath. The trail levels off at a damp area with a boulder field, and at 4.1 miles approaches close to Stonetown Road. From here, the trail turns right across a small freshet, climbs a short knoll, and descends to join a woods road bearing right away from the road. At 4.2 miles, the trail turns right off the woods road to cross two boulder fields and an associated stream. After this crossing, the trail turns left back toward the road and proceeds through the woods to return to its trailhead at 4.4 miles, where your first car is parked in the lot above Mary Roth Drive across Stonetown Road.

The east-facing view from the last viewpoint on Windbeam Mountain. (Note the New York City skyline in the background). Photo by Daniel Chazin.

Buck Mountain Loop

4.5 miles • 3¾ hours

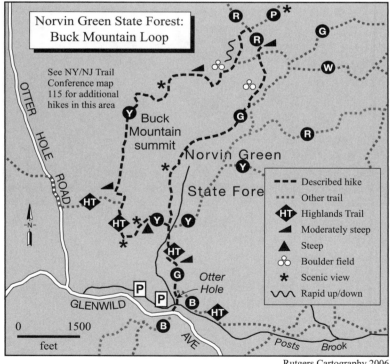

Norvin Green State Forest:
Buck Mountain Loop

See NY/NJ Trail
Conference map
115 for additional
hikes in this area

Buck
Mountain
summit

Norvin Green

State Fore

OTTER HOLE ROAD

-N-

Otter
Hole

GLENWILD

0   1500

feet

AVE

Posts Brook

Legend:
- – – – Described hike
- ········ Other trail
- **HT** Highlands Trail
- ◀ Moderately steep
- ▲ Steep
- ⚮ Boulder field
- ✳ Scenic view
- ∿∿ Rapid up/down

Rutgers Cartography 2006

*The blaze circles marked in primary colors (e.g., "R" for red) may represent a color on
a white background (e.g., red triangle-on-white), as noted in the hike description.*

ELEVATION: Low: 840 feet; High: 1,245 feet.

BLAZES: Blue, green, Highlands Trail teal diamond, yellow, red-on-white, green, and finally blue again.

CLIMBING: About a half an hour from the start, you find a steep 200-foot climb up the east side of Buck Mountain. Near the top of the scramble, you creep four or five feet up a diagonal crack in the rock face. Because the rock face leans comfortably away from the vertical, it isn't very difficult or dangerous. The descent from the summit of Buck Mountain is more moderate. After that descent, a sequence of typical Highlands 40-foot ups and downs and boulder fields, the trail leads to the shoulder of Assiniwikam Mountain and to the return on Otter Hole Road. After the Otter Hole Road junction, the climbs are short and moderate.

PERMITTED USES: Hiking only.

This is a Highlands Trail hike.

OVERVIEW

The Buck Mountain Loop crosses the highest point in the Wyanokie region. Although that summit is thoroughly surrounded by trees, there are four open lookouts with rewarding views on these trails. The first two overlooks are reached less than an hour from the start. The third outlook is on the descent from Buck Mountain and faces toward Assiniwikam Mountain, and the last one is on the return and looks toward the slope of Buck Mountain, which you climbed at the outset. You will also have the opportunity to take a side trip on the new Will Monroe Loop to viewpoints on Assiniwikam Mountain.

Although the hike crosses lively Posts Brook and four seasonal streams, there are no standing ponds along the route, so perching birds, the colorful songsters, don't particularly seek to rest or nest here. However, you will hear an occasional wood thrush, or red-eyed vireo, perhaps a woods-loving scarlet tanager in May or June, or at any season the red-tailed hawk's "keeerr" cry overhead.

ACCESS: Approaching Butler heading west on NJ 23, turn north at the Boonton Avenue/County 511 Exit into the center of town. Boonton Avenue heads downhill, makes a small circuit near its end, turns right onto Park Place, and at 1.0 mile crosses a railroad track, ending at a T-intersection with Main Street.

Approaching on NJ 23 east, take the Kinnelon Road/Kiel Avenue Exit north into Butler. The street ends at a crossroads where you turn left onto Park Place to cross railroad tracks at a T-intersection with Main Street.

In either case, turn right onto Main Street and, at another T-intersection where Main Street ends, turn left onto Hamburg Turnpike. In about 50 yards, take the next right turn (uphill) onto Glenwild Avenue. Continue on Glenwild Avenue for 3.2 miles to the Otter Hole parking area on the right at the top of the hill. If this one is full, continue north for another 0.2 mile to a second parking area on the right.

HISTORY AND TERRAIN

This loop hike through the western edge of the Wyanokie Plateau meets, follows, and crosses many old woods roads. These are not signs of Native American activity or Colonial settlement, however. The land was originally purchased from the East Jersey Board of Proprietors in 1767 by Peter Hasenclever, manager for a syndicate of wealthy Englishmen, to provide wood to make charcoal for smelting iron. The Proprietors found the land too mountainous for farming, "unfit for any purpose but that Mr. Hasenclever proposed."

To fuel the iron industry and to provide timber for local construction, these mountains have been cut over not once, but probably three times, since Colonial days. The largest woods roads, such as the one followed by the green-blazed Otter Hole Trail, brought supplies to and from the iron industry for more than 100 years. Smaller ones crossing the ridgetops were probably logging roads. On this hike, you do not find the long stone fences that would be associated with efforts at farming. The trail winds through a forest of third- or perhaps even fourth-growth trees that have sprung up since the iron industry closed down.

DETAILED DESCRIPTION

The hike begins a few steps east of the parking area, on the blue-blazed Hewitt-Butler Trail heading into the woods to Otter Hole, a picturesque falls of Posts Brook. Look for pink lady's slippers (the Highlands woodland orchid) to the right of the path in late May or early June, and on the margins of the stream, tall scarlet cardinal flowers bloom in late August. You reach Posts Brook 100 yards from the road.

Crossing the boulder-strewn brook requires judgment and care, and a pair of wide-lugged sneakers or hiking boots. Ancient glaciers and the subsequent hundreds of centuries of flowing water and winter freezes have rounded the boulders, some of them refrigerator-sized; moss and algae make some of the lower rocks slippery. During high water or icy weather, the smart hiker may cross farther upstream or choose another trail.

On the other side, the trail leaves the brook over a small ridge of bedrock decorated with a blue blaze. You are now on a wide, eroded woods road, which quickly reaches a Y-intersection, where the Hewitt-Butler and the Highlands trails come down from the right. Turn up to the left, following the green-blazed Otter Hole Trail, which begins here and is co-aligned with the Highlands Trail and its teal-colored diamond blazes.

This section of the Highlands Trail begins here.

Proceed north (uphill) on a wide woods road following both green blazes and teal blazes past blueberry thickets and mountain laurel alleys, and crossing two seasonal streams along the top of the rise. After 0.5 mile, you come to an intersection with the yellow-blazed Wyanokie Crest Trail. Leave the Otter Hole Trail here, turn left (west) downhill, and follow the yellow blazes together with the teal diamonds of the Highlands Trail. Descend briefly to a moist hollow, where you cross a small tributary of Posts Brook.

You have now reached the base of Buck Mountain and will begin a steep 200-foot climb with a rock scramble near the top. As you near the end of the climb, you come face-to-face with two slabs of Highlands bedrock: the first with a vertical crack to follow, and the

Climbing the rock crevices in the east face of Buck Mountain.

second with a shoe-sized crack leading up to the left just where the trail wants to go. Place your foot carefully in the slot, lean against the slope of the rock, and creep up one step at a time. When you stand up on the level spot just beyond these rocks, there is a long and wide view back eastward towards Carris Hill over the knoll from which you just came. In the distance, a viaduct of I-287 is visible, and, on a clear

The view from the south face of Buck Mountain, looking southeast. On a clear day, the New York City skyline is visible.

day, you can see the New York City skyline. On these ledges in late spring and summer, look for the blue-green finely divided leaves and the pink and yellow tubular blossoms of pale corydalis springing from cracks in the rocks.

The joint trail then levels gradually over glacially rounded ridges, in a typical ridgetop forest of chestnut oak, red maple, hickory, and black birch, with an understory of blueberry and laurel. Follow the yellow blazes heading south to two bedrock outcrops at 0.8 mile. The view from the first ledge to the left of the trail is obscured by trees, but the next one is wide open, facing south and a bit east, with a spectacular view of Wyanokie Torne to the south, the southern Wyanokie Plateau to the southeast, and on a clear day, the New York City skyline in the distance. The bedrock on this ledge has a pink color in spots, some of which are from crystals of feldspar, and some from oxidized iron. The rock also has fractures peeling off in sheets as the rock has been relieved of pressures under which it was formed, 20 miles deep in the earth. This is a good place for a rest and a drink, or an early lunch if you're ready for it. As you step down off this ledge, you come immediately to another view more to the south and southwest of the Torne and Kampfe Lake, with Kanouse Mountain and the southern ridge of Bearfort Mountain and its fire tower to the southwest. At these overlooks, you will notice many "snags," the bare standing trunks of trees killed by recent long-term drought and/or infestations of gypsy moths.

Leaving the overlooks, the yellow-blazed Wyanokie Crest Trail turns back north past two large glacial erratics and a bedrock ridge on the left. At 1.0 mile, the Highlands Trail turns off to the left (notice the two teal turn blazes leaning left on a tree and a rock cairn on the ledge), while the yellow trail continues straight ahead (a single yellow blaze on the same tree).

This section of the Highlands Trail ends here.

If you wish to cut short your hike here, you can follow the Highlands Trail teal diamonds easily down the west shoulder of Buck Mountain to Otter Hole Road. Then turn left to walk the paved road back to the parking area, which you should reach in about 30 minutes.

To continue the Buck Mountain Loop, follow the Wyanokie Crest Trail's yellow blazes straight ahead; in another 120 yards, an ATV track comes in from the right and ruts the yellow trail. ATV activity is evident in this area, sometimes using old woods roads, sometimes following the hikers' trail, and sometimes making their own tracks with occasional rough orange blazes. The yellow trail then bears left until it meets a woods road, which it follows to the right (uphill) to a fork with another woods road. Follow the yellow blazes on the left fork gradually uphill, until you come to a glacially smoothed rock outcrop surrounded by trees, at 1.4 miles. Although there is no dramatic viewpoint, this is the summit of Buck Mountain; at an elevation of 1,245 feet, it is the highest point in the Wyanokie Plateau. As you start down off the ridge, a bedrock opening offers a

A view of Assiniwikam Mountain from a rock outcrop on the descent from the summit of Buck Mountain.

good view to the north of the ledges and summit of Assiniwikam Mountain.

As you descend, the yellow trail merges with a woods road veering to the left, then leaves the woods road heading down (east) into a shady ravine, with beech, tulip poplar, a few hemlock trees, and richer soil for wildflowers and flowering shrubs. Along here in June, we found many Indian cucumber plants, with their whorls of several leaves at mid-stem and, at the top of the stem, a smaller whorl of three leaves, which supports two nodding, greenish-white flowers. The trail crosses three strands of a brook at 1.7 miles and parallels a fourth, larger branch before fording it. As the trail starts up on the other side, it passes a large boulder on the right, torn from the ridge above and split in two by freeze-thaw weathering. Here the trail begins a short steep climb and then levels gradually through boulder fields left by glaciers. At 2.2 miles, there is an intersection with a woods road where on the right you may see an unmarked trail. The yellow blaze you are following is on the trunk of a large tree that

The view to the southwest from the second rock ledge on Buck Mountain.

seems to stand in the middle of the track. Continue straight ahead on the yellow trail, cross a woods road at 2.4 miles, and, after a climb in two stages, at 2.7 miles arrive at a T-intersection with the Wyanokie Circular Trail, blazed with a red-dot-on-white circle. Here the yellow-blazed Wyanokie Crest Trail ends, and the Buck Mountain Loop continues to the right on the red-dot Wyanokie Circular Trail.

Before you leave this intersection, notice a trail with a bright pink blaze leading uphill straight ahead across the way. This path is the new Will Monroe Loop, named after a Montclair State University professor who in the 1920s popularized hiking in the Wyanokies. The Will Monroe Loop is a 1.0-mile horseshoe-shaped hike over the summit of Assiniwikam Mountain, with several long lookouts. It ends at a junction with the Wyanokie Circular Trail (red dot blazes), from which you would have a 0.3-mile moderate climb to return to the trailhead of the yellow-blazed Wyanokie Crest Trail where it started.

At the intersection of the yellow trail with the red-dot trail from the Buck Mountain side (coming from the south), you turn right onto the red-dot blazed Wyanokie Circular Trail. Now heading southeast, you begin a steep descent into a shady ravine and, as you climb out, pass near a smooth rock outcrop with a view of Buck Mountain to the south. In a few minutes, at 2.9 miles from the start, the trail crosses an unmarked woods road (at a rock cairn), and passes over a seasonal rivulet. Beyond the damp spot, you begin to climb past a large glacial erratic. Walking here in the first week of June, we heard and saw a scarlet tanager. In this section, you travel through a maze of rounded boulders, dropped here by a melting glacier or tumbled down bare, scraped hillsides by the action of meltwater; however, you stay between 1,000 and 1,100 feet elevation. At 3.1 miles, you descend to intercept the green-blazed Otter Hole Trail; turn right by a rock cairn onto a wide woods road, following the green blazes south back toward Otter Hole. At 3.5 miles, the green trail crosses a small seasonal stream on stepping stones. Just beyond this stream we passed a 5-foot-long black rat snake (a harmless constrictor) lolling under the blueberry bushes just off the trail. He was sluggish and fat in the middle, probably digesting a recent meal of mouse or shrew.

A little farther along, at 3.8 miles, off the trail to the right, there is a wide rock ledge with a westward viewpoint where you can see the forested bulk of Buck Mountain, which you climbed a while ago. At 4.0 miles, the trail crosses the yellow-blazed Wyanokie Crest Trail at the intersection where you first turned off to face the Buck Mountain ascent. From this point, retrace your steps straight ahead, descending towards Otter Hole and following two blazes, the green of the Otter Hole Trail and the teal diamonds of the Highlands Trail, which you have rejoined. You meet the blue-blazed Hewitt-Butler Trail at the bottom of the hill. Turn right to follow the blue blazes back across the sometimes slippery boulders of Posts Brook to the parking area 0.1 mile away, completing the 4.5-mile circuit.

Terrace Pond Loop

5.0 miles • 4¼ hours

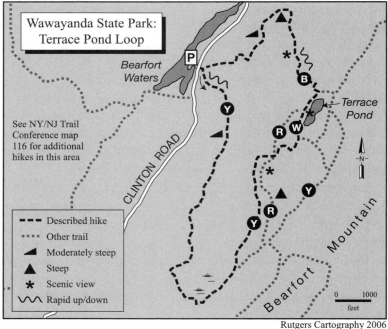

Wawayanda State Park:
Terrace Pond Loop

Bearfort
Waters

See NY/NJ Trail
Conference map
116 for additional
hikes in this area

CLINTON ROAD

Terrace
Pond

Bearfort Mountain

- - - Described hike
..... Other trail
◀ Moderately steep
▲ Steep
✻ Scenic view
〰 Rapid up/down

0   1000
feet

Rutgers Cartography 2006

ELEVATION: Low: 1,060 feet; High: 1,440 feet.

BLAZES: Yellow, white, blue.

CLIMBING: For the first half of the hike, the trail climbs gradually on a path through wetlands and ridges, follows the contour of the south end of Bearfort Ridge, and shortly meets mostly level woods roads. At 2.7 miles, the trail climbs a series of ridges and hollows with some brief rock scrambles, and follows exposed pudding-stone ledges. On the way back from Terrace Pond, the trail descends steeply off four ridges and a slope of loose rock along a gas pipeline. Thereafter, the descents are easy, with some wet areas toward the end.

PERMITTED USES: Hiking only.

OVERVIEW

Terrace Pond, on the southern arm of Bearfort Mountain, was a favorite hiker destination as early as 1923, when the first edition of the New York-New Jersey Trail Conference's *New York Walk Book* was published. That book's description of the Terrace Pond hike includes a sketch showing a young woman in a dark swimsuit and a cap diving off a high cliff into the pond. Swimming is now forbidden at Terrace Pond, but the sights have not changed much in 80 years. It is still a deep, glacially scoured mountain lake surrounded by steep cliffs, a beautiful goal for a popular and strenuous hike. There are two wide lookouts, one on the way up, facing east toward the Wyanokies, and the other on the way down, facing west toward the Wawayanda Plateau.

ACCESS: From NJ 23, 6.5 miles west of the Kinnelon Road traffic light in Butler, take the Clinton Road Exit north. Drive 7.4 miles to a parking area for about ten cars on the left, designated P7 on Trail Conference Map #116. If you pass an area cleared for a gas pipeline, you've gone too far.

DETAILED DESCRIPTION

The Terrace Pond overlook, at 3.2 miles into the hike, is a magnificent spot for lunch and a rest. We recommend you get an early start, no later than 10 a.m., to reach the overlook when you need it most. The trailhead, marked with a sign for Terrace Pond, is across the road from the parking area. Here both the yellow-blazed Terrace Pond South and the blue-blazed Terrace Pond North trails begin on a moderate uphill grade. In about twenty feet, at a Y-intersection, the Terrace Pond North Trail (blue blazes) goes left, and the Terrace Pond South Trail (yellow blazes) goes right. We have chosen to start with the yellow-blazed trail, taking on the uphill walking and rocky climbing when fresh and ready.

Turning right, you follow the yellow-blazed trail on a footpath (uphill) through a laurel grove, with low-lying fragrant-leaved wintergreen plants along the path. This is moderate walking through some 10- to 20-foot ups and downs, with frequent bright yellow plastic trail markers on trees. On the slopes, the forest is the upland type, with red and chestnut oak, hickory, some maple, black birch, and an occasional ash. In the moister hollows and north-facing slopes, hemlock trees have been dominant, but they are now being killed off by the woolly adelgid. As a result, white pines and hardwoods are becoming more numerous in these environments, and the understory is thicker with viburnum, spicebush, laurel, rhododendron, wild azalea, and many hardwood saplings. The path crosses a wetland and a small brook on puncheons (board walkways) at 0.1 mile, turns left to parallel the stream, sometimes almost in it, and then curves uphill to the right. At 0.3 mile, the path passes through another dying hemlock grove with white pines interspersed, where in May we heard a pine warbler singing. The trail soon descends into another hollow, crossing a wetland on stone steps and puncheons.

As you leave the wetland, walking is level through mixed conifers and hardwoods. After a short, easy incline, it is level again at 0.5 mile, on a rocky path between a cliff on the left and a forested steep slope to the right. The trail next passes through an arch of mature rhododendrons that bloom at the end of June. In the hardwood forest, beyond the rhododendrons, you may notice a few coppiced trees, with a group of trunks growing from the stump of what was once a very large tree. The new trunks are about a foot in diameter, indicating they began to sprout from the stump perhaps 50 or 60 years ago. The source stump was three or four feet across to support all those new trees, suggesting it was at least 150 years old when cut. These hillsides were clear-cut at least twice during the nineteenth century to supply nearby iron works with fuel; they may have been kept clear for farming or pasture until the end of the nineteenth century. How a few old-growth trees could have escaped cutting into the middle of the twentieth century is a mystery; perhaps they were pasture trees and not part of a mature forest.

At 0.7 mile, the trail climbs diagonally to the right across the contour of the next ridge, with rock outcrops and loose boulders to the left. The rocks dotting the pathway are most often puddingstone, the metamorphosed purple matrix with embedded quartz pebbles that is the bedrock of Bearfort Mountain. The path continues to climb gradually to the right, at 0.8 mile paralleling the northeast to southwest line of the Highlands ridges. The trail then turns left to climb the ridge and soon emerges into a rocky open area at the lower southern end of Bearfort Mountain, where to the left it skirts a bare cliff with large fractured boulders. On this ridgetop, the sparse canopy of chestnut oak admits some sunlight. At 1.0 mile, the path mounts a glacially smoothed puddingstone outcrop, which it follows for about 100 yards as if on an inclined sidewalk. Leaving that ridge, the trail passes a tumbled stone fence built to enclose cattle, a century or more ago, and turns left to follow a wide woods road entering from the right at

1.2 miles. The trail turns left again onto another woods road, now heading east on level ground.

The forest here is mixed conifers and hardwoods, with an understory along the trail dominated by barberry hedge, an alien plant used by nineteenth-century householders to keep small children from escaping, and to prevent animals from entering into a kitchen garden. The trail soon passes a woods road veering off to the left, and meets it again returning from the left a little further on at 1.4 miles. A wide woods road enters from the right at 1.6 miles, and the trail makes a sharp V-turn to the left to join it, heading back north on an almost level track. Through the trees at 1.7 miles, you catch glimpses of a swamp open to sunlight and lined with snags, and the yellow-blazed trail begins to bend left to cross the wetland. Although this is near the top of the mountain, the forest here contains some red maple, hemlock, white pine, and other plants that need a moist environment, and the deeper, richer soil not usually found on dry ridgetops. The presence of the fairly large swamp shows this area to be a catch basin for a small mountaintop watershed. Perhaps a hundred years ago, before the swamp was filled with organic matter and erosion materials, this level hilltop was a productive area for farming and pasturage; the barberry hedges, the stone fence, and the woods roads all had their domestic uses.

A woods road enters from the right at a Y-intersection at 1.8 miles and, the yellow-blazed trail takes the left fork. The trail comes close to the edge of the swamp, and in wet seasons, the road here may be covered with ankle-deep water. At 1.9 miles, the trail leaves the woods road, first turning right and then quickly left to parallel the road. It crosses the outlet of the swamp on stones, continues over two large cement conduits, and clambers over puddingstone ridges and loose rocks. The trail crosses running streams, passes displays of the August blossoms of sweet pepperbush and jewelweed, and then turns abruptly left to return to the road. Back on the woods road, the trail quickly comes to a Y-intersection, where the Yellow-Dot Trail origi-

Climbing up puddingstone bedrock and boulders on the yellow-blazed Terrace Pond South Trail.

nates on a woods road straight ahead, and the yellow-blazed Terrace Pond South Trail continues on the left fork. Following the yellow blazes to the left, still on a grassy moss-covered woods road, the trail passes a small stream feeding into the swamp and an unmarked woods road that leaves the trail to the left. At 2.2 miles, the trail begins a steady climb and zigs to the left to avoid a large puddingstone boulder. At 2.3 miles, the trail encounters ups and downs over rocky ridges, descends a hollow, crosses a running stream, and climbs a long rise, squeezing between lichen-covered puddingstone boulders near the top.

The trail emerges on a rock outcrop, some of it glacially smooth, some littered with loose fractured boulders and cobbles, and all of it likely to be slippery when wet. A little further on this ridge at 2.6 miles, there is a view to the southeast of Kanouse Mountain and some

A grove of rhododendrons surrounds the white-blazed trail as it approaches Terrace Pond.

of the Wyanokies. Turning left onto a lower ridge, the trail leaves the rock outcrop and descends into a gully between ridges. Here the trail runs in a watercourse, which can be six to eight inches deep after a heavy rain. The trail leaves the streambed at 2.8 miles and climbs back up toward the ridge on the right. The yellow-blazed trail is joined in 0.1 mile by the red-blazed Terrace Pond Red Trail, which in about thirty feet leaves to the left. Following the yellow blazes straight ahead, the trail descends into a hollow, climbs up through large puddingstone boulders with their vertical joints eroded and separated, comes to another damp hollow, and turns left uphill through boulders and under a large blowdown. It levels off at 3.1 miles, passing a ridge on the left, and at 3.2 miles comes to the end of the yellow-blazed trail at an intersection with the white-blazed Terrace Pond Circular Trail. Turn left here to follow the white blazes west through a grove of laurel and rhododendron, with branches arching over the trail. The Terrace Pond Circular Trail passes the trailhead of the Terrace Pond Red Trail, bends to the right (north) and, after short climbs over two rock ledges, reaches Terrace Pond at 3.5 miles.

The scenery from this west viewpoint is memorable. An open ledge looks over the pond and wide, level rock terraces provide comfortable resting places all the way down to the water's edge. The water is clear and dark blue; it is so deep, the bottom can be seen for no more than a few feet from the shore. Steep sides of a long geological fold enclose the pond on the east and west. Across the pond, bare rock cliffs sweep straight down to the water. The crest of those cliffs may be reached by a spur from the Terrace Pond Circular Trail. Except for the cliff faces, the pond is completely surrounded by forest.

The white trail leaves the north end of the open ledge overlooking the pond and climbs onto smooth ridges with fractured boulders and cobbles; here, there are some views back toward the pond. At 3.6 miles, it meets the blue-blazed Terrace Pond North Trail at a

A puddingstone rock outcrop provides a good vantage point at Terrace Pond.

A view of Terrace Pond, one of the most popular hiking destinations in the Highlands.

T-intersection. At this point, you turn left onto the westbound leg of the blue trail, and the white trail departs to the right with the eastbound leg of the blue trail. The blue trail heads down through moist hollows crossed by puncheons, then up a steep rock outcrop to a smoothed ledge extending to the left of the trail at 3.8 miles. It's worthwhile taking a few moments to climb the ridge to the left, for a long view to the west overlooking Clinton Reservoir and the Wawayanda Plateau.

Returning to the blue-blazed trail, turn left and climb down a steep ledge, descending through woods, passing a running stream off to the right, and a rounded ridge to the left, and climbing another steep rock outcrop. This ridge to the left might have been an outlook at one time, but now the view is obscured by trees during leafy seasons. An interesting gneiss glacial erratic is perched on the puddingstone bedrock to the left of the trail. Proceeding from this ridge, the blue-blazed trail curves north to a smooth rock outcrop, on which you walk as if on a puddingstone pavement, and then descends a rocky steep, squeezing between two boulders at 4.1 miles. The trail goes up a third ledge, from which there is no clear view, and proceeds to the right, level on a smooth ridge. It crosses a moist area on stepping stones, leading to a puddingstone ridge from which the trail climbs down. At 4.3 miles, the trail skirts a rock outcrop, which, after a short scramble off the trail up to the left, offers the last viewpoint to the west. Returning to the blue trail, you continue down off the ridge as the trail turns to the north on the edge of a steep, forested slope, descending gradually across the contour of the hill with another climb down at 4.4 miles. The trail reaches an open gas pipeline cut at 4.5 miles, and descends down loose rocks and broken bedrock ledges, passing two unmarked woods roads to the left. At the bottom of the incline, you come to a woods road on the left with blue turn blazes marking the trail's re-entry into the woods at 4.6 miles.

The trail shortly passes an unmarked woods road going off to the right, and continues straight ahead uphill. The forest on this side of the hill is mixed hardwoods, with a few conifers; very few trees are over a foot in diameter. However, as the trail descends into moist hollows, hemlocks, white pines, beeches, and maples become more frequent, and the trees are taller and larger in diameter. The trail becomes covered with soft conifer needles and crosses a small stream at 4.7 miles. It passes a still healthy, mature hemlock grove at 4.8 miles, crosses a second stream on two rounded logs and then a wide damp area on large flat stones. The trail climbs slightly out of the wetland and descends gradually, arriving at the trailhead and parking turnout at 5.0 miles.

28. PEQUANNOCK WATERSHED

Hanks Pond Circle

5.7 miles • 4¼ hours

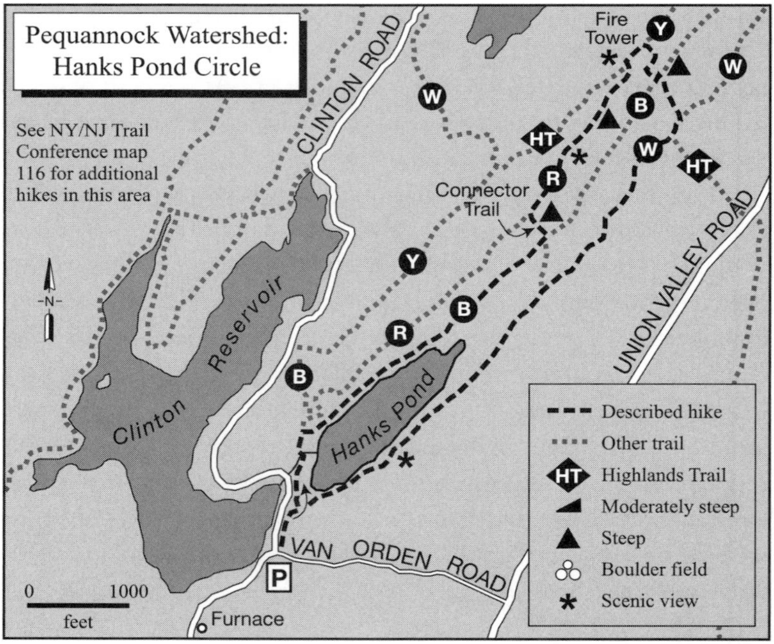
Pequannock Watershed:
Hanks Pond Circle
See NY/NJ Trail Conference map 116 for additional hikes in this area
CLINTON ROAD
UNION VALLEY ROAD
VAN ORDEN ROAD
Clinton Reservoir
Hanks Pond
Fire Tower
Connector Trail
Furnace
P
W
Y
B
R
HT
0
1000
feet
Described hike
Other trail
Highlands Trail
Moderately steep
Steep
Boulder field
Scenic view

Rutgers Cartography 2006

The blaze circles marked in primary colors (e.g., "R" for red) may represent a color over white (e.g., red-over-white), as noted in the hike description.

ELEVATION: Low: 1,000 feet; High: 1,320 feet.

BLAZES: Blue-over-white, blue, red-over-white, Highlands Trail teal diamond, white.

CLIMBING: One steep climb of 140 feet in 0.1 mile on the way north on the blue connector trail. On the last 0.8 mile of the Fire Tower Ridge Trail, a few short, steep climbs down into moist hollows and up again. Returning on the Highlands Trail, there is a climb down a rock ledge from the fire tower, and, after turning south on the Hanks Pond East Trail, about a mile of occasional ups and downs off rock ledges. Lots of ridge walking and old woods roads. At the fire tower, an open field with picnic tables.

PERMITTED USES: Hiking and horses; the horses stay on level woodland roads and paths, and don't go up onto the ridges. No mountain bikes or ATVs.

O V E R V I E W

This hike is "the road less taken" to the Bearfort Ridge Fire Tower and back. It skirts the west shore of Hanks Pond on the way north, climbs on a ridge trail to the fire tower viewpoint and picnic area, and returns on a lower ridge through successional forest along the east shore of the pond. Spring and summer wildflowers are plentiful on the way up, laurel groves and rock ledges with an off-trail view to the east on the way back.

ACCESS: Driving west on NJ 23, turn right onto Clinton Road, 6.5 miles west of the Kinnelon Road traffic light in Butler. Drive 1.7 miles to a parking area at the corner of Clinton Road and Van Orden Road, designated P1 on Trail Conference and Watershed maps. There is a small parking area by a gate on the north side of Van Orden Road, and another turnout on the opposite side of the road. More parking is available in a turnout 50 yards south of this intersection on the Clinton Reservoir side of Clinton Road. A permit is required for adults hiking in the Watershed. An individual (over 18) must have an annual permit (Newark residents $4, non-residents $8), which is issued in person either at the Watershed office on Echo Lake Road, or at the Newark office, 40 Clinton Street. (Permits for senior hikers are half price.) Contact the NWCDC for information: (973) 697-2850; www.nwcdc.net.

HISTORY AND TERRAIN

The Clinton iron furnace, whose remains can be seen on the east side of Clinton Road in a hollow below the dam of the Clinton Reservoir, was one of the most active producers of pig iron (ingots) in the nineteenth century. The forests surrounding the furnace were cleared at least twice before the twentieth century to supply fuel to the furnace, and the woodlands in the watershed now are maturing successional forests. During the iron-mining and lumbering decades, many woods roads crisscrossed these hills, and some of them remained active into the early twentieth century to access subsistence farms and dairies. These trails cross many such roads and follow others. The hike goes out and back along the lower southern ridges of Bearfort Mountain, whose geology is different from other parts of the Highlands. The bedrock outcrops are often puddingstone, the attractive purple rock formed on ancient seashores, composed of fine-grained sand sprinkled with rounded quartz pebbles and heated under pressure into a solid mass deep in the earth. After hundreds of millions of years of erosion and more recent glacial activity, this rock has been exposed in a streak running from Schunemunk Mountain in New York to Bearfort Mountain in New Jersey, called by geologists "The Green Pond Outlier."

DETAILED DESCRIPTION

From the gate at the northeast corner of the intersection of Clinton and Van Orden roads, a wide gravel woods road leads north into the forest. A triple white blaze identifying the trailhead of the Hanks Pond East Trail is found near the gate. Follow the white blazes along the road for 0.2 mile until the blazes fork to the right. This white-blazed trail is the route you will take on your return. However, now continue to the left on the wide woods road (unmarked from this point) which leads to the west shore of Hanks Pond. In spring and summer, you will find interesting wildflowers beside this trail, particularly near clearings, road junctions, and meadows, where the sun's rays slide through the tree canopy. You pass woods roads on your left and right; the one on the right seems to head straight into

The Hanks Pond West Trail is a multi-use trail. Horsemen use the relatively level sec-tions along the pond but don't ride up into the rocky climbs.

the lake. When the reservoir dams were built in the watershed, the water level was raised considerably, covering small farmsteads and roads like this one. When you return on the Hanks Pond East Trail, you will cross a woods road intersection that could well be the continuation of this road. The forest here is the mixed-oak upland type, not the moist hemlock-maple forest you might expect near water. But this terrain was a low hillock, not a moist hollow, before the dam was built; it still retains the features of a well-drained upland. On the left side of the road in early August, there was a wide patch of purple clustered bellflower, a non-native plant which became wild after escaping from nineteenth-century gardens. On the lake side of the road in summer, look for stems of pinesap, a low, yellow-red, non-chlorophyll plant that obtains its nourishment from fungi in the soil near pines or oaks. At 0.4 mile, the road crosses a bridge over the outlet from Hanks Pond into a meadow, where several species of wildflowers grow in summer.

The road soon arrives at an intersection with another woods road bringing the Hanks Pond West Trail in from the left. A blue-over-white double blaze on a tree indicates a turn for that trail, which you join straight ahead on a wide road along the west shore of Hanks Pond. Following the blue-over-white blazes, at 0.5 mile the trail passes a small abandoned building with a puddingstone foundation, about the size of a water pumping station for the Richard F. Cross mansion, whose ruins border the Fire Tower Ridge Trail back toward Clinton Road. Continuing on the level road beside the pond, at 0.8 mile the trail passes the ruins of a large building, also probably part of the Cross complex. At 1.1 miles, near the north end of Hanks Pond, the straight level road bends left and then jogs around a large blowdown. The trail begins to bend away from the pond, climbs a low ledge, and passes a short section where some white blazes mysteriously join the trail for a while and then disappear.

At 1.6 miles, a cliff-like rock ledge appears to the left about 60 feet above the path, and a blue-blazed connector trail comes in from

A steep, rocky climb on the blue-blazed connector trail. These puddingstone rocks still have angular edges, suggesting they were not deposited by glaciers.

the right to join the Hanks Pond West Trail. The two trails run to-gether for a short distance until the blue-blazed connector trail turns left, and the Hanks Pond West Trail with its blue-over-white blazes goes off straight ahead. You leave the Hanks Pond West Trail here and follow the connector trail (blue blazes) to the left, uphill toward the ridge and the Fire Tower Ridge Trail. The trail is now a footpath, and halfway up the hill it runs between two large boulders, one of which is puddingstone. Near the top of the ridge, the trail jogs right to avoid a sheer rock wall, climbs through a small notch, and levels out on top of an outcrop of puddingstone. At 1.7 miles, the blue-blazed connector trail meets the red-over-white-blazed Fire Tower Ridge Trail, which you now follow to the right (north) along the ridgeline. The forest on this dry ridgetop is pitch pine, chestnut oak, black cherry, and scrub oak; down the slope to the left (west) a wet-land hollow supports hemlocks. The blue blazes of the connector

The Bearfort Ridge Fire Tower is on a grassy meadow with open views in all directions.

trail continue for a short distance concurrently with the red-over-white blazes you are following. At 1.9 miles, the trails turn left off the ridge and cross a small stream that seems to emerge right out of the rocks in the hollow. The trails angle slightly west across the narrow ridges, with some ups and downs over rock outcrops. At 2.0 miles, the blue trail leaves to the left, and you continue climbing gradually on the red-over-white trail to the right. The trail arrives on the open meadow around the fire tower at 2.6 miles; this is the high point of the hike (1,320 feet elevation), where there is a fireplace, picnic tables, and a fine view to the east.

To start back, walk to the north end of the fire tower clearing and find the teal diamond blazes of the Highlands Trail as it descends sharply to the right (east) over steep rock ledges. On the ledge just below the fire tower, the trail turns briefly right again (south), and there are good views of Kanouse Mountain to the east and Buck

Mountain to the northeast. The Highlands Trail turns left (east), climbing down to the next ledge, and, descending again, comes to a stone cairn indicating a trail junction 2.9 miles from the start. The blue-over-white-blazed Hanks Pond West Trail leaves here to the south. As you continue to descend on the Highlands Trail, the white blazes of the Hanks Pond East Trail join from the north, at a right turn heading south. These two trails run together until, at 3.2 miles, the trails reach a cairn. At this junction, the Highlands Trail leaves to the left, but you go straight ahead (south) on the white trail that you will now follow all the way back. You may not find white blazes near the cairn; however, as you persist on the southward track, you will find them.

The trail passes a cliff to the right and becomes a rocky footpath

on a ridge of crumbling vertical layers of puddingstone. The rocky path is frequently covered by mats of soft moss. For most of the way, there is only one path visible, and there is a swampy hollow down a slope to the right (west) to keep you oriented. At 3.8 miles, the trail comes to a tall cairn indicating a left turn down a short slope. A

The Hanks Pond East Trail follows a narrow ridge of puddingstone smoothed by glaciers into something like a sidewalk. The layers of the rock have been tilted almost upright by tectonic forces.

white blaze on a tree in the hollow confirms the turn, and the trail is visible through the woods on a moss-covered rocky path. After another bend to the left, in a few minutes the trail turns right (south) again. Follow the mossy track, and the blazes will appear. Just about here in late April, we heard a wood thrush singing and watched him flutter around a nest in a white pine. The trail comes to another large cairn at 4.0 miles; it signals a right turn. You soon enter a laurel grove, almost tunnel-like, with branches arching overhead, and at 4.1 miles meet the trailhead of the blue-blazed connector trail which heads west. You are now about halfway back from the fire tower.

Continuing on the white trail, you come to knobby blowdowns that have to be climbed over because the laurel is so thick you cannot go around. Hanks Pond becomes visible through the trees to the right (west) at 4.7 miles, though the trail doesn't follow close to the shore. The trail soon crosses a wet stretch and, climbing slightly, begins to look more like an old woods road. Just past the wet area, a small patch of trailing arbutus clings to an eroded bank to the left of the trail. As the trail reaches the top of a rise at 5.0 miles, you may see an open ridge through the trees to your left. Though there are no blazed trails to that ridge, a short walk (uphill) to the left will bring you to a pleasant view over Union Valley to Kanouse Mountain. Free of mature trees, the ridge is populated by red cedars, a "pioneer" tree species that, by moving into an abandoned meadow, begins the succession from open pasture land to upland forest. Back on the white trail, as you approach the south end of Hanks Pond, the trees are no more than 6 or 7 inches thick, suggesting that 40 or 50 years ago this was a hillside meadow, although a few minutes farther along, some tree trunks are two feet in diameter, or almost 100 years old. The trail comes closer to the shore of Hanks Pond, circles around its south end in open woods, and, at 5.5 miles, arrives at a T-intersection with the wide gravel road heading back to the gate and your car at 5.7 miles.

Clinton Furnace, along Clinton Road, south of the hike's trailhead. Photo by Daniel Chazin.

Horse Pond Mountain Loop

6.0 miles • 5 hours

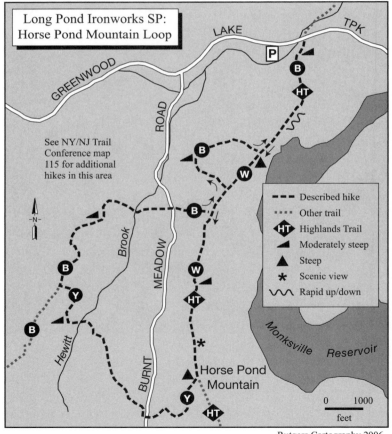

Long Pond Ironworks SP:
Horse Pond Mountain Loop

See NY/NJ Trail
Conference map
115 for additional
hikes in this area

- - - Described hike
········ Other trail
HT Highlands Trail
◀ Moderately steep
▲ Steep
* Scenic view
〰 Rapid up/down

Horse Pond
Mountain

Monksville Reservoir

0   1000
feet

Rutgers Cartography 2006

ELEVATION: Low: 420 feet; High: 945 feet.

BLAZES: Blue and Highlands Trail teal diamond, white and HT teal diamond, yellow, blue, blue and HT teal diamond again.

CLIMBING: A rocky climb of 105 feet to the Horse Pond Mountain ridge. A steep descent from the summit and a moderate 200-foot ascent of Long Hill (a parallel ridge to the west) on the way back.

PERMITTED USES: Hiking only.

This is a Highlands Trail hike.

OVERVIEW

A moderately strenuous hike over Horse Pond Mountain, down across Hewitt Brook, up a parallel ridge and back, briefly through a power line cut. Near the north trailhead, the hike follows an old railroad grade of the nineteenth-century New York and Greenwood Lake Railway. Excellent views of the Monksville Reservoir and Ramapo Mountains from the Horse Pond Mountain ridge on the way up, and also a view from the summit of Horse Pond Mountain.

ACCESS: From the south and east, take I-287 to Exit 55, continuing north through Wanaque on Ringwood Avenue (County 511). In 3.9 miles, at the Wanaque/Ringwood boundary, the name of the road changes to Greenwood Lake Turnpike (it remains County 511). In another 3.2 miles, near the northern end of the Wanaque Reservoir, you will reach a fork where Sloatsburg Road begins to the right. Continue on Greenwood Lake Turnpike for 3.6 miles past Sloatsburg Road, crossing a causeway over the Monksville Reservoir and passing buildings preserved as part of the Long Pond Ironworks site. Parking is available on the south side of Greenwood Lake Turnpike at the junction with East Shore Road.

From the north, take I-87 to Exit 15A (NY 17 North). Proceed north on NY 17 for 1.2 miles to the exit for Ringwood/Sterling

Forest/West Milford. Follow the exit ramp onto Sterling Mine Road (County 72) and continue straight ahead for 4.8 miles to Margaret King Avenue (after 3.3 miles, at the New York-New Jersey state line, Sterling Mine Road becomes Sloatsburg Road). Turn right onto Margaret King Avenue and continue for 2.3 miles to the end of Margaret King Avenue at Greenwood Lake Turnpike. Turn right onto Greenwood Lake Turnpike and drive for 1.3 miles to trailhead parking on the left side of the road opposite the intersection with East Shore Road.

If using public transportation, take New Jersey Transit Bus #197 from the Port Authority Terminal on 42nd Street in Manhattan. This bus will stop at East Shore Road.

DETAILED DESCRIPTION

This section of the Highlands Trail begins here.

To find the trailhead, walk about 70 yards east of the parking area on the south side of the road. The Hewitt-Butler Trail begins with a triangle of three blue blazes on a tree which also has a teal diamond turn blaze of the Highlands Trail. (The blue-blazed Hewitt-Butler Trail is co-aligned here with the Highlands Trail.) The trail heads gently uphill (south) on a footpath and enters the woods. The forest is mixed oak uplands hardwoods, with the largest trunks about 14 inches thick, suggesting this hillside was cleared perhaps 70 years ago. Over the shoulder of the hill, the footpath merges with a woods road and at 0.3 mile leaves the road, heading left down into a hollow with a small brook, to be crossed on stepping stones at 0.4 mile.

The path climbs an embankment to join a railroad grade built for the nineteenth-century New York and Greenwood Lake Railway. The Monksville Reservoir is soon visible to the left through trees. The trail follows an excavated dip in the railroad grade across a cut for a gas pipeline, and at 0.6 mile turns right into the woods on a footpath heading away from the reservoir. This dip is the lowest point of the hike, at 420 feet elevation. The trail passes a couple of large glacial erratics as it climbs, gradually at first, then more steeply up a rocky ledge that can be very slippery in wet or icy conditions. Over the crest of the ledge, the trail descends into a hollow, and, as it climbs up the other side, it reaches the trailhead of the white-blazed Horse Pond Mountain Trail at 1.0 mile. At this junction, the Hewitt-Butler Trail (blue blazes) leaves to the right, but you follow the Horse Pond Mountain Trail's white blazes and the Highlands Trail teal blazes straight ahead steeply uphill on a rocky footpath. The Hewitt-Butler digression is a longer and more gradual climb, which you will travel down on the way back. The white trail you are now following climbs to a ridge in two stages. After the first stage, it reaches a junction where the Hewitt-Butler Trail rejoins the white trail at 1.2 miles.

The Highlands Trail teal diamond turn blaze and the trailhead blaze of the Hewitt-Butler Trail mark the start of the Horse Pond Mountain Loop.

The three combined trails continue to climb almost to the top of the crest and briefly join a woods road. The forest here is the chestnut oak, black cherry, scrub oak, and occasional pitch pine combination, characteristic of Highlands ridgetops.

The trail descends to a power line cut at 1.4 miles, with a limited view of the reservoir to the left. Just beyond, the Hewitt-Butler Trail again departs up to the right, and you continue straight ahead on the combined white-blazed Horse Pond Mountain Trail and teal diamond-blazed Highlands Trail. Soon the trail leaves the woods road, forking to the left on a footpath up over fractured boulders to the top of a rock outcrop (717 feet elevation), with views through the trees over the Monksville Reservoir. After following the ridge for a short distance, the trail briefly rejoins the road, leaves it, then joins it once more. At 1.6 miles, the trail passes within sight of a house and a horse farm through the trees to the west. (At 1.8 miles, a red-blazed private trail forks to the right, leading to the Shiloh Bible Camp on Burnt Meadow Road.) The white-blazed trail follows a level route along the ridgetop, then begins to climb, becoming steeper over gneiss rock outcrops. As you near the summit at 2.0 miles, there is a long view over the Monksville Reservoir to the Ramapo Mountain ridge to the east. This is the one spot where you can view the entire horseshoe-shaped reservoir. At 2.1 miles, the trail reaches the top of Horse Pond Mountain at an elevation of 945 feet, an excellent place for a rest and lunch. From the summit rocks, you can find partial views to the east over the reservoir and clearer views to the west over the valley of Hewitt Brook to Long Hill, whose crest you will skirt on your return.

Farther along the summit ridge, look for three yellow blazes on a large boulder marking the trailhead of the Burnt Meadow Trail, which you follow into the valley of Hewitt Brook. The Horse Pond Mountain and the Highlands trails continue south from this summit. **This section of the Highlands Trail ends here.**

The initial descent on the yellow trail is very steep for 50 feet

A view of one leg of the horseshoe of the Monksville Reservoir from a rock outcrop just before the summit of Horse Pond Mountain.

through fractured boulders, but it begins to moderate as you leave the cliff face. The trail loses 200 feet in 0.2 mile, a net grade of close to 20%, before it begins to level out. At 2.3 miles, the trail joins an old woods road and then leaves the road to turn right on a footpath and meet another road, which it also leaves to turn left. The forest here is uplands mixed oak and hardwoods. The trees are somewhat taller and thicker than others you have seen, perhaps because of the deeper, moister valley soil. The understory is quite open, free of mature shrubs and young saplings. The trail crosses a small tributary brook on stepping stones at 2.5 miles and, at 2.6 miles, meets paved Burnt Meadow Road. It follows Burnt Meadow Road to the right (north) for about 50 yards before turning left (west) into the woods on a wide eroded road. The trail turns off this road onto an older, narrower woods road at 2.8 miles and crosses another road where the intersection is covered with the spring wildflower called lousewort. The trail crosses Hewitt Brook on stones at 3.1 miles, climbs up the opposite

Hewitt Brook full to its banks after a winter rain on the Hewitt-Butler Trail to Horse Pond Mountain.

bank at the foot of Long Hill, and turns right to follow the contour of the hill parallel to the brook. At 3.2 miles, the trail turns left to begin a steeper climb of 170 feet directly up the shoulder of Long Hill. About halfway up at 3.3 miles, it crosses a smooth ledge from which there is a limited view back toward Horse Pond Mountain to the east. The yellow blazes are marked on the rocks, and the trail leads back into the woods (uphill) from the northwest edge of the outcrop. After climbing a bit more and leveling off, at 3.4 miles the yellow trail ends at a T-junction with the Hewitt-Butler Trail, well below the crest of Long Hill.

At this junction you turn right (north) on the Hewitt-Butler Trail, passing on your right a large puddingstone erratic; it must have been carried here by glaciers from the conglomerate summit rock of the Bearfort-Bellvale Mountain ridge, at least five miles to the northeast. The trail descends and then climbs to a crest, turning left at 3.6

miles to descend off Long Hill. It joins a woods road, turning right off the road onto a footpath through a boulder field and laurel grove. The trail passes a large gneiss erratic on the left, enters a small grove of white pine, and continues to descend, crossing two strands of Hewitt Brook on stones at 4.3 miles. It briefly rejoins the same power line you passed on the way in. After a brief descent, Burnt Meadow Road is crossed at a slight diagonal to the right at 4.4 miles. The trail climbs on a footpath, winding through woods to the south of the power lines, and descends to rejoin the combined Horse Pond Mountain and Highlands trails at a T-intersection at 4.6 miles. At this junction, you turn left (north) to follow the three trails as they travel together uphill to a ridge. They then gradually descend on a woods road along a ridgeline, until at 4.8 miles the Hewitt-Butler Trail (blue blazes) forks to the left, while the Horse Pond Mountain and Highlands trails continue straight ahead. Because you skipped this short west loop on the way out, you can now add some variety to your route by turning left here. This trail leads to the west of the ridge within sight of houses, descending easily through a grove of white pines, and passing a puddingstone erratic to the west of the path.

After a 0.3-mile digression, the Hewitt-Butler Trail rejoins the Highlands Trail at 5.1 miles. (The trailhead of the Horse Pond Mountain Trail is at this junction.) Retracing your first steps, you follow the combined Hewitt-Butler and Highlands trails into a hollow, climb to a ridge on the other side, and turn right (east) to descend gradually off the ridge. At 5.4 miles, the trails meet the railroad grade you followed at the start of the hike. From here, continue to retrace your first steps, following the railroad grade for 0.2 mile until the path heads down an embankment to the right, crosses a small stream, and climbs up to meet a woods road. Follow this woods road to the left over the shoulder of a hill, descending to the trailhead at Greenwood Lake Turnpike at 6.0 miles and your car parked nearby.

Skylands–Ramapo Ridgewalk Through Hike

6.2 miles • 5¼ hours

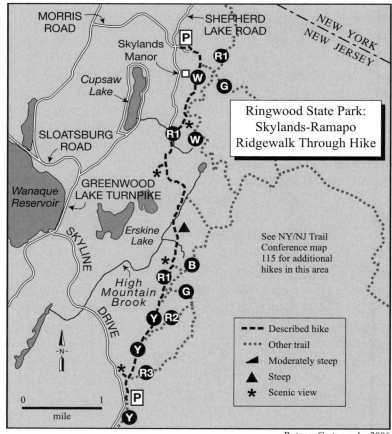

MORRIS ROAD

SHEPHERD LAKE ROAD

NEW YORK
NEW JERSEY

Skylands Manor

Cupsaw Lake

R1

W

G

SLOATSBURG ROAD

R1

W

Ringwood State Park:
Skylands-Ramapo
Ridgewalk Through Hike

Wanaque Reservoir

GREENWOOD LAKE TURNPIKE

Erskine Lake

See NY/NJ Trail
Conference map
115 for additional
hikes in this area

SKYLINE

High Mountain Brook

B

R1

G

Y R2

Y

DRIVE

Described hike

Other trail

Moderately steep

Steep

Scenic view

0   1
mile

-N-

R3

P

Y

Rutgers Cartography 2006

On this map, the blaze R1, on the Ringwood-Ramapo Trail, is a small red rectangle on a white larger rectangle; blaze R2, for the Cannonball Trail, is a white C on a red circle; and blaze R3, the Matapan Rock Trail, is a red square on a white rectangle.

ELEVATION: Low: 550 feet; High: 1,060 feet.

BLAZES: White, red-on-white, green tulip tree leaf-on-white, yellow, white C-on-red, yellow.

CLIMBING: The low point crosses a feeder stream for Cupsaw Lake, reached at 1.4 miles. Just past the mid-point of the hike, a 400-foot-climb winds through a field of large boulders. Most of the other ups and downs are brief or gradual, but there are many of them.

PERMITTED USES: The Ringwood-Ramapo and Hoeferlin Memorial trails are for hiking only. The Crossover Trail is multi-use, as are the woods roads. Woods roads that are part of the Brushwood section of the park are vehicle accessible for hunters and fishermen with annual permits issued at the Ringwood State Park office, (973) 962-7031. Permits are issued only for hunting and fishing in season, not for exploration or off-roading.

O V E R V I E W

This straight through hike begins in the pleasant surroundings of the New Jersey State Botanical Gardens at Skylands Manor. It is rewarding to allow time for a stroll through the gardens. The trail leaves Skylands Manor on the slopes of Mount Defiance and follows the ridgeline of Ramapo Mountain, overlooking Erskine Lakes and the Wanaque Reservoir along the way. There are some all-season viewpoints, especially to the west, from spots on or just off the trail. If you begin the hike by 10 a.m., one of these lookouts provides a fine place for lunch. The rocky Highlands ups and downs pass through a variety of micro-environments, from rich moist stream-sides to dry ridgetop forests. For the last mile, the walking is fairly level.

ACCESS: This through hike will need two cars. Take I-287 to Exit 57 (Skyline Drive). Turn north (uphill) onto Skyline Drive, continuing to a green-and-white 2.4-mile marker at a dirt-and-gravel parking area on the right. You are now in front of a gas pipeline pumping station, with a driveway through a gate to the Oakland Public Works Composting Facility. Park one car outside the gate, but leave plenty of access for town trucks. Do not park inside the gate; it closes at 4 p.m. on weekdays and probably at other odd times, so you might find your car locked inside. Proceed in the other car on Skyline Drive to its end at Greenwood Lake Turnpike (County 511). Turn right (north) here, take the second right turn onto Sloatsburg Road, and then again take a second right turn onto Morris Road, marked by signs to the New Jersey State Botanical Gardens at Skylands Manor. About 1.4 miles up Morris Road, just after crossing Shepherd Lake Road, find Parking Area A on the left.

On weekends from Memorial Day to Labor Day, there is a fee ($5.00 per vehicle) to enter the park's Skylands section, which includes Parking Area A.

D E T A I L E D   D E S C R I P T I O N

As you leave the parking area, turn left (east) onto Morris Road where, on a sign stating "Do Not Enter," a single white blaze marks the Crossover Trail heading south. Twenty yards farther, on the right of the paved road, a sign with symbols designates the Crossover Trail as multi-use: for hikers, bikers, and horses. In 0.1 mile, a grassy trail goes off to the left, but you follow the white blazes of the Crossover Trail as a few steps later, it turns left off the paved road. The forest along the path is mature mixed hardwoods, including maple, red and white oak, hickory, beech, and birch. The understory is full of winged euonymous shrubs, probably escaped from cultivation when Skylands was developed at the beginning of the twentieth century. At 0.3 mile, a gravel road comes in from the right and, in a short distance, a woods road leaves to the right. The trail crosses a stone bridge over a brook and passes the trailhead of the green-and-white-blazed Halifax Trail, with signage indicating that it is for hikers only. With such easy level walking on the gravel road, it's a good idea to make a rapid pace here, since you will be slowed later by occasional rocky slopes. At 0.8 mile, the Crossover Trail passes a grove of hemlocks and some rhododendron shrubs. As we stopped to take a picture of a blossom, a raccoon scurried through the underbrush. The trail soon turns left past a large downed tree and continues for a short distance as a gravel road. The trail narrows, is joined by a woods road from the right, and again becomes a wider road, eroded and rocky, heading uphill.

At the top of this rise at 1.1 miles, the red-on-white-blazed Ringwood-Ramapo Trail intersects the white-blazed Crossover Trail. You now leave the white blazes, turning right (south) to follow the red-on-white blazes on a grassy woodland path. From this intersection to the end of the hike, the trail is for hikers only. The path is on a ridgetop, with rock outcrops and the smaller trees typical of dry, thin-soiled terrain, including chestnut oak, red oak, red cedar, and black cherry. Among the rocks, pale corydalis shows its pink and yellow blossoms, the less common yellow corydalis also blooms here in May, and in late July the bright yellow flower known as butter-and-eggs grows beside the grassy path. At 1.3 miles, the trail crosses a graffiti-covered rock outcrop called Warm Puppy Rock, with a view to the west of the Wanaque Reservoir. Just off the trail to the left, there is also an eastward view of Pierson Ridge.

From the rock outcrop, the trail descends to the left, climbs briefly to a soft grassy meadow, and begins a longer, more gradual descent. At 1.6 miles, the trail meets an old carriage road, where it zigs to the right and quickly zags left, back into the woods; at this point, there is a cement marker stone with the inscription "Y.C.C. 1976-7," indicating that the Youth Conservation Corps probably cut this trail. About 30 yards into the woods, the trail crosses a running stream feeding into Cupsaw Lake at the low point of the hike (550

View of Erskine Lakes and the Wanaque Reservoir from a rock outcrop overlook well off the trail, on an unblazed path at 2.4 miles into the hike.

feet). The bridge is a single stone about eight feet long, which must weigh tons. The path winds between swampy areas to the left and right, where the remains of a bamboo garden, also with large stone bridges, are visible. It soon meets a wide fire road, where a blaze on a sapling on the far side indicates a turn to the left. In about 50 yards, the road passes two inviting, wide unblazed paths on the right, but blazes on nearby trees show that the trail continues straight ahead on the road. Follow the road for a short distance until you see a sign indicating a right turn for the Ringwood-Ramapo Trail leading onto a woodland footpath at 1.8 miles.

The red-on-white-blazed trail now lies in a hollow between two ridges. The young maturing upland forest here contains red oak, chestnut oak, beech, hickory, and yellow birch. The diameter of the largest trees is hardly more than a foot, suggesting these slopes were logged-over fields or pastures 70 years ago. The trail climbs at a 10% grade, then, at 1.9 miles, crosses a brook on a wooden plank bridge, and a companion stream 10 feet ahead, on stepping stones. In a short distance, the trail meets a woods road where it turns left, and again turns left at 2.0 miles onto a long, moderate uphill grade with switchbacks to ease the climb. The path becomes grass-covered as it reaches the crest of the hill. On top of the ridge at 2.4 miles, the trail turns left, and straight ahead you will find an unblazed path, which leads in 0.2 mile to an excellent westward overlook. If you began your walk in late morning, this rock outcrop is a fine place to stop for lunch. On a clear day, you can see Big Beech Mountain to the north near the New York border, Bearfort Mountain on the far side of Greenwood Lake to the west, Horse Pond Mountain a little closer, Wanaque Reservoir and Erskine Lakes nearby, and the Wyanokies to the southwest.

To regain the Ringwood-Ramapo Trail, retrace your steps along the lookout path, turning right (south) when you again see the red-on-white blazes. In July along this ridge at 2.5 miles, we came across

View to the west from just off the Ringwood-Ramapo Trail. The long, high ridge of Bearfort Mountain is seen in the distance.

an uncommon summer wildflower called woodland agrimony, with its six-inch spike of small five-petalled, bright yellow flowers. At 2.6 miles, the trail comes to an intersection, where you should continue straight ahead on a footpath, leaving the woods road. Soon the red-on-white-blazed trail turns left and heads more steeply down off the ridge, passing the Blue Trail (blue-on-white blazes), which leads to the left toward Boy Scout Camp Yaw Paw, about 0.5 mile to the east. You descend easily, until through the woods downhill to the left you see glimpses of High Mountain Brook. The trail approaches and parallels its streambed for about 0.2 mile. As you come closer to the brook, watch for a left turn red-on-white blaze on a slender tree at 3.2 miles, where the trail crosses High Mountain Brook on a woodland path through a damp hollow between two low ridges. The trail crosses another small brook at 3.4 miles, where we heard a scarlet tanager singing in the canopy.

The trail shortly begins a long 400-foot climb, at 3.6 miles angling through a field of large boulders split off by glaciers and weathering from the cliff above. In mid-summer, we found the ghostly gray stalks of Indian pipe and the small white inverted flowers of striped wintergreen beside the trail here. A few switchbacks through the boulders ease the climb, but in some places you may need your hands to scramble over the rocks. As the trail levels out approaching the crest of a ridge, at 4.0 miles it crosses a small stream flowing from the base of a cliff to the left. This brook was still running when we passed in July. The trail continues to climb as the Old Guard Trail, marked with a green tulip tree leaf-on-white, enters from the left at 4.2 miles. Westward views may be possible through the trees at 4.3 miles if you walk a short distance off the trail to a rock outcrop opening over a steep slope.

The Old Guard Trail leaves to the left at 4.4 miles, and the red-on-white blazes you follow continue to the right, where a rock cairn marks the trail. On top of the ridge at 4.6 miles, the path now tracks through more level terrain, with brief rocky ups and downs.

View west from Matapan Rock.

At 5.1 miles, the yellow-blazed Hoeferlin Memorial Trail comes in from the left, and the red-on-white-blazed Ringwood-Ramapo Trail ends at this intersection. You now continue ahead, following the yellow blazes on a path that is well-worn and easily seen. At 5.4 miles, the Cannonball Trail joins from the left with its blaze of a white C-on-red background. The trail here was once a grassy track with rounded boulders hidden underneath, but increased use has worn away much of the grass and exposed the underlying rocks. You will now continue ahead following both blazes to the end of your hike.

A cell phone tower appears on the right of the trail at 5.9 miles, and the trail follows its gravel access road for about 50 yards before turning back into the woods to the right. At the turn, the Matapan Rock Trail, on a woods road blazed with a red-square-on-white rectangle, intersects your trail. To the left, the Matapan Rock Trail leads in 0.7 mile to Camp Glen Gray, a former Boy Scout camp now owned by Bergen County. To the right, in the direction you should follow, it leads to the edge of the ridge, 0.1 mile away. There, a rock outcrop known as Matapan Rock provides an excellent unobstructed year-round view to the west over the Wanaque Reservoir, to Bearfort Mountain in the northwest distance, to Horse Pond Mountain in the near west, and to the Wyanokies in the southwest.

Returning to the combined trails, you turn right and follow both the yellow blazes and the white-C-on-red blazes through level woods to your first car, which you reach at 6.2 miles.

The Ringwood-Ramapo Trail crosses a Cupsaw Lake inlet stream on this eight-foot stone, at the low point of the hike. Photo by Daniel Chazin.

Black River Gorge Loop

6.4 miles • 5¼ hours

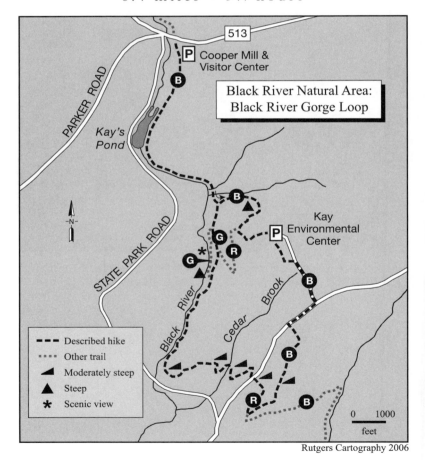

Black River Natural Area: Black River Gorge Loop

Cooper Mill & Visitor Center

Kay's Pond

Kay Environmental Center

PARKER ROAD

STATE PARK ROAD

Black River

Cedar Brook

-N-

Described hike
Other trail
Moderately steep
Steep
Scenic view

0   1000
feet

Rutgers Cartography 2006

ELEVATION: Low: 540 feet; High: 840 feet.

BLAZES: Blue, red, green, unblazed, blue, and the Patriots' Path
blaze, which is a path and tree logo on a white circle, and accompanies all the blue blazes on this hike.

CLIMBING: Long, moderate ascents. Some muddy stream crossings
in wet seasons.

PERMITTED USES: Hiking only.

OVERVIEW

A start at Cooper Mill County Park beside a restored nineteenth-century flour mill, a walk along a railroad grade past Hacklebarney
Mine. Climbs to the Kay Environmental Center and the summits in
the Black River Natural Area, descending to the splashing, boulder-filled Black River Gorge on the way back.

ACCESS: Take NJ 10 to its intersection with County 513 at Morris
County College. Turn southwest on County 513 toward Ironia and
Chester, continuing to the intersection with US 206 in Chester. At
this intersection, continue straight ahead (west) on County 513 toward Long Valley, and drive 1.2 miles to the old mill at Cooper Mill
Park on the left, where you can park in the large lot.

TERRAIN AND HISTORY

Cooper Mill County Park features a restored grain mill built in 1826
by Nathan Cooper. The steel water wheel is an early twentieth-century restoration, but the workings of the mill, with wooden gears and
huge millstone, are original. In Black River Natural Area, the trail in
part follows the railbed of the Hacklebarney Branch of the Central
Railroad of New Jersey, built in 1868 to service the Hacklebarney

Mine, whose location is visible along the trail. The railroad was decommissioned in 1892 when the mine became unprofitable. To the right of the trail near the mine, an old stone and cement dam forms a pond from which a water flume led to the mine. In days before electric refrigeration, the pond was also a source of ice, stored in the small building at the southwest shore. At the top of the first ascent away from the Black River, you pass the Kay Environmental Center, site of the New Jersey Field Offices of The Nature Conservancy, formerly the summer home of environmentalist Elizabeth Donnell Kay. In open fields around this building, summer wildflowers, birds, and butterflies abound. The terrain of this area is formed of typical Highlands crystalline gneissic ridges cut steeply by the Black River. The Black River Gorge, seen on the return trail, is one of the wildest stretches of river in the state. At the south end of the hike, there is a mature white pine plantation at least 70 years old; nearby, an open moist hollow formed by a tributary brook is a good spot for wildflowers.

DETAILED   DESCRIPTION

To complete this hike you will enter the Black River Natural Area, for which a free permit is required. On weekdays, permits are issued at the Kay Environmental Center, which you pass about a third of the way into the hike. On weekends when the Kay Center is closed, the permits are issued at the Cooper Mill County Park Visitor Center, located at the east end of the parking lot.

Begin the hike from the west end of the parking lot; descend a stairway beside Cooper Mill and find the blue blazes of the Black River Trail to your left along the river. The Patriots' Path blaze, a path and tree on a white circle, will accompany all the blue blazes on the hike. The trail winds through moist stretches crossed by puncheons and soon begins to parallel the old Central Railroad railbed off to the right near the river. The trail joins the railbed at 0.3 mile and follows it to the left along the river. On the right at 0.5 mile, you pass Kay Pond, with its old stone and cement dam and the icehouse on the far side.

On the left, you can see where the railbed was blasted through the rock, and you pass a fenced area where the mine was located. At 1.2 miles, after crossing a small brook, the trail comes to an intersection with an old woods road. Here, the blue blazes head (uphill) to the left, paralleling the brook. The trail bends to the right and begins a long steady moderate climb past old stone fences that once surrounded cultivated fields or pastures. The largest trees along here are about a foot or more in diameter, indicating the field was cleared 60 or 70 years ago. At the top of the climb, you come to a grassy clearing where the blue trail meets a red-blazed trail coming from the right,

The restored historic Cooper Mill was built in 1826. The steel water wheel was an early twentieth-century innovation.

Before the days of electric refrigeration, Kay Pond was a source of ice, which was cut and then stored in the icehouse on the far side.

and the two together turn to the left, at 1.9 miles arriving at the Kay Center. On weekdays, when the Center is open, you should request a permit here to continue into the Black River Natural Area.

From the east side of the Kay Center, near the paved parking area, find the blue-blazed Bamboo Brook Trail on a mowed path heading south past a grove of dogwood trees. This trail becomes a gravel road and then joins the paved entrance road at 2.0 miles. Slow down a little here, because along this road on the left, the formerly cultivated fields now overgrown with brambles and shrubs, provide good habitat for summer wildflowers, birds, and butterflies. In September, we saw clematis, blazing star, turtlehead, migrating warblers, and a few fritillary butterflies. Follow the paved road out to Pottersville Road at 2.3 miles, turn right, and in 0.1 mile, opposite a mailbox with the number 230, find a blue blaze on a tree to the left, and follow the trail into the woods. The trail heads south on a level footpath through immature successional forest, until at 2.6 miles it bends right and begins a moderate climb up a rocky hillside. At the top of the ridge, which you reach at 2.9 miles, there is a small outcrop of Highlands gneiss and many small weathered boulders.

Just over the crest as you start down, you see a post marking the intersection with the red-blazed Conifer Pass Trail. Turn sharply right here, and leave both the blue blazes and the Patriots' Path logos, to follow the red blazes down the hill. The trail again crosses Pottersville Road and enters a mature white pine plantation, with trees well over 100 feet tall and two feet thick. They must be at least 70 years old, and are remarkable for their straight, undivided trunks. They have somehow escaped the beetle that attacks the stem buds of East Coast white pines and divides their trunks, diminishing their stately beauty and reducing their value as lumber. At the bottom of this descent at 3.4 miles, you cross a moist treeless hollow formed by Cedar Brook, a tributary of the Black River, where the combination of sun, rich soil, and water produces various wildflowers in all green seasons.

The trail follows the railbed of the nineteenth-century spur of the Central Railroad of New Jersey which served the Hacklebarney Mine.

A waterfall in the Black River Gorge seen from a spur off the Conifer Pass Trail.

Across the brook, the trail climbs in a series of switchbacks through a spruce grove, then, as the grade eases, and as the soil becomes drier, through oak, beech, and hickory upland hardwoods to a forested ridgetop at 3.7 miles. It then descends to the wild and spectacularly beautiful Black River Gorge, where the trail follows the stream north for about a quarter of a mile, sometimes close to the water's edge, sometimes on a narrow footpath on a steep embankment. The trail begins to climb to the right, away from the gorge, although the river is still occasionally visible. At this location, a spur trail forks to the left down to the bank of the river where you can be close to both man-made and natural waterfalls in the heart of the gorge. Green blazes eventually appear on this spur and, if followed, will lead to the woods road intersection with the unmarked trail heading back to the start as described below. However, you can also return by going back up to the red trail just above the riverbank.

At 4.2 miles, the red-blazed Conifer Pass Trail you are following turns sharply right at a T-intersection with a woods road, and then quickly turns back sharply left at a Y-intersection to head north again. At 4.7 miles, the trail arrives at a T-intersection with a wide woods road where the red-blazed Conifer Pass Trail turns right, but you turn left obliquely to follow green blazes slightly downhill. At 5.1 miles, at the next junction, turn left with the green blazes. In about 20 yards, opposite the spot where the green blazes turn left into the woods heading south (this is the green-blazed spur trail described previously) you turn right onto an unmarked woods road. Continue for a short time until the road ends at 5.2 miles at an intersection with the blue-blazed Black River Trail on which you started. Follow the blue blazes back along the river on the railbed, past Kay Pond, to Cooper Mill and the parking lot at 6.4 miles.

32. ABRAM S. HEWITT STATE FOREST

Bearfort Ridge Loop

6.0 miles • 5 hours

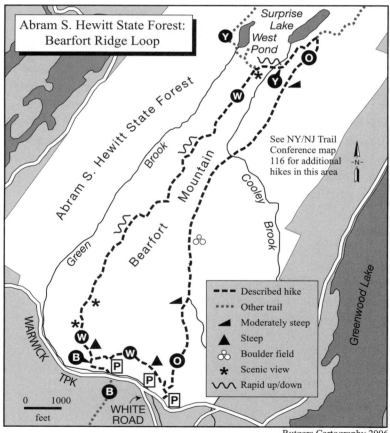

Abram S. Hewitt State Forest:
Bearfort Ridge Loop

Surprise Lake
West Pond

Abram S. Hewitt State Forest

Green

Brook

Bearfort Mountain

Cooley Brook

See NY/NJ Trail Conference map 116 for additional hikes in this area

-N-

Greenwood Lake

WARWICK TPK

WHITE ROAD

0   1000
feet

- - - Described hike
..... Other trail
◀ Moderately steep
▲ Steep
⚬ Boulder field
✱ Scenic view
〰 Rapid up/down

Rutgers Cartography 2006

ELEVATION: Low: 720 feet; High: 1,360 feet.

BLAZES: White, yellow, orange, white.

CLIMBING: From the trailhead, a moderate climb of 300 feet in 0.4 mile, about 15% average grade, with no difficult rocky ledges. After a slight descent, another climb of 350 feet in 0.3 mile, about 20% average grade, with three rock scrambles near the top. Continuing on the ridgetop, a series of 20- to 40-foot rock ledges with scrambles about every 0.2 mile to the mid-point of the hike, each climb not very difficult in itself, but the series can be tiring. The return on the Quail Trail is mostly downhill on woods roads, with some very wet spots at stream crossings about halfway back.

PERMITTED USES: Hiking only.

OVERVIEW

The hike begins with a 300-foot ascent through a dying hemlock forest, and a 350-foot climb through rock outcrops to viewpoints west and south. Along the top of the ridge, the trail works its way east over a succession of short, steep ledges with moisture-loving vegetation, including hemlocks in the hollows, and stunted pitch pines, scrub and chestnut oaks on the ridgetops. Glacially smoothed rock outcrops often provide paths similar to sidewalks, which end in crevices or steep drops. At the hike's north end, the trail reaches the east edge of the mountain, from which there is an excellent viewpoint over little Surprise Lake to the north and spectacular Greenwood Lake to the east. The return is mostly on wide woods roads, with a wetlands crossing halfway back.

TERRAIN AND HISTORY

The bedrock of purple Schunemunk conglomerate, locally known as "puddingstone," thrust upright by tectonic movement and subsequently differentially eroded, has formed a corrugated terrain of short steep ridges and valleys along the crest of Bearfort Mountain. Glaciers have made many of the ridgetops smooth, and weathering has broken some of them into crevices and loose boulders. Since Revolutionary times, Bearfort Mountain had been included in the vast forest holdings associated with the Ringwood Ironworks. The terrain of this part of Bearfort Mountain is too rugged for farming, but it was logged over at least twice to supply fuel and lumber to the nineteenth-century iron industry. In the middle of the twentieth century, the property was deeded to New Jersey by Erskine Hewitt, a descendant of the last operator of the Ringwood Mines, for whose father the state forest containing these trails was named.

ACCESS: From NJ 23, take the Union Valley Road Exit and head north. Follow Union Valley Road as it turns left at the second traffic light in West Milford. From here, drive 1.3 miles, passing Camp Hope on your right and, at a fork, follow Union Valley Road to the right. In 0.4 mile, you arrive at a junction with Warwick Turnpike, where you turn sharply left. There are three parking turnouts on the north side of Warwick Turnpike, each with space for two or three cars. The first turnout is 0.3 mile from the turn onto Warwick Turnpike, a few yards downhill from White Road. The second is about 0.1 mile uphill from the first, and the last, about 0.2 mile farther uphill, gives access to a different trailhead. The trailhead of the Bearfort Ridge Trail is near the first turnout.

Using public transportation, take NJ Transit Bus #197 (from the Port Authority Terminal in Manhattan), which stops at the intersection of Warwick Turnpike and Lakeside Road. From that point, a 0.5-mile walk west on Warwick Turnpike will take you to the trailhead.

DETAILED DESCRIPTION

There are two ways to start this hike, depending on where you park. If you park at the first turnout, you begin the hike at a trailhead next to the parking area at a sign reading "Jeremy Glick Trail" and a triangle of three white blazes on a nearby tree. The sign commemorates the heroism of Jeremy Glick, a West Milford resident, who with others led the successful effort to prevent terrorist hijackers from crashing their airplane into the White House on 9/11/01. He and all the others on board died when the plane crashed into a field in Pennsylvania.

From the next parking area farther up the hill, you will have to walk back to the first turnout to find the trail's triple white-blazed trailhead.

There is also a third parking turnout on the right side of the road 200 yards uphill from White Road, from which you may begin by finding blue blazes leading down to a wooden bridge over Green Brook. The blue trail follows Green Brook uphill through hemlocks and rhododendrons, turning right to meet the white-blazed Bearfort Ridge Trail, where you turn left to continue the hike.

Beginning from the white-blazed trailhead with the "Jeremy Glick Trail" sign (which, at 720 feet elevation, is the low point of the hike) you walk uphill on a wide, eroded footpath, with the rushing Green Brook below and to the left. Over millions of years, the ancestors of this stream have cut the gap in Bearfort Mountain through which Native American Minsis traveled to their settlements on the shores of the upper Delaware River, colonists migrated to the Great Valley farmlands to the west, and we drive along the Warwick Turnpike to reach hikes on Wawayanda Mountain and the Kittatinny Ridge. At 0.1 mile, the white trail meets the orange-blazed Quail Trail on a wide woods road, and in 100 feet it leaves this trail to turn left again into the woods. Follow the white blazes as the trail climbs moderately for about 300 feet through hemlocks and mountain laurel on a footpath covered with soft hemlock needles. In hemlock groves, the forest floor is usually lacking herbaceous plants, which are discouraged by both the soil's acidity and the year-round lack of sun. This hemlock stand is beginning to thin out due to the attack of the woolly adelgid; upland hardwoods, including maple, beech, and oak, are moving in.

At 0.4 mile, the trail crosses a boulder field associated with a seasonal stream and begins to descend slightly, following the contour of the ridge westward. A little farther along, the trail passes a large maple tree with three great trunks, two of them more than two feet in diameter, growing out of the original five-foot old-growth stump. Judging from the size of the stump, the original tree probably was more than two hundred years old when it was logged about a hundred years ago. Along the path, most of the cobbles and boulders you see are a conglomerate formed of quartz pebbles embedded in a purple sandstone matrix along the shore of a shallow sea hundreds of millions of years ago, known locally as "puddingstone." It is the characteristic bedrock of New York

A stunted pitch pine growing in a crack in the puddingstone bedrock of Bearfort Ridge.

A view from a rock outcrop over the ridges of Bearfort Mountain to the east. The pud-
dingstone is dotted with embedded quartz pebbles and streaked with quartz veins.

State's Schunemunk Ridge, of which Bearfort Mountain is the New
Jersey continuation.

At 0.7 mile, a blue-blazed trail terminates at a junction with the
Bearfort Ridge Trail. This blue trail begins at Warwick Turnpike at
a parking turnout uphill from White Road. After this junction, the
white-blazed Bearfort Ridge Trail starts a second fairly steep climb of
350 feet in dry upland chestnut oak forest over a series of three ledges.
The trail climbs the first ledge through clefts in the bedrock. It then
circles a second large outcrop of puddingstone, with many boulders
at its base, some plucked off by the glacier on this southeast ridge and
some by subsequent weathering. The trail crosses a seasonal
streambed and reaches the top of this second ridge through bedrock
notches. At 1.1 miles, the trail reaches the crest of the third ridge,
where just off the trail to the left on a smooth rock outcrop, there is
a view to the west and south, over Upper Greenwood Lake and the

Overlook to the west from a puddingstone rock outcrop. Freeze-thaw weathering and erosion have separated a slab of bedrock from the ridge, creating a yard-wide cleft.

Wawayanda Plateau, with the New York City skyline visible to the southeast. Leaving the viewpoint, the trail bends right, climbs uphill, and arrives at an open view to the east and south.

On the ridgetop, the walking is an interesting mix of easy and difficult. The trail often crosses open level ledges with puddingstone surfaces resembling paved streets. But the mountaintop is not a level plateau; tectonic folding, differential erosion, weathering, and glaciation have formed it into a corrugated series of ridges and small valleys. These forces have also produced frequent breaks in the bedrock, so no matter how the trail winds and dodges, every 100 yards or so the walker must clamber up, over, or down a 20- or 30-foot steep ledge, with occasional longer climbs or scrambles. On ridgetops, the pitch pine and scrub oak forest offers scant protection from chilly winds or summer sun, but larger trees in the hollows, including some hemlocks in moist areas and groves of mountain laurel, provide occasional cover.

As it follows the ridgeline, the trail works its way toward the east, crossing diagonally from one ridge to another through moist hollows. At 2.1 miles, the trail goes through a small hemlock grove and emerges onto a puddingstone rock outcrop overlooking a ridgetop swamp to the west. Weathering and erosion have formed unusual yard-wide clefts in the west edge of the bedrock here. This is a good place to take a break and enjoy these special surroundings.

At 2.4 miles, a rock outcrop offers a limited view to the north and east, though Greenwood Lake is not visible. At 2.7 miles, the trail approaches a 40-foot rocky cliff, where as you climb along its side you can hear water trickling under the rocks. After another steep 50-foot rise, you emerge at 2.9 miles on a rock outcrop offering your first view of Greenwood Lake. Surprise Lake is visible to the north, the Sterling Ridge to the northeast, the Awosting Ridge and Big Beech Mountain to the east, the Wyanokies to the southeast, and the New York City skyline in the background. Just beyond the viewpoint, at 3.0 miles, the Bearfort Ridge Trail ends at the yellow-blazed Ernest Walter Trail, where you turn right and head off the ridge to the northeast.

The Ernest Walter Trail leads down into the woods through a moist area, across a little brook, and up the opposite ridge. At 3.2 miles, the trail passes through a memorable grove of wild rhododendron, which will produce a marvelous bloom at the end of June just after the mountain laurel has passed its peak. When you emerge from the rhododendron thicket, you are close to Surprise Lake, which you may be able to see off to the left. The Ernest Walter Trail (yellow blazes) meets the north trailhead of the orange-blazed Quail Trail at 3.5 miles, where you turn a sharp right and start back south on a very wide, but rocky, woods road. There is a rock outcrop a few yards to the north of this junction, which offers a satisfying view from the shoreline of Surprise Lake, and is worth a few minutes to visit.

At first, the Quail Trail climbs gradually through upland hardwoods past two glacial erratics on the right, until it reaches a forested knoll at 3.7 miles. The trail levels off and at 3.8 miles passes an unmarked woods road on the left. Continue straight on the Quail Trail, which soon runs into a very moist area surrounding Cooley Brook; this is the runoff from Surprise Lake. The orange blazes leave the woods road, heading slightly left on a narrower track, paralleling and then, at 4.2 miles, turning to cross Cooley Brook, which may be a wet project involving more than one running stream in high water. After the crossing, at 4.6 miles the trail follows an exposed ledge of bedrock through a grove of hemlocks, where the southward blazes are more than usually distant from each other. (You can keep on the track by turning to check the blazes going the other way.) By 4.7 miles, you have left the wetlands and hemlock groves and emerged onto a wide and dry woods road headed gently downhill. At 4.9 miles, the trail gets steeper as it continues downhill, and at 5.3 miles you parallel a tributary of Cooley Brook coming down from the right. A woods road soon joins the trail from the left and, at 5.4 miles, you cross the tributary brook. Another woods road joins the trail from the left at 5.7 miles, and, at 5.9 miles, the Quail Trail meets the white Bearfort Ridge Trail on the right, which you should follow back to the first parking turnout to complete the loop of 6.0 miles.

Hiking through a dense rhododendron grove on the Ernest Walter Trail. Photo by Kenny Harcsztark.

Lost Lake Turnaround

6.4 miles • 5½ hours

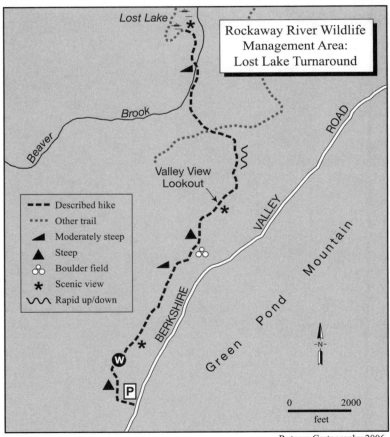

Lost Lake

Rockaway River Wildlife
Management Area:
Lost Lake Turnaround

Brook

Beaver

ROAD

Valley View
Lookout

VALLEY

Legend
- — — Described hike
- ····· Other trail
- ◄ Moderately steep
- ▲ Steep
- ஃ Boulder field
- * Scenic view
- ∿ Rapid up/down

BERKSHIRE

Green   Pond   Mountain

-N-

W

P

0   2000
feet

Rutgers Cartography 2006

ELEVATION: Low: 710 feet; High: 1,200 feet.

BLAZE: White.

CLIMBING: A steep climb of 320 feet in 0.3 mile to the first ridge and lookout. Another climb up slopes and rocky ledges, halfway through. Three stream crossings with associated boulder fields, and a long, moderate upgrade (340 feet in 0.7 mile) on the return.

PERMITTED USES: Hiking only.

ACCESS: From I-80 west, take Exit 34A, or from I-80 east, take Exit 34; from either exit proceed on NJ 15 north toward Sparta. Drive 1.1 miles past the Picatinny Arsenal and turn east onto Berkshire Valley Road. Continue for 1.0 mile and, at the bottom of a gradual incline, cross a bridge over the North Branch of the Rockaway River and immediately find a small gravel parking area on the left side of the road.

O V E R V I E W

This straight out and back hike takes you 3.1 miles from the trailhead to the shore of Lost Lake, a beaver pond of many years standing. If you start by 9:30 a.m., you will reach Lost Lake for lunch. Along the way, viewpoints, somewhat restricted by trees, face southeast toward the west end of Green Pond Mountain in the Picatinny Arsenal. In spring, the long slope away from the first lookout glows with anemones and hepaticas, and intermittent wildflower displays edge the trail in all green seasons. In July, we saw signs of pileated woodpeckers, heard the cries of hunting hawks, and watched a great blue heron fish the water's edge of Lost Lake.

T E R R A I N   A N D   H I S T O R Y

Several woods roads and the young maturing forest 70 to 100 years old indicate the area was logged clean in the nineteenth century to supply fuel and lumber to ironworks nearby in Mount Hope. A leveled stone fence and manmade excavations suggest that the area near Beaver Brook was farmed perhaps 100 years ago.

DETAILED DESCRIPTION

At the southwest end of the parking area near the road, a triangle of three white blazes marks the trailhead of the Beaver Brook Trail. The trail heads into the woods on an almost level footpath for 0.1 mile, passing a coppiced red maple tree with five trunks, two of them a more than a foot in diameter. This tree was cut down 50 to 60 years ago when its trunk was four or five feet thick, and it was then perhaps 200 years old; these several smaller trunks grew out of the same large stump. Because no other nearby trees show similar characteristics, it seems likely this tree was saved from earlier logging for some domestic purpose: to provide shade or the landscaping of a building beside the river. The trail soon meets a wide, eroded, rocky woods road coming in from the left and begins to climb, moderately at first, through a dying hemlock grove and past bedrock ledges and boulders split off by weathering. On this moist lower slope grow many maples, which are not to be found on higher and drier terrains. At 0.3 mile, the grade gets steeper, and at 0.4 mile the trail comes to a cairn, a marker of piled stones, which along with a white blaze on a rock signals a right turn (north) off the road and onto a path climbing steeply through rock outcrops.

The trail begins to level off, following the contour of the hill below a cliff to the left. At 0.6 mile, it crosses a glacially scoured rock outcrop, with one good view to the southeast toward Green Pond Mountain and the hills beyond, and a series of slightly obscured views through maturing trees. This is the high point of the hike (1,210 feet elevation). The trail lies close to a steep eastward slope on

View from the first ridge toward the south end of Green Pond Mountain.

a dry thin-soiled stony ledge with smaller ridgetop trees: chestnut oak, red oak, scrub oak, hickory, and an understory of blueberry shrubs and viburnum. The path soon becomes grass-covered, and at 0.8 mile begins to descend gradually away from the crest of the hill. For about a half-mile along this descent, where the soil is deep, moist, and organically rich, anemone, hepatica, and other wildflowers sprout and bloom in early spring sun before the trees are fully leaved. During summer months, other wildflowers, including yellow star grass, Indian tobacco, false foxglove, white baneberry, enchanter's nightshade, and the orchid called rattlesnake plantain, bloom sporadically beside the trail. In July, we heard the beautiful flute-like song of a wood thrush near the trail.

At 1.1 miles, the trail crosses a boulder field and its associated seasonal streambed. A glacial erratic almost blocks the trail at 1.2 miles, and the path then goes through another dying hemlock grove. It soon turns right onto an old woods road at 1.4 miles and, a few yards later, leaves the road, turning left down into a hollow. The trail crosses a streambed where in July the unseen brook burbled beneath the rocks, then passes a hemlock snag pocked with the typically deep, squared holes made by the big pileated woodpecker. At 1.5 miles, it winds through another boulder field, passes another glacial erratic, and crosses a wide streambed. At this point you are about halfway to Lost Lake.

The trail climbs out on the other side of the streambed and begins a moderate ascent, joining a woods road at 1.6 miles, and meeting a cairn and a blaze signaling a sharp left turn onto a switchback. The trail comes to the crest of the first of a series of rocky ledges at 1.7 miles. On the next rock outcrop, a couple of cairns as well as white blazes mark turns, first to the right, then to the left. To the right, and 25 feet (downhill) from these markers, at 1.8 miles, the Valley View Lookout (1,060 feet) faces southeast through treetops. The view overlooks the valley of the north fork of the Rockaway River and Green Pond Mountain to the east. From the lookout, turn back to the cairn and, continuing straight to the northwest, find a white blaze on a small dogwood tree. The trail follows the west edge of the ledges over another rock outcrop with a view to the east and, at 2.0 miles, crosses a seasonal stream. The trail climbs here, still sticking close to the west edge of the ledge at 1,160 feet elevation, beside a steep west-facing slope. At 2.1 miles, the trail turns left off the ledge; there is no turn blaze, but the path is very easy to follow. It descends over rocks, leveling out into a wide, grassy path. At 2.3 miles, the trail crosses a wide woods road at a smooth rock surface and, at 2.4 miles it passes a tumbled stone fence, an excavated trench, and an excavation the size of a home cellar, the first signs of farming along the trail. After the trail passes a wooden hunter's blind in a tree, views of Beaver Brook open through the trees to the left. The trail passes a large glacial erratic and, at 2.7 miles, crosses a stream feeding Beaver Brook. A circular stone fence at the stream bank was probably long ago the location of either a spring or a contained flowing water source. At 2.8

miles, the trail crosses another woods road that heads downhill to ford Beaver Brook. The trail continues to parallel Beaver Brook, crosses another tumbled stone fence, and emerges into an open meadow thickly overgrown with shrubbery under power lines. Bending left, the trail descends gradually to cross Beaver Brook on rounded boulders.

On the far side, the ground is covered with a layer of very healthy poison ivy, so thick in growing seasons that you can't see the stepping stones beneath. In summer, the undergrowth along the trail is impassable, so there is no way to find a better crossing by bush-whacking through. About 25 feet upstream there is a rickety plank bridge, but heavy thickets make it inaccessible and almost invisible. Probably the best way is to use the marked trail directly through the poison ivy; but watch your footing, just move quickly and carefully to keep your balance.

The beaver dam at the south end of Lost Lake. There was no sign of recent beaver activity when we were there.

A view toward Green Pond Mountain from the last overlook on the return from Lost Lake.

The trail climbs briefly up the opposite bank into the woods, then at 3.0 miles turns right, bending slightly away from the brook. At 3.2 miles, the trail arrives at the shore of Lost Lake beside a long beaver dam about three feet high. This is a good place to rest and have some lunch before you start back. There is no evidence of recent beaver activity around the dam, but the water level is still high and the dam holds pretty well. The water is shallow and almost completely covered by water lilies. Two beaver lodges out in the lake are visible from the shore, and the lake's perimeter is lined with a 20-foot band of bare snags. As we ate, we watched a great blue heron as it fished along the opposite shore.

The return trip retraces your steps on the Beaver Brook Trail. Distances will be given from the start of the hike. You may be surprised at how many new sights you discover looking from the opposite direction. For example, as you approach the turn of the trail left toward the Beaver Brook crossing, you will be able to see the swaying old plank bridge over the stream. The path to and from the bridge is completely overgrown and the bridge itself is so rickety that this is not really a safe option for the crossing.

On the way back, you may want to stop to examine the stone fences and excavations between 0.5 and 0.8 mile from Lost Lake (3.7 to 4.0 miles from the start of the hike) to see if you can figure out the purposes they may have served. As you approach the Valley View Lookout at 4.6 miles from the start, you will see more of the long view from the trail, and the scene seems more attractive from this direction. After descending from Valley View Lookout and crossing the stream at 4.9 miles from the start, you face a long moderate climb of 340 feet in 1.0 mile. This is the last climb of the hike, and you may be surprised at how often you feel like stopping for a drink. If you are hiking in late April or early May, you will have many wildflowers and migrating birds to distract you. When you reach the crest of this climb at 5.8 miles from the start, you are once again at 1,200 feet elevation, the high point of the hike.

You can stop here for a last look east across Green Pond Mountain. You might want to examine the smoothed rock outcrops for signs of northwest-to-southeast glacial score marks. This is not an easy thing to determine, because differential erosion also produces lines in the gneiss (though erosion lines follow grains in the rock, which may not align with the glacial flow). The descent from this overlook is steep; expect to negotiate it at a slow pace until you reach the level stretch approaching the parking area. When you arrive at your car, you will have completed a hike of 6.4 miles.

The Viewpoint Line
Through Hike

6.8 miles • 6 hours

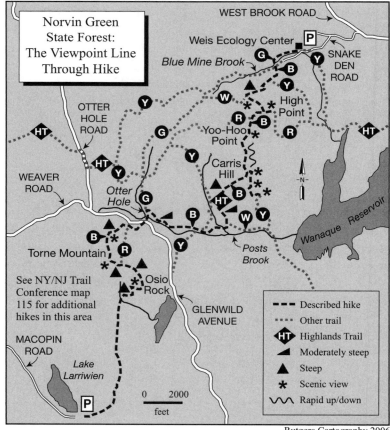

Rutgers Cartography 2006

*The blaze circles marked in primary colors (e.g., "R" for red) may stand for a combina-
tion of a color on a white background (e.g., red triangle-on-white), as noted in the hike
description.*

ELEVATION: Low: 490 feet; High: 1,120 feet

BLAZES: Blue and yellow-dot-on-white, blue, blue joined by Highlands Trail teal diamond and red dot, then blue and HT teal diamond (joined briefly by a yellow blaze), and finally blue alone again to the end.

CLIMBING: A steep beginning to reach Wyanokie High Point, a fairly level stretch then a brief climb to Carris Hill, a short, steep descent off the Carris Hill ridge, a long moderate ascent to Otter Hole, a wide stream crossing at Posts Brook, a steep climb up to the top of the Torne, a scramble down off the Torne, a rocky climb back up to Osio Rock on the summit of South Torne, a rocky switchback descent down the south face of South Torne, and a two-mile pleasant, mostly level walk through woodlands to the end of the trail.

PERMITTED USES: Hiking only.

This is a Highlands Trail hike.

O V E R V I E W

This hike takes you to most of the dramatic lookouts in the Wyanokies. At the beginning, Wyanokie High Point offers a 360-degree panorama from the north side of the Wyanokie Plateau, and Osio Rock on the summit of South Torne near the end provides the same from the south. The topography varies from moist hollows and cool stream crossings to dry open ridgetops, with trees and plant communities to match. There are enough examples of the effects of glacial activity on gneiss bedrock to fill a geology textbook. In spring, you will find many of the region's most beautiful wildflowers on the trail, as well as migrating songbirds preening and singing near the ridgetops. Smaller displays of birds and plants follow the seasons. In autumn, the spectacle of colorful leaves from the viewpoints and in forest glades is unsurpassed. There are plenty of Highlands short steeps and descents, and a few long ones, also. After the last descent from Osio Rock, the final two miles of mostly level walking takes you through a damp maturing forest where you can stretch your tightened muscles and catch your breath.

ACCESS: This straight-through hike requires two cars. To reach the first parking area, turn north off NJ 23 at the Kinnelon Road/Kiel Avenue Exit into the center of Butler. At the end of Kiel Avenue, turn left and cross the railroad tracks. After crossing the railroad tracks, turn right at a T-intersection onto Main Street. At the end of Main Street, turn left onto Hamburg Turnpike. You will soon reach a fork at which you should bear left and continue for 1.3 miles to Macopin Road, where you turn right. After 1.2 miles on Macopin Road, you come to a used car lot on the left and the entrance to Camp Vacamas on the right. Turn right into the gravel entrance road of Camp Vacamas, and find a parking place in the lot on the left. Note the sign with parking instructions for hikers. Leave one car here.

In the other car, return by Macopin Road to Hamburg Turnpike, turn left, and drive 0.8 mile to an intersection with Delazier Place. Turn left onto Delazier Place and continue to its end at Glenwild Avenue. Turn left here and continue on Glenwild Avenue for 3.4 miles to an intersection with Weaver Road, where the road you are traveling on is now signed "Otter Hole Road." Continue ahead on Otter Hole Road for 3.1 miles, passing Mt. Glen Lakes and Lindy's Lake on the right and arriving at an intersection with West Brook Road. Turn right onto West Brook Road and drive for 3.8 miles to Snake Den Road (East), marked by a sign for the Weis Ecology Center. Turn right onto Snake Den Road (East), and travel 0.6 mile to a wide parking lot on the right. Leave your second car here.

DETAILED DESCRIPTION

From the large open lot, you will find the trailhead of the green-blazed Otter Hole Trail at the beginning of the Weis Ecology Center entrance road at the end of the lot. Follow the green blazes along Blue Mine Brook, under a row of spruces, past a brick pump house, and up a rocky rise (joined here by green-W-on-white blazes) beside the Highlands Natural Pool to a sturdy bridge over the brook at 0.3 mile. At this bridge, the trail is joined by orange-L-on-white blazes. From the bridge, continue straight ahead on the green-blazed Otter Hole Trail, as the L Trail leaves to the left, and the "W" Trail leaves to the right. From this junction, the Otter Hole Trail leads through the woods to the unpaved extension of Snake Den Road, formerly known as the "Winfield Farm Road," where there is a kiosk. At this intersection at 0.4 mile, the trail to High Point is marked with two triangles, each one composed of three blazes. These are the trailhead signs for the co-aligned Hewitt-Butler (blue blazes) and Mine (yellow-dot-on-white blazes) trails.

Follow both blue and yellow-dot blazes to the left of the kiosk (uphill), leaving the Otter Hole Trail which turns right on the woods road. You will follow the blue-blazed Hewitt-Butler Trail (sometimes co-aligned with other trails) all the way to the end of the hike. The trails climb a rocky hillside with stone steps, cross a rocky outcrop, and descend through a grove of mountain laurel. Shortly, the Mine Trail (yellow-dot-on-white blazes) leaves to the left (southeast) and you follow the Hewitt-Butler Trail over a patch of exposed bedrock. Your trail turns sharply left, drops down around another rock outcrop, squeezes through a narrow defile between two massive rock exposures, and continues (uphill) into the woods. The trail climbs steeply until it reaches the top of the ridge, where a rock outcrop to the right of the trail offers the first of many good views, toward Assiniwikam Mountain to the northwest.

Shortly after that viewpoint, a triangle of three white blazes

Wyanokie High Point summit, with Windbeam Mountain directly to the west beyond the Wanaque Reservoir.

marks the trailhead of the Macopin Trail heading off to the right. You continue straight ahead on the blue trail, at 1.0 mile reaching another rock outcrop with a large glacial erratic perched on its top. During leafy seasons, the view here is to the north and east, but in winter it is clear in every direction. Coming off this overlook, the trail levels out along the crest of the ridge, where exposure to wind, cold, recent drought, gypsy moth infestations, and poor, thin soil prevent most trees from achieving mature growth. The largest trees, whose trunks have reached 8 to 12 inches in thickness, though gnarled and stunted, are probably over 100 years old. During spring bird migrations we have seen bluebirds, indigo buntings, thrushes, and a variety of warblers on this ridge.

This section of the Highlands Trail begins here.

Just below High Point summit at 1.2 miles, the Hewitt-Butler Trail is joined by the red-dot-on-white Wyanokie Circular Trail coming from the left, and the teal diamonds of the Highlands Trail. You will follow the three trails together to the right. But first, a sign painted on the bedrock points to High Point, one of the great viewpoints on this hike. Climb the short, steep rock scramble to the glacially-smoothed summit at 960 feet elevation, with its 360-degree view of the Wyanokie Plateau. Wanaque Reservoir lies to the east, with the New York City skyline beyond visible on a clear day. Windbeam Mountain is to the northeast, Assiniwikam and Buck mountains to the west, and Carris Hill to the south. After appreciating the view, climb back down to the intersection and follow the co-aligned Wyanokie Circular, Highlands, and Hewitt-Butler trails to the south.

In descending terrain, the trail soon crosses a seasonal stream on stepping stones, and, at 1.4 miles, the red dots of the Wyanokie Circular Trail leave to the right. You follow both blue and teal diamond blazes straight ahead, heading gently down, then climbing back up to a rock outcrop, Yoo-Hoo Point (1,000 feet elevation), at 1.5

Looking toward Wyanokie High Point from Yoo-Hoo Point.

miles. Looking back the way you came, High Point is visible to the north. Continuing south and descending along the ridgeline for a while, at 1.9 miles the trail begins the ascent of the rock ledges on the north face of Carris Hill, at 2.0 miles reaching the summit at 1,040 feet elevation. From this second great lookout of the hike, there are dramatic views of High Point to the northeast, Assiniwikam Mountain to the north, and Buck Mountain to the west.

On the bedrock at the summit, you will find the trailhead of the Carris Hill Trail, with yellow blazes arrowed to show a way southeast off the ridge. On that trail, a series of open ledges offers excellent views: the first to the south and west, succeeding ones to the south and east over the Wanaque Reservoir to the New York City skyline, and the last one at 0.4 mile below the summit. This down and up side trip will add almost a mile to your walk, but if you have the time and

Climbing from Yoo-Hoo Point to Carris Hill.

energy, and want to bag all the possible viewpoints on this Viewpoint Line, it is a worthwhile option.

From Carris Hill summit, the Hewitt-Butler and Highlands trails you are following on the Viewpoint Line lead south over a descending series of ledges lined with typical ridgetop vegetation: scrub oak, chestnut oak, some pitch pine, shrubby black cherry, blueberry underbrush, and pale corydalis, with pink and yellow flowers growing out of crevices in the rock. At 2.1 miles, the trail enters a grove of laurel and bends to the left, reaching the top of a steep slope at 2.5 miles. From here, the trail climbs down over loose boulders fractured from the bedrock, dropping 200 feet of elevation in 0.2 mile. At the bottom of the cliff, the trail turns left and briefly joins what looks like a woods road but is actually the path of the nation's first oil pipeline, built in 1880 from Olean, New York, to Bayonne, New Jersey. The trail next winds through a boulder field and turns right on a gradual descent through open upland forest, at 2.8 miles meeting the white-blazed Posts Brook Trail, which comes from the left and ends at the crossing of a tributary of Posts Brook. Here you follow the Hewitt-Butler Trail's blue blazes and the teal diamonds of the Highlands Trail as they turn right and head towards Otter Hole.

The trail begins to climb gradually, and at 3.1 miles the yellow-blazed Wyanokie Crest Trail joins from the right and very soon leaves to the left. The Hewitt-Butler Trail continues generally uphill, paralleling Posts Brook, which you may hear and sometimes see through the trees. This stretch of trail is on a woods road whose surface in spring is below the water table, which makes the going very muddy. In earlier times, travelers put logs across the wet spots, making it a "corduroy" road. The dampness encourages spring ephemeral wildflowers, including some scarce varieties that can be plentiful here alongside the trail. For this reason, it helps for hikers to keep to the middle of the road, even if it's muddy, because, in most seasons, even though you might not be able to see the plants, their root structures are vulnerable to boot soles.

The summit of Carris Hill looking north over High Point to Assiniwikam, Saddle Mountain, and West Brook Mountain, with Horse Pond and Harrison mountains in the middle distance, and the long ridge of Bearfort Mountain to the northwest at the horizon.

At 3.3 miles, a woods road joins from the left; the trail widens and soon begins to climb more steeply. The crest of the rise is reached at 3.6 miles, where you can hear the Otter Hole cascade ahead at 3.7 miles. At an intersection just before Otter Hole, the Highlands Trail turns right onto a woods road heading uphill, along with the green-blazed Otter Hole Trail that begins here.

This section of the Highlands Trail ends here.

Following the now solitary blue blazes straight ahead over rock outcrops, you must cross the wide Posts Brook on large rounded boulders. This is easy enough most times of the year, but during high water we have had to seek safer crossings farther upstream. Otter Hole exhibits beautiful wildflowers in most seasons, including pink lady's slippers in spring and cardinal flowers in late August. After crossing the brook, however, keep to the footpath to avoid the thick poison ivy beside the trail.

The Hewitt-Butler Trail crosses Glenwild Avenue at 3.8 miles, where blue blazes on a post on the south side of the road lead steeply on a rocky footpath (uphill) toward Wyanokie Torne. After reaching the crest of a bedrock outcrop, the trail descends gradually through laurel and blueberry shrubs in dry upland forest. Although it stays in the woods, the trail basically parallels the road until, at 4.0 miles, it reaches a junction at the trailhead of the red-blazed Torne Trail. You follow the blue blazes up a steep incline on a woodland path, gaining 200 feet in 0.2 mile. Near the top of the ridge at 4.2 miles, the trail passes over glacially scoured gneiss outcrops, typically smooth on the north end of the ridge, where the ice pushed against the rock. On the

On the way up to Osio Rock, a rounded knob of bedrock gneiss with many boulders fractured by thaw-freeze weathering.

south end, you will see how the ice clawed the rock away, fracturing parts of it into rough surfaces as it pulled toward the southeast. The top of this ridge, at 1,120 feet, is the highest point of the Viewpoint Line. It provides the third great view of the hike, to the north toward Buck Mountain and west toward Kanouse Mountain in the Pequannock Watershed. In late May beside the trail here, we have seen pink lady's slippers growing among the rocks. In summer, we have heard the high-pitched "keeeer" cry of the red-tailed hawk as it glided over the treetops below us. The trail follows the contour of the hill just below the ridgeline southward along the edge of the steep western slope of the Torne, offering frequent views westward even in leafy seasons. At 4.4 miles, the trail bends left (east) to circle the south end of the ridge, where the gneiss outcrop is rough and fractured. Here, too, is a great view of Kanouse Mountain to the west and, on a clear day, the New York City skyline to the southeast.

From this point, the trail descends a steep rocky cliff, where you may feel a method other than walking is required. At the bottom of this slide at 4.5 miles, the Hewitt-Butler Trail meets the trailhead of the red-blazed Torne Trail, which heads left up a boulder-filled rock outcrop. You follow the blue-blazed Hewitt-Butler Trail as it turns right to climb steeply eastward through boulders split off from rock outcrops on both sides of the trail. As the trail climbs, it passes through a dense laurel grove, then levels twice to follow the contour of the northwest face of South Torne. At 4.7 miles, the trail bends to the southeast on a grassy path and continues to climb through snags and boulders, emerging into the open sun with views west and south. The trail reaches the summit of South Torne at 4.9 miles, atop Osio Rock, a smooth round knob where the view is unobstructed in every direction. This is the last great overlook of the hike, from which you can see northeast over the Wyanokie Plateau which you have walked across.

From the summit, the trail climbs down to the south, passing a small bedrock enclosure where there are signs of cook fires, perhaps made by the young campers at Camp Vacamas. They call Osio Rock "suicide hill" because it kills them to climb it from their location two miles to the south. In about 30 yards more, the trail turns right, due west, beginning a switchback descending across the south face of the ridge through rock outcrops and loose boulders, where you need to step carefully. The trail soon turns left again, heading south. This part of the mountain is completely open to the sun, all the trees having been killed by drought, weather, or gypsy moth infestation. At 5.1 miles, the trail turns right, descending on another switchback to the west toward a hollow, where it reaches healthy woods with a shady canopy.

At the bottom of the hollow at 5.3 miles, the trail turns left, crosses a wide running stream on large stones, and on the other side joins a woods road heading almost due south. The trail parallels a small tributary brook and then heads uphill on a badly eroded road with ruts and loose rocks. In this cooler, moist hollow many maple trees flourish; these are not found in the drier, warmer hillsides. At 5.5 miles, the blue trail passes a rock outcrop on the left with boulders split off by glacial action or weathering. At 5.7 miles, the trail runs between two cliffs with associated boulders. This is fairly level walking, with occasional gentle grades on easy paths. Then, at 5.9 miles, the trail makes a sharp right turn, descends into a hollow, and climbs up the other side to meet a wide eroded woods road. The trail descends and bends to the right around a knoll, at 6.1 miles turning left off the road into a woodland path. There is no turn blaze here, but a clear blaze on a tree seems to lead into the woods, where you can find the next blaze. The trail widens into a road and descends into a clearing, where three wide white blazes in a line are painted on trees. These may be for mountain bikers, whose trail arrives from the east and turns here onto the path we have followed.

The blue-blazed trail continues south across the clearing, passing a Camp Vacamas sign posted on a tree, and crossing a small brook on tree trunks. At 6.2 miles, the trail leaves the woods road it has been

The summit of Osio Rock, with a 360-degree viewpoint, from which you can look back over the entire Wyanokie Plateau.

following and turns onto a path up a boulder-strewn ledge. Although there is no turn blaze here, a blaze on a tree 30 feet into the woods helps. You will soon notice there are no blazes at all on the woods road straight ahead. The trail climbs about 80 feet, reaching a wooded ridgetop at 6.3 miles. The trees on this dry ridge are mostly stunted and gnarled chestnut oaks and red oaks. The trail soon comes to a steep 40-foot descent, and then descends more gradually through rounded boulders. At 6.5 miles, you climb again, but the path averages a gradual descent. At 6.6 miles, the trail comes to a fork, with a double blaze on a tree, suggesting that the narrower path straight ahead is the right one; on this narrow trail you will find a blue blaze 40 feet in from the fork. The trail descends through moist woods, at 6.8 miles reaching the parking lot at Camp Vacamas where you left your first car.

A coppiced tree, one whose wide old-growth trunk was cut long ago, but then grew these new trunks from its old root structure. Using a rough estimate of two-and-a-half feet thickness of trunk per hundred years of age, we guess the tree was cut a century ago, and at the time was perhaps 200 years old. You will notice other coppiced trees on this hike, though none as large as this one. Photo by Daniel Chazin.

Split Rock Loop

11.1 miles • 8 hours

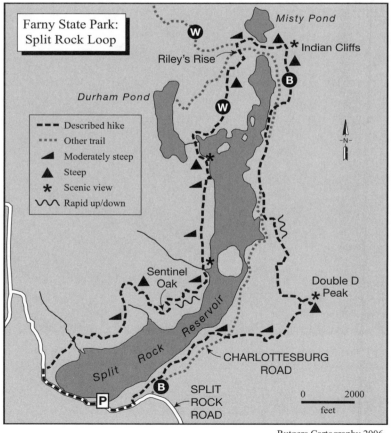

Farny State Park:
Split Rock Loop

Misty Pond

W

Indian Cliffs

Riley's Rise

B

Durham Pond

W

- - - Described hike
...... Other trail
◀ Moderately steep
▲ Steep
* Scenic view
〰 Rapid up/down

-N-

Sentinel
Oak

Double D
Peak

Split Rock Reservoir

CHARLOTTESBURG
ROAD

P

B

SPLIT
ROCK
ROAD

0   2000
feet

Rutgers Cartography 2006

ELEVATION: Low: 820 feet; High: 1,110 feet.

BLAZES: Blue, white.

CLIMBING: The elevation gain is only a small part of the story. In the 11.1 miles of this circuit, you will encounter climbs going up and down over rocky knolls, some fairly steep, at least eight times. You will pass through dozens of boulder fields, a few rock scrambles, and every kind of topography found in the Jersey Highlands, from rocky cliffs to wetlands.

PERMITTED USES: Hiking only.

OVERVIEW

This hike is a serious challenge to fit hikers. Although, according to the map the maximum elevation gain is only 290 feet, there are many ups and downs over steep rocky terrain from shoreline to high ridge. It circles Split Rock Reservoir, with two excellent high lookouts on the east side, and two long shoreline views of the reservoir on the way back on the west side. The first half of the hike heads north on the Split Rock Loop Trail, concluding with Indian Cliffs overlook and Misty Pond with its beaver activity. The second half returns on the Four Birds Trail, with many ridge climbs, stream crossings, and boulder fields.

ACCESS: From I-80 West, take Exit 37 (Rockaway/Hibernia). Turn right at the traffic light at the end of the exit ramp. In 20 yards, you come to another traffic light, where you turn left onto Morris Avenue.

From I-80 East, take Exit 37 (Rockaway/Hibernia) and, at the traffic light at the end of the ramp, turn left under the highway. In 30 yards, you come to a traffic light, where you turn right onto Morris Avenue.

From the Morris Avenue traffic light, drive 0.9 mile, passing

Morris Catholic High School on your left. At the intersection where you pass Kitchell Road, which turns acutely left uphill, make the immediate next left onto the continuation of Morris Avenue. From this intersection, drive 0.8 mile to a T-intersection at the end of Morris Avenue. Turn left onto Diamond Spring Road (called Rockaway Valley Road in Boonton Township) and drive 3.5 miles, passing the beautiful early nineteenth-century Dixon Farm with a pond and historic home on your left. Take the next left (uphill) onto Split Rock Road. Follow Split Rock Road, bearing right at a fork with Decker Road at 0.8 mile. Continue on Split Rock Road, bearing left at a junction with Charlottesburg Road, where it becomes a dirt road, and arriving at a gravel parking area on your right at 2.6 miles.

TERRAIN AND HISTORY

This hike circles Split Rock Reservoir, a five-mile-long supplementary reservoir for Jersey City's water supply that is the centerpiece of Farny State Park.

One hundred fifty years ago this area was alive with iron mines, smelters, forges, railroads, and the communities and activities that grew up around them. These included logging and charcoal production that denuded the hillsides, as well as subsistence and small market farms. That activity ceased entirely by the second decade of the twentieth century, and the logged and farmed hillsides have returned to successional upland forest. A short walk west from the parking lot toward the dam will reveal a nineteenth-century iron furnace in the woods on the south side of the road. The roads that serviced these communities are now unmarked and sometimes obscure woodlands tracks. At the northwest end of Split Rock Reservoir, you are at least two miles from any human habitation, with no quick exit available in case of need. For these reasons, this hike should be walked by fit and experienced hikers with good boots, a trail map, plenty of water, and a backpack with the standard emergency equipment.

DETAILED DESCRIPTION

To find the trailhead, turn left as you leave the parking lot, walking east (uphill) for 0.3 mile, until you reach the second crossing of the power line. The Split Rock Loop Trail (blue blazes) crosses the road here. You will find a blue blaze on a tree on the left (north) side of the road. The trail enters the woods heading slightly downhill toward the lake shore. The forest here is typical Highlands upland hardwood, with chestnut oak, red and white oak, black and yellow birch, hickory, some maple and beech, and an understory of shade-loving viburnum and spice bush. The hillside is fairly moist, with occasional seasonal brooks feeding into the lake. Here and there, bedrock outcrops protrude.

About fifty yards after entering the woods, the trail turns right through such an outcrop, with boulders split off from the bedrock by weathering. After crossing an old woods road (probably used first by loggers and then by subsistence farmers) at 0.8 mile, the trail briefly parallels the shore of the reservoir. It soon bends away from the shore, passes through a boulder field, and turns again towards the reservoir, this time coming even closer to the shoreline. The trail then leaves the shore and climbs gradually, crossing a seasonal brook and a small boulder field.

At 1.2 miles, the trail crosses Charlottesburg Road. This unpaved road heads toward what was once an active settlement near the most productive iron furnace of the Revolutionary years. On its way to the north end of Split Rock Reservoir, the trail will cross Charlottesburg Road four times.

Across the road, the trail heads uphill. It bears left and levels off for a section of easy walking. At 1.3 miles, the trail crosses a distinct woods road. To the right, this road leads to a grassy knoll lightly cov-

A group of large boulders across the trail. The one on the left was apparently split from the one on the right by thaw-freeze weathering, and then moved away by soil creep.

ered with red cedars and small saplings, suggesting that the hilltop was pasture not long ago.

Avoiding that unmarked road, continue following the blue blazes uphill until the trail levels out for a section of easy walking. You shortly come upon a group of boulders, where the trail goes through a split between them at 1.4 miles. After passing through a grassy area, the trail heads uphill, reaching a rocky outcrop, with views of the valley below, at 1.5 miles. Here, the trail bends to the left and continues to climb to another outcrop. Watch for the double blaze turn indicator here; this turn is easy to miss. A vague path straight ahead leads to a grassy knoll, with several small glacial erratics and another view of the valley below. Just beyond, at 1.6 miles, the trail crosses another outcrop with a huge glacial erratic perched on top. A short distance ahead, you can see piles of mine tailings and remnants of old mine pits to the left of the trail.

This is typical Highlands terrain, with quick ups and downs

through rock outcrops and boulders either left by glaciers or split off by weathering. The trail follows the ridge with twists and turns until, after a short descent at 1.9 miles, it comes upon a spur trail down to the right. This short (0.1-mile) unmarked spur trail descends to a hollow, then climbs on switchbacks to the top of Double Peak, with its year-round 360-degree views of the Farny Highlands. This is a worthwhile digression, and a good place for a rest, a drink, and a snack.

Returning from the Double Peak spur, turn right onto the blue-blazed Split Rock Trail, which descends to cross a small stream and then begins to gently climb. At 2.1 miles, a woods road joins from the right and soon leaves to the left, as the blue trail turns right. The trail passes an interesting overhanging ledge and continues across a relatively flat area, crossing several rock outcrops along the way. Then, at 2.6 miles, the trail turns sharply right and descends off the ridge into a hollow, with a ridgetop wetland to the right of the trail. After crossing a stream and its associated boulder field, the trail bears right and climbs along the edge of a rock ledge. At the top, it bears sharply left and follows along the top of the ledge, the first of three ridges that you will encounter along this stretch of trail. Watch carefully for a turn where the trail bears left and descends rather steeply off the ledge, crossing another stream at its base, at 3.0 miles.

After crossing a woods road, the trail continues to climb, reaching the top of the second ridge, with a good view of the Split Rock Reservoir at 3.2 miles. The trail now passes through a thick stand of mountain laurel, with intermittent views over the reservoir to the west. It descends on switchbacks towards the reservoir and continues along a fairly flat, but often rocky, route, following the contour of the hill, with large homes visible to the right of the trail.

Until recently, the Split Rock Trail headed to the right and proceeded to climb the third in this series of ridges. At one time, there was a panoramic view over the reservoir from the summit of the third ridge. However, several years ago, the trail was relocated fur-

The view from Indian Cliffs at the northern end of Split Rock Reservoir.

ther down the ridge, eliminating this view. Large homes have recently been constructed on top of the ridge, immediately adjacent to the trail route. The climb of this ridge has become largely pointless and, as a result, Trail Conference maintainers have decided to avoid it. A permanent reroute is in the planning stages; however, as a temporary measure, the trail now heads north along Charlottesburg Road until, at 4.6 miles, it turns left, leaves the road, and heads west towards the reservoir, descending gradually. Hikers should be alert for the new blazes.

The section of trail between Charlottesburg Road and the reservoir follows a tranquil, beautiful route which comes near the shore of the reservoir. This stretch is a welcome respite from the walk along the road and from the new construction along the trail in an area that, until recently, was a wilderness, far from any sign of civilization.

After climbing slightly and recrossing Charlottesburg Road at 4.8 miles, the trail heads into the woods and begins to climb on a rocky footpath. It then descends gently, crosses a stream, and levels off. Soon, it joins an orange-blazed woods road. The trail follows the road for only about 100 feet and then leaves to the left. It now begins a steady climb up Indian Cliffs, gradually at first and then more steeply. There are views of the reservoir from rock ledges to the left, but the best view is from a large rock outcrop at the very top of the climb, reached at 5.3 miles. The entire Split Rock Reservoir is visible to the south, and Misty Pond may be seen to the north. You are now almost at the halfway point of the hike. If you began early in the morning, this panoramic viewpoint, probably the most outstanding viewpoint on the entire trail, is a good place to rest and have lunch.

The descent from Indian Cliffs is rocky and, in a few places, steep. As it descends, the trail passes through a large laurel grove, which is beautiful in early to mid-June. At 5.5 miles, the trail crosses Charlottesburg Road for the last time. Just beyond, there is a forest of larch trees (the deciduous conifer that loses its needles in fall) to the left of the trail. At 5.8 miles, the trail passes the south shore of Misty Pond, which was an active beaver pond when we last saw it. An old stone fence here suggests this was a nineteenth-century farm. The blue-blazed Split Rock Trail climbs from Misty Pond to its terminus, 6.0 miles from the start of the hike, at a junction with the white-blazed Four Birds Trail.

At the junction with the Four Birds Trail, you turn left and follow the white blazes south on a wide woods path with easy walking. The trail shortly crosses a woods road marked with red blazes and showing signs of ATV activity. If followed to the right, this road, bearing left (west) at a Y-intersection, in 1.5 miles joins paved Timber Brook Road where houses are in sight. Straight ahead you face Riley's Rise, a fairly steep 200-foot hill with thickets and rocky ledges barring the way. Your white-blazed trail circles to the left toward the reservoir and around the east face of the hill where the climbing is easier. On the way up, you can see Indian Cliffs across the reservoir, but there are no views from the top of the rise. Near the top, the

A view of Split Rock Reservoir from the west shore near its north end.

grassy path is foot-trodden; by following this visible track and finding white blazes, you can easily stay on the trail. The summit of this hill is at 6.3 miles.

Coming off the summit of Riley's Rise, the trail heads down through a field of blueberry shrubs, at 6.5 miles turning steeply down to the west away from the reservoir. The trail then turns left, heading south at a fairly level grade along the contour of the hill. You may see some blue blazes on trees near the trail, but these blazes indicate property boundaries and are not trail markers. At 6.9 miles, the trail approaches the reservoir and follows close to its shore. After crossing a woods road that leads to the reservoir, the trail goes through a boulder field and crosses a stream. Then, at 7.3 miles, you come to a rocky point that juts out into the reservoir, another great place for rest and a snack.

After passing this point, the trail heads up into the woods away from the reservoir, generally following the traces of an old logging road. The trail continues along this ridge for 1.1 miles, with occasional brief rocky climbs and descents. At 8.4 miles, the trail descends to cross a woods road and a stream. A short distance beyond, it crosses a dirt road known as Durham Road. Continuing close to the shore, the trail comes to another rock outcrop that extends into the reservoir, with more good views over the water. The trail again bears away from the lake and climbs 100 feet to the top of a ridge where it is well out of sight of the water. After nearly a half mile of fairly level walking, at 8.9 miles the trail comes to a wide hollow where it bends to the right around a large white oak approximately 150 feet tall with a diameter of about five feet. This is the "Sentinel Oak," which must be at least 200 years old. There are a few other large oaks in the area, though none as large as the Sentinel. It is a mystery how this tree and its slightly smaller companions have survived intact, when the whole

The Sentinel Oak, the largest old-growth tree in Farny State Park, is about 150 feet tall, has a diameter of five feet, and is at least 200 years old.

area has been logged at least twice, possibly three times, since Colonial days.

After passing the Sentinel Oak, the trail climbs west away from the reservoir, at first gradually, and then more steeply. The ascent up a rocky ledge gains 100 feet in 0.1 mile, and you arrive at the crest of a hill that is just over 1,100 feet elevation, where a cairn marks the summit at 9.4 miles. At the top, the trail turns left and descends, reaching a ledge where there is a view (in leafless seasons only) to the southeast. From the ledge, the trail descends into a hollow and crosses a woods road and a seasonal creek bed at 9.7 miles. You are now approaching a ridge overlooking the reservoir, where the trail turns right and passes a viewpoint (again, only when leaves are down) off the trail to the left. The trail descends from that ridge, crosses a running stream near the reservoir at 10.1 miles, climbs to a rocky ledge, and then descends steeply to Split Rock Road at 10.6 miles. Turn left onto Split Rock Road and walk back across the dam, passing the remains of a Civil War-era iron furnace in a hollow on the south side of the dam, and reaching your car at 11.1 miles.

A winter view of Split Rock Reservoir from the Four Birds Trail. Photo by Daniel Chazin.

THE FRINGED GENTIAN

Walking into the October woods I look
for the fringed gentian my grandfather loved
by the spring the years have covered over,
though I remember where it was. My wistful
mother said they survive even frost, blood blue
against the dead brown in high hidden meadows,
where she and my father tramped so painfully
toward their griefs, taking almost a century to leave me,
a grizzled child searching for a small joy in the leaves.
But, of course, it's not there, wasn't last year either,
though my cousin says he saw one near the swamp,
the seeds are tiny and easily wash that way;
and I push through thickets and blow-downs,
relishing the knocks and scratches, the stiffening gusts
and the crackle of coming frost that remind me I'm alive,
till standing in the muck, the cool fire of age
creeping slowly over my ankles, my fingers numb
like leaves dying back from the edges,
I believe my cousin never saw a gentian here,
and only I care that it might—must—have ever been,
wondering not that I doubt there is one
in these woods, but that I know surely there is not,
and every year, following the old steps, I try to find it.

—George Petty

from *Boulder Field*
Finishing Line Press, 2004

THE
HIGHLANDS TRAIL
IN NEW JERSEY

New Jersey's Millennium Legacy Trail

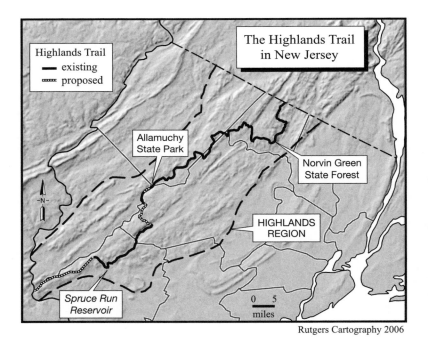

The Highlands Trail in New Jersey

Highlands Trail
- — existing
- ▬▬ proposed

Allamuchy State Park

Norvin Green State Forest

HIGHLANDS REGION

-N-

Spruce Run Reservoir

0   5
miles

Rutgers Cartography 2006

One day soon, hikers will walk the Highlands Trail (HT), New Jersey's Millennium Legacy Trail, from Big Beech Mountain at the New York State border to the Delaware River, at a spot perhaps near where the Musconetcong River empties into the Delaware. They will have tramped through a 120-mile continuous greenway of wild woodlands, rocky hills, and pristine lakes and streams. It cannot be done today because there are gaps in the trail, but every year some of those gaps are closed. By early 2007, nearly 90 miles of the Highlands Trail have been built and blazed. Hikers who complete the trek can give credit to their physical stamina, their love of the wilderness, the public spirit of many state and federal officials, and the patience and dedication of the visionary leaders, trail builders, and maintainers of the New York-New Jersey Trail Conference.

The New York-New Jersey Trail Conference has always enthusiastically backed the development of long-distance trails. The organizers of the Trail Conference were early supporters of the

The Highlands Trail blaze is a teal diamond, or a plastic blue-and-white diamond with a logo, as pictured above.

establishment of the Appalachian Trail (AT) when it was proposed in 1921. In 1924, the Trail Conference opened the first 20-mile section of the AT through Harriman and Bear Mountain parks. Decades later the Trail Conference conceived and built the Long Path from the George Washington Bridge to Albany. The Trail Conference naturally gravitated toward the idea of a hiking trail through the geological continuity of the Highlands of New York and New Jersey.

The concept of a Highlands Trail from Storm King Mountain at the Hudson Gorge near Cornwall, New York, to the Delaware River near Phillipsburg, New Jersey, arose in 1992 during discussions between officials of the Trail Conference and the National Park Service Rivers, Trails and Conservation Assistance Program (RTCA). Working together, the two organizations took on the task of coordinating the project with interested public and private organizations. In 1993, in cooperation with the New Jersey Conservation Foundation (NJCF), the Trail Conference and RTCA convened meetings to develop a vision for the trail, explore potential trail linkages, and produce working base maps. In 1994, they selected a feasible trail corridor, established guidelines for trail development, and designed an HT trail marker. The Trail Conference, the only hiking organization among the groups, undertook to locate, build, and maintain the trail, and to take the lead in negotiating trailways through public and private lands. The NJCF devoted its efforts to finding landowners willing to sell for conservation purposes, and arranged purchases, often with the assistance of the publicly funded New Jersey Green Acres Program. In 1995, the Trail Conference obtained access to key trail sections and dedicated the first section of the New Jersey portion of the Highlands Trail, which it celebrated with a "cannonball relay" hike, where hikers carried a historic cannonball made of iron mined in the Highlands.

The concept of the HT continues to grow. In October 2006, the Trail Conference Trails Council approved an extension of the trail from the east shore of the Hudson River to the New York-

Connecticut state line. Further extensions into Connecticut and Massachusetts are possible.

At the urging of the Trail Conference, the Highlands Coalition, a group of Highlands conservation organizations of which the Trail Conference was a founding member, adopted the Highlands Trail as an important part of their public and political advocacy for protection of the area. The Highlands Coalition supported the development of the trail, believing it would be the "spine" of public recreation in the Highlands and would encourage the preservation of a continuous swath of Highlands terrain from unrestrained development. The route of the Highlands Trail and the scenic views from its overlooks, were included in brochures and maps published by the Highlands Coalition, and because 120 miles of its proposed 150-mile total was to be in New Jersey, the New Jersey section of the Highlands Trail became prominent in these displays.

Since its inception, the physical growth and maintenance of the Highlands Trail has been the responsibility of the Trails Council of the Trail Conference, and particularly of Trails Council member Robert Moss, who in 1995 was designated Trail Supervisor for the Highlands Trail. At the time of his appointment, most of the New York section of the trail had been completed, but he directed the fieldwork for the New Jersey section. Finding land to put the trail on was the job of Trail Conference Land Acquisition Director, John Myers. Moss, the trail builder, and Myers, the land access negotiator, were the leaders in the routing and construction of the New Jersey section of the trail. Though they had different responsibilities, they often found themselves wearing each other's hat: Moss sitting in on negotiations with private landowners and public land managers, and Myers doing trail scouting in the woods. They combined existing marked and maintained trails, unmarked woods roads, old railbeds, and even an old canal towpath, with new trails cut through public lands and, where permission could be obtained from landowners, through private property. When woodland trails were unavailable, they included walks on country roads. In four years, from 1995 to 1999, with the help of volunteers from member hiking clubs and Trail Conference trail maintainers, they created a New Jersey Highlands Trail 75% complete from the New York State border to the Delaware River.

In 1999, the Trail Conference proposed the Highlands Trail for designation as New Jersey's Millennium Legacy Trail, under a nationwide outdoor recreation program initiated by President Bill Clinton. On October 22nd of that year, the formal announcement of its designation as the state's Millennium Legacy Trail made headlines in New Jersey newspapers. There are still places where the continuity of the trail is broken by problems such as obstruction by private development, safety issues involved in crossing public highways, closure of reservoir lands to the public since 9/11, and the difficulty of negotiating trail easements through private woodlands. But the Highlands Trail is very near to completion, which in these times is remarkable, and every year there are fewer gaps needing to be closed.

This achievement is a monument to the great public and private support for the idea that the Jersey Highlands, from one side of the state to the other, should be open for passive recreation to all. In the words of the Trail Conference's petition nominating the Highlands Trail for designation as New Jersey's Millennium Legacy Trail: "The Highlands Trail offers New Jersey communities along its way a recreational resource, and it offers the public organized access to a rich wildlife habitat."

HIKING DIRECTIONS

Big Beech Mountain to Black Brook Road
89.3 blazed miles of the Highlands Trail

The hikes in this book have been selected to include the most dramatic views and natural scenery of the HT, and arranged so as to be walked from north to south. When the guide that follows refers to HT sections described in detail as part of the hikes in this book, it will refer to these hikes by name and number. The reader will find complete north-to-south hiking directions for the HT section included in those hikes, with prominent notations where the HT enters and leaves the described hike.

For sections of the HT not included in the hikes in this book, hiking directions have been inserted from the trail notes of the author, from the *Highlands Trail Guide* with updates provided by the Highlands Trail Supervisor, Glenn Oleksak (available online at www.nynjtc.org), and from the description of the HT in the *New Jersey Walk Book*. As trails are improved or altered, new directions are included on the Trail Conference website: www.nynjtc.org. Hikers may also call the office, (201) 512-9348, for the latest information.

Throughout its length, the HT is blazed with teal-colored diamonds; plastic blue-and-white diamond markers with a printed HT logo are found at many trailheads, intersections, and kiosks. Where the HT is co-aligned with another trail, both blazes are maintained. Hikers should be careful at intersections where the HT may leave one trail to join another.

We have arbitrarily considered a short roadwalk (less than 2 miles), whether blazed or not, to be part of the HT for the purpose of calculating section length and total trail distance. Roadwalks are infrequent; only four are more than a mile: 1.3, 1.3, 1.1, and 1.6 miles, respectively. Roadwalks that are longer than 2 miles were counted as gaps in the HT, and were not included in the distance calculations. We have been careful to make note of these in the HT descriptions, not to discourage HT hikers from extending their walks, but to show it can readily be done. Distance is not always the most important consideration; walking a mile on a shady country road can be a pleasant interlude, but crossing a busy highway or marching through a shopping center can be a drag. The Trail Conference tries constantly to obtain new permissions from public and private landowners to close such gaps. Where substitutions of new woodland paths for road walks are planned for the future, we have included comments about the proposed changes.

S E C T I O N   1

State Line to Weis Ecology Center
LENGTH: 11.5 miles

The HT in New Jersey starts at the New York-New Jersey boundary line on Big Beech Mountain in Passaic County. There is no close access to that crossing; for New Jersey hikers, the best way to get there is to walk Hike #21 (Long Pond Ironworks State Park: Big Beech Mountain Turnaround). That hike takes you north 2.2 miles to the summit of Big Beech Mountain, where you are about 400 yards south of the New York-New Jersey boundary. A sign on the trail marks the state line. As you turn around and complete that hike by returning south, you are walking the first north-to-south steps of the HT in New Jersey.

Another way to get to the beginning of the HT in northern New Jersey, without duplicate mileage, is to walk the Lake-to-Lake Trail in Sterling Forest State Park for 2.3 miles from its east trailhead on Long Meadow Road in New York to the intersection with the Highlands Trail, 0.1 mile north of the state line.

From the end of Hike #21, the HT continues south over Horse Pond Mountain, described in this book as Hike #29 (Long Pond Ironworks State Park: Horse Pond Mountain Loop). The HT leaves that hike at the summit of Horse Pond Mountain, 4.4 miles from the state line.

From the summit of Horse Pond Mountain, the HT is co-aligned with the white-blazed Horse Pond Mountain Trail. The trail descends moderately through woods over the south shoulder of Horse Pond Mountain, crosses a brook feeding the Monksville Reservoir at 4.9 miles, and, heading southeast, ascends Harrison Mountain. Near the summit, the HT leaves the Horse Pond Mountain Trail at 5.2 miles, turning left along with the Stonetown Circular Trail (STC) and its red-triangle-on-white blazes. (The white-blazed Horse Pond Mountain Trail continues over Harrison Mountain, crosses a marvelous viewpoint on a rock outcrop under a power line, and descends for another 0.6 mile, to end at Lake Riconda Road, where limited parking is available.)

The HT, now co-aligned with the Stonetown Circular Trail (red-triangle-on-white blazes) gradually descends northward to the shoreline of the Monksville Reservoir. Turning right along the shore, the trails follow a woods road out to Stonetown Road at its intersection with Ricker Drive. Although space seems to be available, as of spring 2007, parking is not permitted here.

The HT/STC trails re-enter woods on the east side of the road, descend immediately to cross a stream, and then ascend to enter the property of the North Jersey District Water Supply Commission. At the top of a hill, the trails turn sharply right to head south to an intersection with the Ricker Hill HT-Connector Trail. Here, the HT/STC bears left to climb Board Mountain. Hikers who want an early exit may turn right to follow the black-diamond-on-teal-diamond blazes out to White Road and limited parking.

For a detailed description of the Bear, Board, and Windbeam mountains section, check Hike #25 (North Jersey District Water Supply Commission: Windbeam Mountain Through Hike). The Highlands Trail section of that hike ends on the south face of Windbeam Mountain, 10.4 miles from the state line.

As noted in the description of Hike #25, the HT leaves the Stonetown Circular Trail 0.1 mile downhill from the south summit of Windbeam Mountain, bearing left away from the STC and proceeding steeply down the mountain to meet Stonetown Road at 10.7 miles, close to its intersection with West Brook Road. The HT proceeds on West Brook Road (with blazes on telephone poles on the left side of this road), crosses West Brook, and turns left into the woods after 0.1 mile of road walking. The HT continues on a level track, emerging from the woods into an open meadow, where it crosses a running brook on a plank and reaches Townsend Road at 11.0 miles, a few yards from West Brook Road.

Note: A new HT section from Townsend Road over Ball Mountain to the Wyanokie Circular Trail (WCI) at the Blue Mine has been flagged, but not yet cleared and blazed. When this section is completed, the HT will continue across Townsend Road, climb Ball Mountain and descend to meet the Wyanokie Circular Trail (red dot-on-white blazes) near the Blue Mine. Those two trails then proceed co-aligned up the north shoulder of Wyanokie High Point and over its summit toward Yoo-Hoo Point and Carris Hill. For the status of this connection, check with the Trail Conference: (201) 512-9348, www.nynjtc.org.

For a temporary unblazed continuation, hikers should walk to the right out to West Brook Road, turn left, and, after a few yards, turn left again onto Snake Den Road. Follow Snake Den Road, staying to the left at the first fork, until you come into sight of a large parking lot at 11.5 miles.

Beyond the parking lot, a gravel road leads to the Weis Ecology Center of the New Jersey Audubon Society. For through hikers, camping is available on Wednesday through Sunday nights when NJAS staff people are present. For information, either call the Weis Ecology Center, (973) 835-2160, 8:30 a.m. to 4:30 p.m., Wednesday through Sunday, or email weis@njaudubon.org.

Weis Ecology Center to Newark Watershed Conservation and Development Corporation Office on Echo Lake Road

LENGTH: 10.5 miles, ending 22.0 miles from the state line

To continue on the HT, before you get to the parking lot you will find the red-dot-on-white triangular trailhead blazes of the Wyanokie Circular Trail (WCI), as well as the yellow-dot-on-white blazes of the Mine Trail, on a tree on the left side of the road. Turn left on the red-dot-blazed WCI into the woods between houses. Follow the red dots through a damp boulder field, over a short rise, and down to a long level stretch. You will pass intersections where the yellow-dot Mine Trail leaves to the right, crosses from the right to the left, and finally rejoins at 0.5 mile (12.0 miles on the HT). The trail next descends on a wide rocky eroded old mine road to the mouth of the Blue Mine and turns right across a wooden bridge over Blue Mine Brook. (A short reroute, parallel to this road, is planned.) From this point, the HT teal blazes resume, co-aligned with the Wyanokie Circular Trail and the Mine Trail. The Mine Trail leaves to the right at 12.5 miles. The two trails, HT and WCI, together climb the northeast shoulder of Wyanokie High Point, at 13.2 miles reaching the summit, where views in all directions are spectacular.

From the High Point summit, a short steep climb down over glacially smoothed rock outcrops brings you to an intersection with the blue-blazed Hewitt-Butler Trail coming from the right. The joint HT, WCI, and Hewitt-Butler trails now proceed southwest towards Yoo-Hoo Point and Carris Hill. For hiking directions, see the Highlands Trail section of Hike #34 (Norvin Green State Forest: The

Viewpoint Line Through Hike).

The WCI Trail leaves to the right in 0.8 mile, and then, just north of Otter Hole, 4.2 miles from Weis Ecology Center and 15.7 miles from the state line, the HT turns right, leaving the Hewitt-Butler Trail.

From the intersection, follow the directions in Hike #26 (Norvin Green State Forest: Buck Mountain Loop) for 0.9 mile, to the point where the HT leaves that hike, 16.6 miles from the state line.

From the rock cairn and teal diamond turn blaze where the HT leaves the Buck Mountain Loop, the HT follows its own route, marked only by teal diamond blazes. It descends easily down the west shoulder of Buck Mountain, following woods roads and foot-paths, and passing within sight of houses before reaching Otter Hole Road, 0.4 mile from the cairn, where a small hiker parking area is available. The HT turns right onto Otter Hole Road, follows it for 0.2 mile, and turns left onto Crescent Road. At a T-intersection, it turns right and follows Newton Road to Algonquin Way. At the end of Algonquin Way there is a parking turnout for two cars. Here, the trail re-enters the woods where three boulders block a wide eroded woods road, 1.1 miles from the cairn on Buck Mountain and 17.7 miles from the state line.

From this point, follow the description of Hike #12 (Pequannock Watershed: Echo Lake East), which begins at the end of Algonquin Way and ends at the Pequannock Watershed office on Echo Lake Road, 22.0 miles from the beginning of the New Jersey HT.

From the beginning of Hike #12 until the second crossing of paved Rock Lodge Road south of NJ 23, a distance of 16.2 trail miles, the HT traverses the Pequannock Watershed, where a hiking permit is required, and hiking west of Clinton Road is limited to Sundays during hunting seasons. Permits are issued at the office of the Newark Watershed Conservation and Development Corporation, 223 Echo Lake Road, West Milford, NJ 07480. The office is 1.1 miles north of the Echo Lake Road Exit from westbound NJ 23. For information on permits and hunting dates, contact NWCDC, (973) 697-2850, www.nwcdc.net.

Newark Watershed Conservation and Development Corporation Office to NJ 23

LENGTH: 13.8 miles, ending 35.8 miles from the state line

From the end of Hike #12 at the Pequannock Watershed office on Echo Lake Road, follow Hike #11 (Echo Lake West Turnaround) for 1.9 miles to where the HT leaves the Echo Lake West Trail.

From the Echo Lake West Trail at the base of Kanouse Mountain, the HT turns northwest away from Echo Lake, following its own teal-diamond-blazed route diagonally up the east side of the mountain, reaching unpaved and deeply eroded Kanouse Road at 2.0 miles from the watershed office on Echo Lake Road. It turns right and follows Kanouse Road for 500 feet, then turns left into the woods, descending through a hemlock grove with an understory of mountain laurel. The trail crosses Gould Road at 3.2 miles, a power line at 3.8 miles, and Union Valley Road at 4.0 miles. From Union Valley Road, the trail heads west and begins a steep climb across several ridges and up the east face of Bearfort Mountain. At a junction with the Hanks Pond East Trail (white blazes) there is an open rock ledge providing a long view east over Union Valley and Kanouse Mountain. The HT turns right onto the Hanks Pond East Trail (white blazes) for 250 feet, then left up a rocky ridge to the Hanks Pond West Trail (blue-over-white blazes). It turns left onto the Hanks Pond West Trail for 100 feet, then turns right up the last steep pitch to the Bearfort Ridge Fire Tower (manned seasonally), where there is an open grassy meadow with picnic tables at 5.2 miles from Echo Lake Road.

The HT turns right at a cement pillar just south of the fire tower, and in 50 feet turns left (south) onto the Fire Tower West Trail (yellow blazes). Descending gradually along the ridge of Bearfort Mountain, it reaches a junction with the Two Brooks Trail (white blazes) in 0.8 mile. Here, the HT bears right and follows the Two Brooks Trail 1.0 mile to Clinton Road, 7.2 miles from Echo Lake Road. Parking is available here at Pequannock Watershed parking area P4, 4.5 miles north of NJ 23 on Clinton Road.

From parking area P4, the HT turns left onto Clinton Road for 400 feet, crossing a bridge over Mossmans Creek. It then turns right into the woods to join the Clinton West Trail (white blazes) on a woods road. The co-aligned trails pass through a grove of hemlocks and some white pines, turn left onto a footpath and in two stages climb a steep 200-foot ridge of Bearfort Mountain in 0.2 mile. At 7.5 miles, the trails reach a rock cairn marking a junction where the Clinton West Trail and the HT turn left (south) and a blue-blazed connector trail begins straight ahead.

Following the two co-aligned trails south, the path traverses the ridge with occasional ups and downs, reaching a high point with limited views at 8.3 miles, and an open rock outcrop at 8.5 miles with better views of Clinton Reservoir. The HT and Clinton West Trail cross the Buckabear Pond Trail (red-triangle-on-white blazes) at 8.7 miles. From this point, follow the detailed description in Hike #14 (Pequannock Watershed: Buckabear Pond Loop) for 1.4 miles, until the HT departs across a bridge over the dam at Buckabear Pond.

On the other side of the dam, the yellow-blazed Bearfort Waters/Clinton Trail begins to the right, and the HT (teal diamonds) and Clinton West Trail (white blazes) turn left (south) along the west shore of the reservoir. The trails pass by plaques which commemorate the trailbuilders of the Pequannock Watershed, and join a horse/bike trail built by the Civilian Conservation Corps in the 1930s. At 11.0 miles from Echo Lake Road, the HT leaves the Clinton West Trail, turning right and following its own route across an area of abandoned farmland with broken stone fences and old farm roads. At 11.8 miles, it turns right onto Lud Day Road for a short distance, then turns left and begins to ascend, with a pine forest to the left. Reaching the crest of the rise at 12.0 miles, the trail begins to descend. At the base of the descent at 12.2 miles, it turns left, joins a woods road for 150 feet, and turns right onto a footpath. Continuing to descend, the trail goes through a hemlock grove at 12.6 miles and soon reaches Dunker Pond. It turns left to parallel the narrow rocky gorge of the outlet stream that drains the pond, then turns right and crosses the stream. It turns right onto a woods road, climbs to the crest of a rise, and descends to reach Canistear Road at 13.8 miles from Echo Lake Road. Here the trail turns left and proceeds through a one-lane stone underpass beneath the tracks of the New York, Susquehanna & Western Railroad to reach a parking area on the east side of the road, just north of NJ 23, 35.8 miles from the state line.

SECTION 4

NJ 23 to NJ 15

LENGTH: 15.7 miles, ending 51.5 miles from the state line

To reach this section of the HT, take Exit 52 from I-287 and proceed west towards Butler on NJ 23. The northern end of this section is at the intersection of NJ 23 and Canistear Road, 13.1 miles west of I-287, where parking is available. To reach the southern end of the section, continue west on NJ 23 for another 1.5 miles to Holland Mountain Road (reached shortly after NJ 23 becomes an undivided highway). Turn left and follow Holland Mountain Road south for 3.7

miles to Ridge Road. Turn left onto Ridge Road for only 0.2 mile, and turn right onto Russia Road. Follow Russia Road for 1.4 miles and turn right onto Weldon Road. The south end of the section is at the picnic parking area for Mahlon Dickerson Reservation, 1.9 miles south of Russia Road, on the right side of the road. (The south end of this section can also be reached from I-80 and NJ 15; see directions in the following section.)

This section of the HT is remarkably free from visible intrusions of civilization. From the parking area on Canistear Road just north of NJ 23, the HT crosses to the south side of NJ 23, turns left and heads east along the road shoulder. At 0.3 mile, immediately after NJ 23 crosses a bridge over the Pequannock River, the trail turns right, leaving the road and entering the woods on a footpath. For the next 4.7 miles, the trail traverses the Pequannock Watershed, where hiking is by permit only.

The trail heads steadily (uphill) through an open deciduous forest until it gains the crest of the ridge at 0.7 mile, proceeds along the ridge in a long level walk, and crosses two stone walls. After a short climb, at 1.8 miles it reaches a rock ledge with views through the trees to the left over the Oak Ridge Reservoir. The trail descends steadily from the ridge, reaching a woods road at 2.3 miles. It turns right, follows the road for 250 feet, and turns right again, leaving the road. The trail soon begins to climb Green Pond Ridge, steeply in places, crossing several woods roads on the way. There are limited views from the rocky summit, reached at 2.7 miles.

Now descending, the trail traverses a mixed pine and deciduous forest and crosses several woods roads. At the base of the descent, at 3.1 miles, the trail turns left onto a woods road, crosses a stream, then turns right and climbs another hill. From the top of the hill, it descends gradually, reaching paved Holland Mountain Road at 3.8 miles.

The HT turns to the right, follows the road for 150 feet, then turns left and re-enters the woods. It soon turns right onto a narrow dirt road, which it follows for 0.2 mile. Watch carefully for a double blaze marking the point where the trail turns left and leaves the dirt road. The trail descends to cross a stream and turns left onto a graded path, which it follows across a second stream. Just beyond the second stream crossing, the trail turns right, leaving the graded path, to climb through the woods and cross paved Rock Lodge Road at 4.6 miles.

Here the trail ascends gradually on a footpath. After passing two large glacial erratics to the right at 4.8 miles, the trail reaches the crest of the rise and begins to descend. It turns left onto a woods road and again reaches Rock Lodge Road at 5.0 miles, leaving the Pequannock Watershed. The trail then turns right and follows the paved road to an intersection at 5.2 miles. Here, the trail bears left, continuing to follow Rock Lodge Road, as Fall Drive continues straight ahead. At 5.3 miles, the paved road ends at a turnaround.

The HT continues ahead, following a woods road (the extension of Rock Lodge Road), which may be rutted and muddy in places, for the next 1.2 miles. It runs through a young, but maturing upland mixed oak, hickory, and beech forest, with a section of sugar maples as it approaches Glen Road. The grades are fairly gentle all the way to Ryker Lake. At 6.5 miles after the road begins to descend, and before reaching a large wetland, the HT turns left, leaves Rock Lodge Road, and enters property of the New Jersey Audubon Society. For the next 1.3 miles, the trail is also blazed with the bird symbol blazes of the Audubon Society.

For a detailed description of the next 1.2 miles, see Hike #9 (Sparta Mountain Wildlife Management Area: Ryker Lake Circle).

After the HT leaves the Ryker Lake Circle, it turns left at a T-intersection and descends to a Y-intersection where it bears right. The trail reaches a wide woods road at 7.8 miles, where there are Audubon blazes again. Take care to follow the teal diamond blazes (which cross the road and continue ahead through the woods), as the bird-symbol Audubon Society blazes turn right onto the woods road.

Just beyond, the HT crosses Russia Brook on rocks. This crossing may be difficult at times of high water, but there is an old bridge farther downstream to the left. At 7.9 miles, the trail crosses paved Ridge Road and then continues under a power line.

The trail now begins to traverse the property of the Missionary Society of St. Paul the Apostle (Paulist Fathers). It gradually climbs a hill and descends rather steeply to a col, where it turns right and briefly follows a faint woods road. Leaving the road to the left, it steeply climbs a second hill, and descends to reach a woods road at 9.1 miles. It turns right onto the woods road and almost immediately bears left at a Y-intersection onto another woods road. After crossing a stream, the trail bears right at a fork at 9.3 miles, continuing to ascend on a woods road. At 9.6 miles, the HT turns left, leaving the woods road. After a brief but steep descent over rock ledges, the trail reaches Sparta Mountain Road with limited parking, at 10.0 miles.

The trail crosses the road, entering Mahlon Dickerson Reservation, where camping is available, and turns left to join the Pine Swamp Loop Trail (white blazes). It follows the Pine Swamp Loop Trail for 1.2 miles, then turns left and proceeds for 0.2 mile to the picnic parking area, reached at 11.4 HT miles from the start of this section, and 47.2 HT miles from the state line.

SUBSECTION: *Weldon Road to NJ 15*
LENGTH: 4.3 miles

For a detailed description of this section of the HT, see Hike #7 (Mahlon Dickerson Reservation: Highlands Trail–Headley Overlook Through Hike) up to the junction with a short spur trail that leads to the Saffin Pond parking lot.

From this junction, the HT bears left and follows along the southern end of Saffin Pond. At the southwest corner of the pond, it turns left onto the railbed of the abandoned Sussex Mine Railroad. The HT turns right and leaves the railbed 3.3 miles from the picnic parking area at the start of Hike #7, immediately crossing Weldon Road. After passing a gate, the trail turns right onto a woods road, passing several fenced-in mine shafts up the hill to the right, and crossing a stream. At 3.8 miles, it crosses a power line right-of-way, where it bears left to re-enter the woods. After approaching near to NJ 15, the trail turns away from it, recrosses under the power line, and reaches Winona Trail (an unpaved road) at 4.3 miles. In spring 2007, there is a gap in the HT to the west of this point. To the left, Winona Trail may be followed back to Weldon Road. This section of the HT ends near NJ 15: 15.7 trail miles from NJ 23, and 51.5 trail miles from the state line.

SECTION 5

NJ 15 to US 46

LENGTH: 12.7 miles, ending 64.2 miles from the state line

In spring 2007, a gap exists in the HT between NJ 15 and US 46. There is now no safe crossing of NJ 15, and the HT resumes from the parallel road, NJ 181, at the north end of Lake Hopatcong, and continues through the woods 8.6 miles to Roseville Road. After a road-walk of 1.3 miles, another 2.0-mile section parallels the massive Cutoff of the Delaware, Lackawanna & Western Railroad from Lake Drive in Lake Lackawanna to Mansfield Drive in Byram Township. Following that woodland path, there is a 0.8-mile roadwalk to US 46 where the next section begins.

SUBSECTION: *NJ 181 to Roseville Road*
LENGTH: 8.6 miles

Alert: The Hudson Guild Farm part of this section is open during daylight hours only, March 1 to November 30.

This section of the HT begins on NJ 181 heading west (uphill) at the north end of Lake Hopatcong. Just past a dock and a marina on the left, limited parking is available under a power line on the southbound side of the road. To find the trail, walk west (uphill) along the road for about 600 feet until you see the teal diamond blaze on a tree on the south (left) side of the road, where the trail enters the woods to the left, ascending a hill. Cross a woods road and, at 0.2 mile, enter a low, wet area bounded on the west by a steep rise, which may be an old quarry wall. At 0.4 mile, turn right onto a grassy woods road, then bear left, crossing an exposed rock surface. At 0.6 mile, turn left between two rocks, each about ten feet high, skirting a wetland. Cross a faint woods road at 0.7 mile. At 0.8 mile, there is a view of the Kittatinny Ridge from the power line to the left. At 0.9 mile, you scramble down a rocky slope to a low, wet area, which takes the trail under the power line. At the top of the next ascent at 1.1 miles, a fence joins from the left, which the trail follows with a power line on the right. At the end of the fence, turn left onto a faint track at 1.6 miles. Join a grassy woods road for a short distance before bearing right through sparse oak cover and rocky ground. Descend to a mountain laurel stand on the right and a small rocky rise on the left. A faint woods road joins from the left. At 1.8 miles, the Anderson Bypass, a 1.7-mile alternate route blazed with teal diamonds with black centers, begins and continues on this faint woods road. At 2.2 miles, turn right and shortly cross a stream. To follow the main trail, turn left to ascend a rocky hill with sparse oak cover. At 2.5 miles, there is a limited view to the south. Turn right and descend past a vertical rock face on the right, to a mixed hardwood forest, reaching a woods road designated Eves Mountain Road, at 2.6 miles.

A convenient terminus with parking may be reached by turning left on Eves Mountain Road. The road forks immediately, but the two forks shortly rejoin. At 0.2 mile from the junction with the HT, bear left where there is an exposed rock surface on the right. At 0.3 mile, turn left where the Hopatcong Nature Trail (yellow blazes) joins from the right. Cross a footbridge but avoid both a trail and a fainter woods road, which diverge to the left. At 0.4 mile, a bypass with a bridge takes you around a wet area. Continue past the start of a gravel surface and two driveways, which join from the left, reaching Roland May Eves Mountain Inlet Sanctuary on Northwood Road, where there is parking (0.6 mile from the HT).

Back at the Eves Mountain Road junction, to continue on the HT, pass through patches of mountain laurel and over low hills to reach the south junction with the Anderson Bypass, which, at 3.1 miles, joins the main trail from the right. At 3.3 miles, enter the private property of the Hudson Guild Farm. From this point to Roseville Road, the HT is on Hudson Guild Farm property. Hudson Guild Farm is a private estate. Please respect the privacy of the owners, who have graciously allowed the HT to cross their land. At 3.8 miles, reach an old woods road and an old water pump. Turn left and descend to Bear Pond, then follow the trail to the right as it parallels the shoreline of Bear Pond, passing over a spillway and along a woods road. The trail turns right into the woods and travels over some small hills before going downhill to the Hudson Guild Farm driveway. Turn left into the driveway and reach County 605 (Sparta-Stanhope Road) at 4.8 miles.

Turn right onto County 605 and walk 0.7 mile to where limited parking for the next section is available on the left, passing over a bridge and then a small culvert. At the top of a rise in the road, the trail enters the woods to the left at 5.5 miles. After a short distance paralleling the road, it ascends steeply, crossing under a power line to a woods road and the junction of two rock walls. Continue through an opening in one wall into a former agricultural area, and ascend a little further to a rocky, sparsely wooded ridgetop. The trail meanders through miniature valleys and alternating sparser and thicker tree cover, passing many interesting erratics of varying sizes, and two viewpoints. It then descends on a long, relatively gentle slope, ending at an old woods road near some abandoned mines. Turn left and walk down to the gate at Roseville Road at 8.6 miles. There is limited parking available on Roseville Road across from the gate. Do not park in front of the gate.

From this junction, a 1.0-mile walk to the left (southwest) on Roseville Road, through a tunnel under the Delaware, Lackawanna & Western Cutoff, leads to Lackawanna Road. Here you turn left for another 0.3 mile to Lake Drive on the right. Walk downhill and across a new bridge to find the teal diamond HT blazes on the far end of the bridge where the next 2.0-mile section of the HT begins.

SUBSECTION: *Lake Drive to Mansfield Drive*
LENGTH: 2.0 miles

Much of this section parallels the Lackawanna Cutoff. This is a massive cut-and-fill rail line built about 1910 by the Delaware, Lackawanna & Western Railroad to create a nearly straight, low-grade route across the ridges and valleys from Netcong to the Delaware Water Gap. The line was abandoned in 1980, but plans are underway to restore its rail passenger service to Scranton, Pennsylvania.

The trail leads to the left into the woods from the west end of the bridge on Lake Drive, climbing on an ATV track and turning right before reaching the old railbed.

Almost immediately, the trail bears left, crosses a rocky hilltop at 0.2 mile, and descends to cross a stream in a wet area. It then climbs through a rocky area, with the towering embankment of the Cutoff on the left. The HT crosses an ATV track at 0.6 mile, a rocky stream at 0.8 mile, and continues through a generally rocky area. At 1.6 miles, the trail reaches a woods road and turns left, joining an un-paved section of Mansfield Drive at 1.8 miles. The HT turns right and follows the road, which shortly becomes paved. The section ends at the Byram Township Intermediate School at 2.0 miles, where parking is available. To reach the next blazed section of the HT, walk 0.4 mile north from the school to Lackawanna Drive, turn left, and walk another 0.4 mile to US 206. This completes the 12.7 miles of this section, of which 10.6 miles is blazed woodland trail. You are now 64.2 HT miles from the state line.

SECTION 6

US 206 to US 46

LENGTH: 8.2 miles, ending 72.4 miles from the state line

Alert: The property of the Hackettstown Municipal Utilities Authority, which covers the last 1.1 miles of this section from Mine Hill Road to US 46, has been closed to the public since 9/11. As of spring 2007, this section cannot be completed as blazed. Hikers should plan to stop at the parking area in Stephens State Park, or, when they reach Mine Hill Road, follow it to US 46, which requires 2.4 miles of roadwalk, as described below. Because it is possible that, at some time in the future, the ban will be lifted, a complete description of the trail is included here. For the latest information on the status of this property, check with the Trail Conference: (201) 512-9348, www.nynjtc.org.

To begin this section from US 206 opposite the shopping center north of Lackawanna Drive, proceed along Hi Glen Drive about 300 feet. Turn left onto Francis Terrace and follow it to the right, as it becomes Drexel Drive. Bear right after a sign stating "Norman Terrace," to reach a parking area at 0.2 mile. Turn right into the woods, crossing well-preserved rock walls and small rocky ridges. At 1.2 miles, enter the north fringe of a mining area with many large rocks and some tailings and pits. At 1.5 miles, cross a 30-foot-wide stream on numerous rocks, reaching the Sussex Branch Trail (no blazes) at 1.6 miles. Turn left onto the Sussex Branch Trail and, at about 100 feet bear right onto a narrow, level trail. In another 100 feet, turn right onto a narrow footpath and ascend a hill. At 1.9 miles, cross a dirt road, skirt a large depression, and continue to a multi-use trail at 2.5 miles. Turn left onto this trail, follow it for 0.1 mile, and turn right, crossing a dirt road at about 250 feet. Cross a stream, skirt a wetland on the right, and continue to a multi-use trail at the top of an ascent, at 3.3 miles. Continue straight ahead. This section is open to bicycles, and old white blazes appear along with the HT blazes. At 3.5 miles turn left, and leave the white blazes, which bear right. Descend about 200 feet to a lookout, where you can see Waterloo Lake and the Musconetcong River. To the left is the International Trade Center; to the right the Pohatcong and Jenny Jump ridges are visible. Make a sharp right, and continue along the face of the mountain, descending to Waterloo Road at 4.4 miles, where there is parking.

Turn right and follow Waterloo Road as it goes under I-80. At 5.0 miles, there is parking. In another 300 feet, bear left onto the Morris Canal Towpath. In this section, the Musconetcong River is on your left and the old canal bed is on your right. Cross Kinny Road at 5.2 miles. At 5.7 miles, turn right off the towpath, reaching Waterloo Road in about 100 feet. Turn left onto Waterloo Road. At 5.9 miles, a parking turnout appears on the downhill side of the road; on the uphill side, you pass the trailhead of the green-blazed Waterloo South Trail. At 6.0 miles, bear right (uphill) onto a woods road which 150 years ago was the old Waterloo Road. In this section, the canal and towpath have been obliterated by the present Waterloo Road. Yellow hexagonal plastic blazes of the Morris Canal Greenway join the HT teal diamonds on this path, and the trail joins the (new) Waterloo Road at 6.2 miles. On the road, telephone poles are marked with HT blazes. At 6.8 miles, the HT turns left (watch for the turn blaze on a pole) off Waterloo Road onto paved Colony Road (no sign) heading toward the Musconetcong River. The trail follows the road, turning right at 6.9 miles, and leaving the pavement on a footpath to the left down to the river's edge at 7.0 miles. The path turns right at the river to follow the old canal towpath, reaching the Saxton Falls dam and historic site at 7.5 miles, where there is a large parking area. Here the HT returns to Waterloo Road, until at 8.2 miles it turns left into Stephens State Park, crossing a bridge and turning right to a parking area. At this turn, a brown tree-and-path logo on a white circle (the blaze of the Patriots' Path) joins the HT teal diamonds. Because of a trail interruption at Mine Hill Road, described below, this section ends here, 72.4 miles from the state line.

It is still possible to follow the blazed HT/Patriots' Path past a small island, and at 8.5 miles bear right on three co-aligned trails: HT/Patriots' Path/red trail. After a short distance, you leave the Patriots' Path/red trail and turn left, climbing up a few steps to the HT/yellow trail, where you turn right. Follow the HT /yellow trail out to its trailhead at a second parking lot at 9.1 miles. Pass a small ranger station and gate, and follow the park road with both the Patriots' Path logo and the HT teal diamonds to where the pavement ends at 9.6 miles. Continue through the picnic area onto a narrow trail along the river to a Y-intersection at 10.2 miles. Bear left following only HT blazes, and angle up the hill along an old road. Then turn left and continue straight up, reaching a level area at 10.7 miles. Cross a faint woods road and reach Mine Hill Road (unpaved) at 10.9 miles.

Note: This is the boundary of the Hackettstown Municipal Utilities Authority area, now closed to hikers. In the event that it will be re-opened, the trail through this HMUA property is described as follows: Cross Mine Hill Road, and another dirt road, and then pass under a power line at 11.2 miles. Continue through a stand of evergreens, turn right and descend to a stream at 11.5 miles. Ascend an old woods road to a plateau, make a sharp left and continue to US 46 at 12.0 miles. The HMUA property ends here. Follow US 46 left to the light at Naughright Road, 12.3 miles from US 206. Across US 46 is a shopping center where there is parking.

As long as the HMUA property remains closed, hikers may turn right at Mine Hill Road and descend 2.0 miles to US 46, where they turn left for another 0.8 mile on US 46 to reach a light at Naughright Road, at the shopping center and parking. This long roadwalk is not true hiking, and hikers might be happier to plan to stop at Stephens State Park.

This section ends at Stephens State Park, 8.2 blazed trail miles from US 206, and 72.4 HT miles from the state line.

As of spring 2007, there is a long gap in the HT between US 46 and Long Valley. This gap will eventually be closed by a combined Patriots' Path/HT route to Long Valley, through Schooley's Mountain County Park. For the present, the blazed HT resumes at Long Valley, 6 road miles away.

SECTION 7

Long Valley to Van Syckels Road

LENGTH: 16.9 miles,
ending 89.3 blazed HT miles from the state line

From Schooley's Mountain Road (County 517) in Long Valley, the HT proceeds south for 9.0 miles on the Columbia Trail. To reach this section of the trail, take NJ 10 to the Dover-Chester Road (County 513) Exit. Turn south toward Chester on County 513, and continue for 12.8 miles to the intersection with Schooley's Mountain Road in Long Valley.

The HT teal blazes begin on the west side of Schooley's Mountain Road, where the trail enters the old railbed of the High Bridge Branch of the Central Railroad of New Jersey. This railroad was completed in 1876 to service the area's iron mines, and was finally abandoned in 1975. The HT/Columbia Trail soon crosses a triple-track rail bridge over a stream and continues on the level railbed, crossing Middle Valley Road at 3.1 miles. At 3.3 miles, the trail crosses a 200-foot rail bridge over the South Branch of the Raritan River. Reaching West Mill Road (County 513) at 4.0 miles, the trail turns right to detour along the road to avoid a commercial nursery, which has taken over the railbed. The HT/Columbia Trail turns left just before a fence, skirts the nursery, and turns right to regain the railbed.

At 4.7 miles, the trail crosses Valley Brook Road near the intersection of Vernoy Road (where parking is available), and enters Hunterdon County. For the next 4.5 miles the trail closely parallels the South Branch of the Raritan River, which flows to its right. Entering the small town of Califon at 6.4 miles, the trail, still on the railbed, crosses Main Street and then Academy Street (County 512), where the original stone station still stands, housing the museum of the Califon Historical Society. According to local historians, the town was named California for a citizen who struck it rich in the 1848 California gold rush; however, to fit the rail station sign, the town's name was shortened.

For a detailed description of the HT from this point to Voorhees State Park, see Hike #10 (Ken Lockwood Wildlife Management Area: Ken Lockwood Gorge). That hike arrives at County 513, from which intersection the HT continues south (uphill) on the road to Voorhees State Park, 4.0 miles from the Califon station and 10.4 miles from Long Valley.

Enter Voorhees State Park on the main entrance road from County 513, opposite Voorhees High School. There is parking here. At 0.5 mile into the park, turn left off the road and cross a wooden bridge, reaching the Brookside Trail in about 250 feet. Jog right slightly, then continue on, crossing stone walls, and winding through black raspberry patches. At 1.5 miles, turn right and continue under a power line for 250 feet, then turn left and re-enter the woods. (Note: It is difficult to position blazes in the cleared area under the power line, so look carefully for the turns.) Continue to Observatory Road, where there is parking, at 1.7 miles.

Turn right onto Observatory Road, and at 0.3 mile make a sharp left onto Buffalo Hollow Road. After another 0.2 mile, Poplar Road bears off to the left. Bear slightly to the right, reaching NJ 31 at 2.7 miles. Turn left and proceed 0.2 mile to the traffic light at the junction with Van Syckels Road. Turn right across NJ 31 and follow Van Syckels Road for 0.1 mile to the entrance of Union Furnace Nature Area, 3.0 miles from County 513.

Turn right into the Union Furnace area, then left. Ascend the embankment of an old millrace and go right along the top of the embankment for about 0.1 mile. Turn left and cross the bottom of the millrace. Proceed up the hill and descend to emerge on a cul-de-sac, Serpentine Drive, at 3.9 miles. Follow Serpentine Drive 0.3 mile down to Van Syckels Road. There are no utility poles and therefore no blazes on this roadwalk.

At Van Syckels Road, turn left, then bear right into a parking area. Proceed to the water and make a sharp right into Spruce Run Recreation Area. Here you will traverse meadows, a pine plantation, and dense autumn olive thickets. Cross the boat launch road near the boat launch area at 4.7 miles, then emerge onto the same road near the group picnic area, 5.1 miles from County 513, 15.5 trail miles from Long Valley, and 87.9 blazed HT miles from the state line.

Turn left onto the boat launch road and continue to the Spruce Run headquarters. There, turn right and proceed to the Spruce Run entrance at Van Syckels Road. Turn left and follow Van Syckels Road for about 400 feet. Turn right onto a gated gravel road, which takes you into Clinton Wildlife Management Area (the blazes resume here). Where the gravel road turns left, continue straight on a dirt road. Pass through a series of fields separated by hedgerows, with many mowed paths at right angles to each other. The trail turns left, jogs right, then left, and finally reaches a T-intersection, 0.6 mile beyond the entrance to Spruce Run. Turn right and follow a woods road into a mixed hardwood forest with an understory of widespread multiflora rose and other invasive plant species. At a fork bear right up a hill. At 1.0 mile from the Spruce Run entrance, turn left onto a narrow footpath, descending to Black Brook Road, an old woods road, at 1.4 mile. The HT temporarily ends here, 16.9 trail miles from Long Valley, and 89.3 HT miles from the New York-New Jersey state line. To the right, Black Brook Road leads out to Polktown Road.

SECTION 8

Unfinished Portions of the Highlands Trail

Planning and/or construction are proceeding on various sections of the remainder of the HT. From Allamuchy State Park, two alternatives are being considered:

1. The Hunterdon Highlands route includes the completed sections from Stephens State Park to US 46, and Long Valley to Black Brook Road. From there, the proposed route continues north to Charlestown Reservation, then south again through the Musconetcong Gorge. The location of the terminus on the Delaware River near Phillipsburg is presently undecided.

2. The proposed Warren Highlands route heads west from Allamuchy State Park to Jenny Jump Mountain, then south to Buttzville, Merrill Creek Reservoir, and Scotts and Marble mountains, reaching the Delaware River at Phillipsburg.

Organizations of Interest to Highlands Hikers

New York-New Jersey Trail Conference
    156 Ramapo Valley Road (Route 202)
    Mahwah, NJ 07430
    (201) 512-9348
    www.nynjtc.org

New Jersey Department of Environmental Protection
    401 East State Street (7th Floor)
    P.O. Box 402
    Trenton, NJ 08625
    (609) 777-DEP3
    www.state.nj.us/dep

New Jersey DEP, Division of Fish and Wildlife
    501 East State Street (3rd Floor)
    P.O. Box 400
    Trenton, NJ 08625
    (609) 292-2965/(609) 984-0547
    www.njfishandwildlife.com

New Jersey State Parks
www.njparksandforests.org

Abram S. Hewitt State Forest
See Wawayanda State Park

Allamuchy Mountain State Park
c/o Stephens State Park
800 Willow Grove Street
Hackettstown, NJ 07840
(908) 852-3790

Farny State Park
See Ringwood State Park

Hacklebarney State Park
See Voorhees State Park

Hopatcong State Park
P.O. Box 8519
Landing, NJ 07850-8519
(973) 398-7010
Entrance fee: Memorial Day to Labor Day.

Jenny Jump State Forest
P.O. Box 150
Hope, NJ 07844
(908) 459-4366

Long Pond Ironworks State Park
See Ringwood State Park

Norvin Green State Forest
See Ringwood State Park

Ramapo Mountain State Forest
  See Ringwood State Park

Ringwood State Park
  1304 Sloatsburg Road
  Ringwood, NJ 07456
  (973) 962-7031
  Entrance fee: Memorial Day to Labor Day.

Stephens State Park
  800 Willow Grove Street
  Hackettstown, NJ 07840
  (908) 852-3790

Voorhees State Park
  251 County Route 513
  Glen Gardner, NJ 08826
  (908) 638-6969

Wawayanda State Park
  885 Warwick Turnpike
  Hewitt, NJ 07421
  (973) 853-4462
  Entrance fee: Memorial Day to Labor Day.

Morris County Park Commission
  53 East Hanover Avenue
  P.O. Box 1295
  Morristown, NJ 07962
  (973) 326-7600
  www.morrisparks.net

Morris County Parks:
  Cooper Gristmill/Black River County Park
  (908) 879-5463

Mahlon Dickerson Reservation
(973) 663-0200

Pyramid Mountain Visitors Center
(973) 334-3130

Morris County Park Police
(973) 326-7632

Morris Trails Partnership
Greg Murray, President
(973) 829-8256
info@morristrails.org

Newark Watershed Conservation and Development Corporation
223 Echo Lake Road
West Milford, NJ 07480
(973) 697-2850
www.nwcdc.net

North Jersey District Water Supply Commission
One F.A. Orechio Drive
Wanaque, NJ 07465
(973) 835-3600
www.njdwsc.com

Hunterdon County Department of Parks and Recreation
P.O. Box 2900
Flemington, NJ 08822
(908) 788-1158
www.co.hunterdon.nj.us

FOR INFORMATION ON HUNTING DATES AND REGULATIONS:

NJ State Parks:
Call the numbers given above for the state parks, or
NJ DEP Division of Fish and Wildlife
(609) 292-2965
www.njfishandwildlife.com

Morris County Parks:
(973) 326-7600
www.morrisparks.net

Morris County Park Police
(973) 326-7632

APPENDIX B

Sources Consulted in Preparing this Book

Baker, Donald R., and A. F. Buddington. *Geology and Magnetite Deposits of the Franklin Quadrangle and Part of the Hamburg Quadrangle*, New Jersey. Geological Survey Professional Paper #638. Washington, DC: U.S. Government Printing Office, 1970.

Chazin, Daniel, editor. *New Jersey Walk Book*, 2nd ed. Mahwah, NJ: New York-New Jersey Trail Conference, 2004.

Collins, Beryl Robichaud, and Karl H. Anderson. *Plant Communities of New Jersey: A Study in Landscape Diversity*. New Brunswick, NJ: Rutgers University Press, 1994.

Daniels, Jane, et al. *Day Walker: 32 Hikes in the New York Metropolitan Area*, 2nd ed. Mahwah, NJ: New York-New Jersey Trail Conference, 2002.

Dann, Kevin, and Gordon Miller. *30 Walks in New Jersey*. New Brunswick, NJ: Rutgers University Press, 1992.

Dixon, Dougal. *The Practical Geologist*. New York: Simon and Schuster, 1992.

Lenik, Edward J. *Iron Mine Trails*. Mahwah, NJ: New York-New Jersey Trail Conference, 1999.

Moss, Robert, and John Myers. *Highlands Trail Guide*. Mahwah, NJ: New York-New Jersey Trail Conference, 2003.

Newcomb, Lawrence. *Newcomb's Wildflower Guide*. Boston, MA: Little, Brown and Company, 1977.

Scofield, Bruce, Stella J. Green, and H. Neil Zimmerman. *50 Hikes in New Jersey: Walks, Hikes, and Backpacking Trips from the Kittatinnies into Cape May*. 3rd ed. Woodstock, VT: Backcountry, 1997.

Scofield, Bruce. *Circuit Hikes in Northern New Jersey*. Mahwah, NJ: New York-New Jersey Trail Conference, 2001.

Skinner, Bryan, Stephen C. Porter, and Jeffrey Park. *Dynamic Earth: An Introduction to Physical Geology*, 5th ed. Hoboken, NJ: Wiley, 2004.

Wolfe, Peter Edward. *The Geology and Landscapes of New Jersey*. New York: Crane, Russak, 1977.

Wessells, Tom. *Reading the Forested Landscape*. Woodstock, VT: The Countryman Press, 1997.

Wyckoff, Jerome. *Reading the Earth: Landforms in the Making*. Mahwah, NJ: Adastra Press, 1999.

INDEX

Page numbers in **bold** refer to trial descriptions.

PHOTO CREDITS

COLOR INSERT:

BW–Bob Whitney; LH–Lee Hoentz; BS–Brian Strauss; MS–Matt Singer; MK–Marilyn Katz; GP–George Petty

Spring: 1. Wood anemone: BW; 2. Rue anemone: BW; 3. Trailing arbutus: GP; 4. Canada mayflower: MK; 5. Bloodroot: GP; 6. Dwarf ginseng: MK; 7. Early saxifrage: BW; 8. Solomon's seal: MK; 9. False Solomon's seal: MK; 10. Dutchman's breeches: MK; 11. Spring beauty: MK; 12. Deerberry: GP; 13. Large-flowered trillium: GP; 14. Mountain shadbush: BW; 15. Mayapple: MK; 16. Foamflower: MK; 17. Starflower: BW; 18. Spicebush: GP; 19. Wild oats: BW; 20. Trout lily: GP; 21. Lousewort: MK; 22. Marsh marigold: BW; 23. Downy yellow violet: BW; 24. Golden Alexander: MK; 25. Wild geranium: MK; 26. Herb Robert: MK; 27. Pink lady's slipper: MK; inset photo: BW; 28. Toadshade: MK; 29. Fringed polygala: BW; 30. Wild columbine: MS; 31. Pinesap: BW; 32. Pinxster flower: GP; 33. Round-lobed hepatica: LH; 34. Common blue violet: BW; 35. Forget-me-not: MK; 36. Wild sarsaparilla: MK; 37. Jack-in-the-pulpit: MS; 38. Indian cucumber root: GP.

Summer: 1. American fly honeysuckle: MK; 2. Wild madder: MK; 3. Black snakeroot: MK; 4. Bouncing Bet: MK; 5.White campion: MK; 6. Bristly sarsaparilla: GP; 7. Garlic mustard: MK; 8. Strawberry: MK; 9. Hedge bindweed: MK; 10. Tall meadow rue: MK; 11. Meadowsweet: MK; 12. Hoary mountain mint: GP; 13. Indian pipe: MK; 14. Striped wintergreen: MK; 15. Daisy: BW; 16. Sweet pepperbush: BW; 17. Turtlehead: LH; 18. White water lily: BS; 19. Whorled aster: BW; 20. Daisy fleabane: MK; 21. Tall buttercup: GP; 22: Dwarf cinquefoil: MK; 23. Cypress spurge: MK; 24. Evening primrose: BW; 25. Fringed loosestrife: MK; 26. Butter-and-eggs: MK; 27. Hawkweed: GP; 28. Panicled hawkweed: BW; 29. Agrimony: BW; 30. Thin-leaved coneflower: GP; 31. Whorled loosestrife: BW; 32. Jerusalem artichoke: BW; 33. Yellow stargrass: MK; 34. Spotted jewelweed: MK; 35. Black-eyed Susan: GP; 36. Canada lily: GP; 37. Frostweed: GP; 38. Cynthia: GP; 39. Yellow sorrel: GP; 40. Rattlesnake weed: GP; 41. Nodding bur marigold: GP; 42. Purple gerardia: MK; 43. Winged monkey flower: GP; 44. Bull thistle: BW; 45. Crown vetch: BW; 46. Purple loosestrife: BS; 47. Wandlike bush clover: LH; 48. Bee balm: BW; 49. Chicory: BW; 50. Pokeweed: BW; 51. Stout blue-eyed grass: GP; 52. Indian poke: BW.

Fall: 1. Pearly everlasting: GP; 2. Sweet everlasting: BW; 3. Nodding ladies' tresses: LH; 4. White wood aster: LH; 5. Goldenrod: BW; 6. White snakeroot: GP; 7. Silverrod: LH; 8. Cardinal flower: BS; 9. False Solomon's seal (fruit): GP; 10. Jack-in-the-pulpit (fruit): MK; 11. Partridgeberry: MK; 12. Bottle gentian: MK; 13. Great lobelia: MK; 14. Wavy-leaved aster: GP.

Black-and-white photos accompanying the text were taken by Bob Whitney, Marilyn Katz, George Petty, unless otherwise specifically credited.

We invite you to join

the organization of hikers, environmentalists, and volunteers whose skilled efforts have produced this edition of *Hiking the Jersey Highlands*.

The **New York-New Jersey Trail Conference**, founded in 1920, is a federation of member clubs and individuals dedicated to providing recreational hiking opportunities in the New York-New Jersey region, and to representing the interests and concerns of the hiking community. The Trail Conference is a volunteer-directed public service organization committed to:

- Developing, building, and maintaining hiking trails.
- Protecting hiking trail lands through support and advocacy.
- Educating the public in the responsible use of trails and the natural environment.

Join now and as a member:

- You will receive the *Trail Walker*, a bi-monthly source of news, information, and events concerning area trails and hiking. The *Trail Walker* lists many hikes in the New York-New Jersey metropolitan area, led by some of our more than 100 member hiking clubs.

- You are entitled to purchase our authoritative maps and books at *significant discounts*. These highly accurate, up-to-date trail maps, printed on durable Tyvek, and our informative guidebooks enable you to hike with assurance throughout the region.

- You are also entitled to discounts of 10% (and sometimes more!) at most local outdoor stores and at many mountain inns and lodges.

- Most importantly, you will become part of a community of volunteer activists with similar passions and ideas.

Your membership helps give us the clout to protect and maintain more trails. As a member of the **New York-New Jersey Trail Conference**, you will be helping to ensure that public access to nature will continue to expand.

New York-New Jersey Trail Conference
156 Ramapo Valley Road ✦ Mahwah, NJ 07430 ✦ (201) 512-9348
www.nynjtc.org ✦ info@nynjtc.org

Other Hiking Books Available From the Trail Conference!

Authoritative Hiking Maps and Books
by the Volunteers Who Maintain the Trails

CIRCUIT HIKES
IN NORTHERN NEW JERSEY
Fifth Edition (2003), Bruce Scofield
Revised and expanded, the book describes 25 hikes in
the New Jersey Highlands that can be walked without
the need for a car shuttle or significant retracing of
steps.
sc. 176 pp., 4¾ x 6¾, B&W photos with a map for each hike

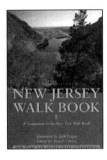

NEW JERSEY WALK BOOK
Second Edition (2004), Edited by Daniel Chazin
Illustrations by Jack Fagan
Essential source book for the New Jersey hiker.
Indispensable reference book, full trail descriptions,
illustrations, color maps, ecology, geology, and history.
Companion to the *New York Walk Book*.
sc. 442 pp., 5³/₈ x 8¹/₈, B&W illus.

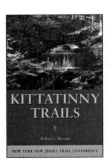

KITTATINNY TRAILS
First Edition (2005), Robert L. Boysen
Complete guide to Kittatinny Trails from the Delaware
Water Gap to the ridgeline summit at High Point. Day
hikes to enjoy the natural wonders of northern New
Jersey. Discover interesting geology and great views,
glacial lakes and waterfalls, long views of valley farmlands, and a unique Atlantic White Cedar forest—all on
trails along the Kittatinny Ridge.
sc. 219 pp., 5³/₈ x 8¹/₈, B&W photos & maps